CHANNELING THE APOCALYPSE
From the Eighteenth Dynasty to the Current Incarnations
Volume One

BY
Arthur Earl Jones, Ph. D.

In God We Trust
Mount Shasta
California

CHANNELING THE APOCALYPSE
From the Eighteenth Dynasty to the Current Incarnations
Volume One
Copyright © 2007 Dr. Arthur Earl Jones

All rights reserved. No portion of this book may be reproduced in any form,
except for brief quotations in reviews, without the written permission of the publisher.

Library of Congress Cataloging in Publication Data:
Jones, Arthur Earl, 1928 -
Channeling the Apocalypse: From the Eighteenth Dynasty to the Current Incarnations, Vol. 1
ISBN 978-0-6151-6204-1
1. History-Egypt-Eighteenth Dynasty. 2. Akhenaten. 3. Moses. 4. Archangel Gabriel.
5. Journal of Dr. Arthur Earl Jones for 2006-2007. 6. Channeling. I. Title.

Publisher: In God We Trust

Distributor: Liberty Rising Productions
P.O. Box 204264
Austin, Texas, 78720

Website: www.fearorlove.com
Order by email: fearorloveorders@austin.rr.com.

Retail price: US $29.95 plus shipping

Item 1: Sphinx with Khafre Pyramid at Giza

Table Of Contents

DEDICATION	5
LIST OF ITEMS	12
PREFACE	13
PROLOGUE	13
INTRODUCTION	21
BACKGROUND	21
PRELUDE	27
CHANNELING	38
ILLUSTRATIONS	44
CONTROVERSIES	46
CONFIRMATION	53
REFINEMENT	92
REJECTION	95
PUBLICATION	99
RECONFIRMATION	113
REVIEWERS	118
PREVIEWS	141
NEFERTITI	153
OSAMA	161
COMPLETION	172
CONCLUSION	216
EPILOGUE	217

APPENDICES:

Appendix A	Operation Apocalypse: End Timers & End-Game Strategy	222
Appendix B	A Message from God	225
Appendix C	Prophetic Message #1 from Kryon	233
Appendix D	Prophetic Message #2 from Kryon & Hatonn	237
Appendix E	Business Proposal	241
Appendix F	Admiral Fallon versus General Petraeus	243
Appendix G	Message from Adama	246
Appendix H	Letter to Lulu.com	248
Appendix I	How to Destroy a Nation	249
Appendix J	Update from the Galactic Federation	254

Item 2: Arthur Earl Jones, Ph. D.

DEDICATION

Life in this polarized world of illusion is essentially a contest
between civilized lightworkers, who love the truth,
and uncivilized darkworkers, who fear the truth.

This book is humbly dedicated to all those who love the truth.

It was the German philosopher Arthur Shöpenhauer who
observed that "All truth passes through three stages:
first, it is ridiculed;
next, it is violently attacked;
finally, it is held to be self-evident."

"You shall know the truth, and
the truth shall make you free."
– *John* 8:32

May all of humanity awaken by making the empowering choice
to become lovers of truth.

Item 3: WHAT IS A DARKWORKER?

A darkworker may be defined as an uncivilized person who practices deception and coercion for the purpose of subjugating others. In other words, darkworkers are psychopaths who derive conscious pleasure from deceiving, subjugating, and destroying other human beings.

Whether they realize it or not, the ultimate aim of all darkworkers is to create Hell on Earth. This has the effect of inviting and provoking the judgmental emotions of others, which results in the contraction and imprisonment of the collective consciousness of humanity.

The spawning ground for darkworkers may be found in the legions of unenlightened people who do not acknowledge or align to the Source of their being. Thus, like all unenlightened people, darkworkers are incarnations of the One Universal Being that we are who have temporarily chosen to live in a negative state of disacknowledgement and denial regarding their true identity.

The basic characteristic of all unenlightened people is separation consciousness, which consists in the illusion created by a closed heart chakra that causes them to experience themselves as separate from one another as well as separate from their Source. Whereas enlightened people in unity consciousness are by nature lighthearted, spontaneous, and characterized by positive feelings of love, joy, enthusiasm, and gratitude, unenlightened people in separation consciousness are by nature heavyhearted, calculating, and characterized by negative judgmental emotions of fear, anger, grievance, and guilt.

As is the case with all unenlightened people, the outer minds of darkworkers are not in alignment with their inner beings. Consequently, they do not know the truth, they do not love the truth, and they do not speak the truth. Indeed, it is precisely because they are not blessed with divine guidance in the form of intuitive knowing that they inevitably lose their way in the labyrinth of polarized illusion. What is more, darkworkers are by their very nature conspirators who fear and hate the truth because of its capacity to expose their nefarious schemes.

Like all unenlightened people, darkworkers perceive themselves as disempowered creatures and act like self-imprisoned victims of circumstance. However, unlike most unenlightened people, darkworkers seek to gain power over others in an effort to compensate for their disempowered condition. And it is precisely because they seek to subjugate others that darkworkers constitute the supreme example of God disacknowledging God.

Unlike lightworkers, who derive satisfaction and fulfillment from unselfishly serving others, darkworkers are totally selfish in that they derive satisfaction and fulfillment only from serving themselves. Although it is possible for a darkworker to evolve from the third dimension through the fourth into the fifth dimension on the service-to-self path, darkworkers who have succeeded in becoming black magician adepts on the fifth dimension of consciousness discover to their consternation that they cannot graduate into the sixth dimension until they exchange their unenlightened service-to-self orientation in separation consciousness for an enlightened service-to-others orientation in unity consciousness. It thus becomes clear that the path of the darkworker is a dead-end road.

Item 4: WHAT IS A LIGHTWORKER?

A lightworker may be defined as a civilized person who, having renounced both deception and coercion, practices the love of truth for the purpose of educating others. In other words, lightworkers are enlightened people who have made the empowering choice to help others become enlightened.

Being spiritually awake, lightworkers are fully aware of the fact that their ultimate aim is to create Heaven on Earth. By choosing to practice unconditional forgiving love in every situation, lightworkers are able to embrace and transmute negative judgmental emotions so as to facilitate the expansion and liberation of the collective consciousness of humanity.

The spawning ground for lightworkers may be found in the multitudes of enlightened people who acknowledge and align to the Source of their being. Thus, like all enlightened people, lightworkers are incarnations of the One Universal Being that we are who have made the positive choice to acknowledge and affirm their true identity as the Children of God.

The basic characteristic of all enlightened people is unity consciousness, which is the natural state that occurs when our heart chakra is open, and which consists in the absolute knowing that we are all connected with one another because the reality is that we are all part of one whole. Whereas unenlightened people in separation consciousness are by nature heavyhearted, calculating, and characterized by negative judgmental emotions of fear, anger, grievance, and guilt, enlightened people in unity consciousness are by nature lighthearted, spontaneous, and characterized by positive feelings of love, joy, enthusiasm, and gratitude.

As is the case with all enlightened people, the outer minds of lightworkers are in alignment with their inner beings. Consequently, they are able to know the truth, to love the truth, and to speak the truth. Indeed, it is precisely because they are blessed with divine guidance in the form of intuitive knowing that they are able to find their way through this wondrous world of polarized illusion without getting lost in the labyrinth.

Like all enlightened people, instead of regarding themselves as human beings who are having some spiritual experiences, lightworkers regard themselves as spiritual beings who are having some human experiences. However, unlike most enlightened people, lightworkers have arrived at the point in their spiritual evolution where they use their power of choice to make the empowering choice to be one with their Creator Source by choosing to be lovers of truth.

Unlike darkworkers, who perceive themselves as disempowered creatures and act like self-imprisoned victims of circumstance, lightworkers perceive themselves as empowered creators who use their power of choice to create their experiences for the purpose of gathering wisdom. Thus, whereas darkworkers seek external power over others as a means of compensating for their disempowered state of being, lightworkers cultivate their internal power as a means of claiming their mastery. And it is precisely when they become ascended masters as a consequence of making the empowering choice to return home to Source through the process of God Realization that lightworkers constitute the supreme example of God acknowledging God.

Item 5
DIMENSIONS OF CONSCIOUSNESS

Descension ↓ / **Ascension** ↑

12. Creator Source

11. Archangels

10. Angels

9. Lords of Creation

8. Oversouls

7. Ascended Masters : Crown Chakra (Violet Ray)

6. Light Body : Brow Chakra (Indigo Ray) knowing (WISDOM)

5. Etheric Body: : Throat Chakra (Blue Ray) creation (POWER)

4. Causal Body : Heart Chakra (Green Ray) cooperation (LOVE)

3. Mental Body : Solar Plexus Chakra (Yellow Ray) competition

2. Emotional body : Sacral Chakra (Orange Ray) subjugation

1. Physical body : Root Chakra (Red Ray) destruction

Item 6: THE DIVIDING OF THE WAYS

With humble gratitude and profound love, I wish to acknowledge the archangel Gabriel and the ascended master Saint Germain, who have been my spiritual guides, mentors, and companions during this and many previous lifetimes.

Whatever I am able to accomplish for the benefit of humanity in this or any other incarnation would not be possible without their inspiration and assistance, which mean more to me than words could ever express.

It was on 11 November 1981 that Germain first began to make his presence known to me; and it was on 28 October 1982 that Gabriel spoke unexpectedly through the vocal cords of one of my patients while she was undergoing deep-trance therapy to inform me that humanity would pass through a time of worldwide tribulation and planetary transformation which would begin in 1987. (Francuch and Jones, *Intensive Spiritual Hypnotherapy*, 1983, p. 477)

As you may know, it was the I AM Presence of the ascended master Saint Germain, speaking through his dedicated full-body channel Azena at a series of five public presentations on the slopes of Mount Shasta during Harmonic Convergence in August of 1987, who first confirmed the recently-published prediction by Dr. Jose Arguelles in his scholarly book, *The Mayan Factor*, that a 25-year process of planetary transformation begun in August of 1987 would be completed in December of 2012, and then went on to explain that this planetary transformation would be nothing less than a process of planetary ascension from the third dimension of consciousness to the fourth dimension, which he called "superconsciousness". (Saint Germain channeled by Azena, *Earth's Birth Changes*, 1993, Chapters 4-6).

I shall now reveal that between 17 June 1987 and 1 August 1990, I had twenty-four private sessions with Saint Germain through his dedicated full-body channel Azena, which had the effect of greatly expanding my consciousness, and between 9 June 1997 and 23 March 2006, I had fourteen telephone consultations with Archangel Gabriel through his dedicated full-body channel Karen Cook, all of which have proved to be extremely informative and highly reliable.

In any case, what I would now like to share with you is the fact that, during the past several consultations, Archangel Gabriel has consistently confirmed one particular prediction that is worthy of our top-priority attention at this point.

Archangel Gabriel has consistently predicted that only those human beings who have opened their heart chakras before the end of 2006 (by releasing all judgmental emotions of fear, anger, grievance, and guilt through the practice of unconditional forgiving love) will be able to continue living on Planet Earth as she ascends from the third dimension of unenlightened separation consciousness into the fourth dimension of enlightened unity consciousness before the end of 2012.

When I asked Gabriel for reconfirmation of this prediction on 23 March 2006, he replied: "That is correct, and you are going to see a lot of people opting out."

When I then said: "So, basically, this year is the dividing of the ways", Gabriel replied: "Yes, it is... This is the deciding year for a lot of things."

For those of you who find this radical prediction difficult to believe, I recommend that you simply regard it as a working hypothesis which is about to be put to the test.

Item 7

Message from SaLuSa of Sirius
channeled by Mike Quinsey on 12 April 2006

It is time to make your minds up. Do you allow just anyone to make decisions in your name that have the potential to plunge the whole world into war? Nuclear devices have an effect that is far reaching. Can one nation subject all others to their madness and intention to use them? The use of such weapons will soon polarize people throughout the world, and you have the ingredients for a long drawn out war. It is not just up to the people to show their dissent, but this is a glorious time for other nations to insist on having a say in the matter. If you were ever to see genuine efforts to bring peace to a troubled world, this is the opportunity for it to take place. **It is decision time** for many leaders, and if sufficient of them voiced their opposition to attacking Iran, it could be stopped.

Where are the United Nations, and what has happened to the voices of other leaders who are quietly voicing their concern? It is not a time for fickle and hesitant people, it is a time for firm outspoken opposition to the idea of introducing nuclear weapons in any circumstances. Where is diplomacy when threats rarely work and only produce more rhetoric and defiance? A handful of leaders have the future of the world in their hands, albeit they are unaware that **we of The Galactic Federation will not allow the use of nuclear weapons**. When will people be led in the right direction, one that brokers peace that can bring an end to all wars? It could realistically happen, as war has so many unwanted repercussions all around the world. No one would be unaffected, and you have only to look at one example of the difficulties and rising costs of fuel as a result of the Iraq war.

We know that more of you are pleading for an end to the madness of your leaders. The last stronghold of the dark forces is determined to go ahead with their plan, yet they know it will be short lived. The clamor and determination of those opposed to all forms of violence is rapidly gaining ground. This enables us to enter the arena, and those who oppose us will find a different proposition. We have no need to use any form of violence, our methods are ones of control and prevention that will contain the present situation. However, that action will only be known to a few, and the vast majority will have no idea of our presence.

How can you help as individuals? We would say that you must pressurize your representatives to reflect the view of those who demand peace. The past is littered with corpses and broken promises, and it is time that once and for all that a new path is taken. Other nations would respond if it was seen that they were not asked to do what privileged nations were not, and fairness and above board dealings are essential. No one should be disadvantaged when it comes to policing the world, and one nation cannot impose itself upon all of the others.

The current period will give a pointer as to how much you have learned from the last century of almost continual war. Those who see another way busily gather together to influence the proceedings, and much needed light and love is being spread throughout the world. It certainly helps, and as it grows so it dampens down the enthusiasm of those who push for warlike aggression to subdue others. The Lightworkers have more power than would seem apparent to them, and their continued actions are essential to a peaceful outcome. **It does however present every soul on Earth with a challenge to choose which side they are on, either peace or war, and it will determine their future path. Those who seek peace cannot much longer be subjected to the choice of those who have lost their way. A stop will be brought to their actions and plans, and they will continue their dark activities elsewhere until they too understand creation and the responsibility of all souls to each other.**

The dark, in their eagerness to control the world, are prepared to go against all advice to the contrary. They reckon without our presence and ability to stop them dead in their tracks. They know we are waiting to come to Earth, but still believe they can keep you in a lower vibration through fear and undo the good that has seen a great uplift in positive vibrations. We will not allow that to happen, and have **a divine decree** that allows our influence to maintain the higher vibrations. Historically, the dark have been trying for millennia of time to subdue and control you to imprison your souls. They have failed, but will not accept defeat, and in their minds still believe they can achieve their aims. **You have but the one last cabal that is reluctant to give up, and it is inevitable that we will have to be party to any action to remove them.**

The events taking place on Earth are too serious to be called a game, but nevertheless it is akin to one, as once it is over, all move in their chosen directions to further their experiences. The soul is immortal and will survive all of its experiences, but it is not for nothing and will result in growth and understanding that will carry it ever upwards. The dark learn harsh lessons from their experiences and will eventually also return to the Light. You wonder why you would have volunteered for such a cycle that has set man against man. It is all part of the understanding of duality, the positive and negative, and being able to handle the energies within the Universe. To experience everything, and still reclaim your Light to become the Master that you always were.

I am SaLuSa, and I see the victory that is yours, but I also see the need for your continuing efforts to support each other in these final hours. You have in a manner of speaking done the hard work, but need to concentrate your efforts to bring more light to bear upon those who are enshrouded in the dark energies. Soon you will be able to release the tension that has built up, and **with our arrival you will know that a new era has begun**. I will echo the sentiments of my colleagues and express the need for much love and light to be spread around you. Many are naturally concerned with the state of affairs upon Earth, and need the comforting and assurances that all will be well. We do our part to help, and the Heavenly forces behind us also direct much beneficial energy to you. Mother Earth is being embraced in beautiful light that can lift up your hearts and souls.

List of Items

Item 1:	Sphinx with Khafre Pyramid at Giza	2
Item 2:	Arthur Earl Jones, Ph. D.	4
Item 3:	What is a Darkworker?	6
Item 4:	What is a Lightworker?	7
Item 5:	Dimensions of Consciousness	8
Item 6:	The Dividing of the Ways	9
Item 7:	Message from SaLuSa of Sirius channeled by Mike Quinsey on 12 April 2006	10
Item 8:	George W. Bush	14
Item 9:	Quotations from the Bush Dynasty	15
Item 10:	David Rockefeller	16
Item 11	The Confession of David Rockefeller	17
Item 12:	Dick Cheney	18
Item 13:	The Solution to Our Problem	19
Item 14:	Captain Eric H. May	20
Item 15:	Claire Heartsong	22
Item 16:	Laurence Gardner	24
Item 17:	Ahmed Osman	25
Item 18:	Mount Shasta	26
Item 19:	Grace of Mount Shasta	28
Item 20:	Resurrection: a poem by Grace of Mount Shasta	30
Item 21:	Psychoanalyzing the Apocalypse	32
Item 22:	Surfing the Ascension Wave with Germain	40
Item 23:	Mike Quinsey	42
Item 24:	Dr. Joann Fletcher	48
Item 25:	The three controversial mummies in King's Valley tomb 35	48
Item 26:	Head of the mummy of Queen Nefertiti, revealing postmortem wound.	49
Item 27:	Dr. Zahi Hawass	50
Item 28:	Press Release for "The Bible's Cover-Stories Revealed"	100
Item 29:	Did You Know...?	132
Item 30:	Message from the Galactic Federation channeled by Sheldan Nidle	144
Item 31:	Message from Ker-On of Venus channeled by Mike Quinsy of England	146
Item 32:	Queen Nefertiti	160
Item 33:	Jeroboam Rothschild (alias Georges Mandel) with Paul Reynaud	164
Item 34:	Osama bin Laden	168
Item 35:	Admiral William Fallon	176
Item 36:	Twelve Steps to God-Realization	180
Item 37:	Aung San Suu Kyi	184
Item 38:	October 2007 meeting of Aung San Suu Kyi with UN envoy Ibrahim Gambari	196
Item 39:	General Than Shwe, Burmese tyrant	197
Item 40:	Thousands of protesters executed in Burma	198
Item 41:	Buddhist monk murdered by the Burmese military junta	200
Item 42:	The ascended master Saint Germain	208
Item 43:	Aurelia Louise Jones	210
Item 44:	Truth: a poem by Robert Howard Jones	214
Item 45:	A poem for Darkworkers	218
Item 46:	A poem for Lightworkers	219

CHANNELING THE APOCALYPSE
From the Eighteenth Dynasty to the Current Incarnations
Volume One

Copyright © 2007 Dr. Arthur Earl Jones

PREFACE

My immediate purpose in writing this book is to make full use of my personal experience as an effective means of validating my illustrated historical treatise, *The Bible's Cover-Stories Revealed: The Golden Keys That Unlock History.*

Thus, the ultimate purpose of this book is the same as that of my treatise: namely, to facilitate the awakening and enlightenment of humanity at our present pivotal point in human history by revealing the truth of what really happened during that previous pivotal point in human history known as the Eighteenth Dynasty of ancient Egypt.

The relevance of that pivotal point to this pivotal point will be demonstrated when it becomes apparent that there are many fear-based darkworkers at the present time who are doing all they can to prevent this revelation of the truth about what happened during that earlier time.

PROLOGUE

With the illegitimate election of George W. Bush in the year 2000, the dark cabal of international bankers known as the Illuminati, who constitute the psychopathic core of the global elite, hijacked the United States federal government for the ultimate purpose of enslaving humanity in the guise of protecting humanity through the uncivilized use of deception and coercion to create their so-called "New World Order."

Following their contrived terrorist attack against the World Trade Center and the Pentagon on 11 September 2001, the so-called Patriot Act and the criminal invasions of Afghanistan and Iraq by the armed forces of the United States completed the century-long process of transforming our American Dream into the American Nightmare.

Whereas it was easy to see that the Dark Illuminati were motivated by a desire to gain control of the oil fields in Iraq and Iran, what most people failed to realize is that the Illuminati were also motivated by a determination to punish Iraq and Iran for refusing to allow them to establish their fraudulent banking system in those nations.

Not to be overlooked is the crucially important fact that, by paying their fundamentally unconstitutional and increasingly exorbitant income taxes, the subjugated American people were giving their "voluntary" consent to an increasingly oppressive government that was systematically enslaving them in the guise of protecting them while simultaneously committing increasingly outrageous war crimes in their name.

Item 8: George W. Bush

Item 9

QUOTATIONS FROM THE BUSH DYNASTY

"Everything that I am, I owe to David Rockefeller."

– George Bush the First (c. 1988)

"If the American people ever knew what we have done, we would be chased down the street and lynched."

– George Bush the First (1992) to journalist Sarah McClendon

"If this were a dictatorship, it would be a heck of a lot easier, just so long as I'm the dictator."

– George Bush the Second (18 December 2000)

"Our enemies . . . never stop thinking about new ways to harm our country and our people, and neither do we."

– George Bush the Second (2004)

"Stop throwing the Constitution in my face. It's just a goddamned piece of paper!"

– George Bush the Second (November 2005)

Item 10: David Rockefeller

Item 11

The Confession of David Rockefeller

David Rockefeller became the chief architect of the Dark Illuminati's New World Order agenda by working, first through the Council on Foreign Relations, and later through the Trilateral Commission and the Bilderberg Society.

In the following passage on page 405 of his Memoirs, which was published in 2002, David Rockefeller makes a transparent attempt to exonerate himself by using a false political spectrum to imply that he is a moderate rather than an extremist, but then goes on to unwittingly incriminate himself by first summarizing the charges that have been directed against him as an international banker, and then acknowledging that he is guilty as charged of "conspiring", the dictionary meaning of which is, "secretly agreeing together to do something wrong, evil, or illegal."

"For more than a century ideological extremists at either end of the political spectrum have seized upon well-publicized incidents such as my encounter with Castro to attack the Rockefeller family for the inordinate influence they claim we wield over American political and economic institutions. Some even believe we are part of a secret cabal working against the best interests of the United States, characterizing my family and me as 'internationalists' and of conspiring with others around the world to build a more integrated global political and economic structure—one world, if you will. If that's the charge, I stand guilty, and I am proud of it."

Item 12: Dick Cheney

Item 13

THE SOLUTION TO OUR PROBLEM

We hold these truths to be self-evident, that all men are created equal, that they are endowed by their Creator with certain unalienable Rights, that among these are Life, Liberty and the pursuit of Happiness. – That to secure these rights, Governments are instituted among Men, deriving their just powers from the consent of the governed, – That whenever any Form of Government becomes destructive of these ends, it is the Right of the People to alter or to abolish it, and to institute new Government, laying its foundation on such principles and organizing its powers in such form, as to them shall seem most likely to effect their Safety and Happiness. Prudence, indeed, will dictate that Governments long established should not be changed for light and transient causes; and accordingly all experience hath shewn, that mankind are more disposed to suffer, while evils are sufferable, than to right themselves by abolishing the forms to which they are accustomed. But when a long train of abuses and usurpations, pursuing invariably the same Object evinces a design to reduce them under absolute Despotism, it is their right, it is their duty, to throw off such Government, and to provide new Guards for their future security.

The Declaration of Independence

– Thomas Jefferson

4 July 1776

Item 14: Captain Eric H. May

It is no exaggeration to say that, when viewed from the perspective of an enlightened civilization such as Arcturus, Planet Earth looked very much like an insane asylum being run by the inmates. (See Appendix A: Operation Apocalypse by Captain Eric May.)

By October of 2006, the United States Constitution had been thoroughly trashed and replaced with a mafia-like fascist dictatorship disguised as the Bush Administration.

At this point in the rapidly-accelerating downward spiral, it was beginning to look as though there was no hope for the future of humanity.

INTRODUCTION

It was precisely at this point that I made a conscious decision on 8 December 2007 to invite the Holy Spirit to use me as a channel for the purpose of helping to awaken and enlighten humanity.

When my sixth-dimensional higher self responded instantaneously to my humble offer by inviting my third-dimensional mind to serve as a channel for the specific purpose of birthing an apocalyptic revelation titled *The Bible's Cover-Stories Revealed*, I was not only surprised but absolutely astounded by what then transpired.

To my utter amazement, I was blessed with the miraculous gift of absolute knowing, which enabled me to solve the mysterious puzzle of what really happened during the Eighteenth Dynasty of ancient Egypt prior to the exodus of the Israelites, and then to resolve the perplexing riddle of Judeo-Christian religion, exemplified by the contest between the Pharisees and the Essenes which culminated in the crucifixion of Jesus.

In what follows, I will share the highlights of my experiences immediately before, during, and after the process of channeling the information contained in my illustrated historical treatise titled *The Bible's Cover-Stories Revealed: The Golden Keys That Unlock History*.

For those of you who wish to learn more about my spiritual journey during this lifetime, I have written a brief autobiographical account titled *Illustration of Spiritual Awakening* by Arthur Earl Jones (2001).

For those of you who wish to explore my website, which I began in May of 2002 using my spiritual name All-is-one Heartsong, I refer you to www.planetaryascension.net

BACKGROUND

Before I provide you with a precise account of exactly what I experienced during the two months immediately preceding the channeling of my treatise in December of 2006, let me pause for a moment to explain that, prior to participating in a memorable group tour of Egypt in November 1996, I knew absolutely nothing about the Eighteenth Dynasty in general or the Pharaoh Akhenaten in particular.

Item 15: Claire Heartsong

When a wealthy friend by the name of Joan Reddish invited me and my twin-flame soulmate Claire Heartsong to accompany her on a two-week tour of Egypt facilitated by the unorthodox Egyptologist John Anthony West, I accepted her invitation without knowing in advance what a profoundly enriching experience it would turn out to be.

It is worth noting that by 1996, John Anthony West had become famous throughout the world for daring to assert that the Sphinx at Giza was much older than the age specified by orthodox Egyptologists, who continued to insist that both the Great Pyramid and the Sphinx had been created around 2550 BC during the Fourth Dynasty.

It is also worth noting that, by this time, Claire Heartsong had developed into one of the most extraordinary channels on Planet Earth, with virtually unlimited access to all dimensions of consciousness.

Thus it was that, when I asked Claire to channel the ascended master Saint Germain for me just prior to our trip to Egypt, Germain confided that at the appropriate time he would reveal to me who I had been during a previous incarnation in ancient Egypt — a promise that was not fulfilled until several years later.

As a consequence, the only clue that I experienced during our trip to Egypt occurred at the Luxor Museum where, upon viewing a large sculptured head of Akhenaten, I experienced a sense of instant recognition accompanied by a profound feeling of love.

During the following year, I had occasion to examine Laurence Gardner's first book, *Bloodline of the Holy Grail*, which had been published in 1996 and which I immediately recognized as politically motivated disinformation regarding Akhenaten and Moses as well as Jesus and Mary Magdalene, his primary thesis being that modern European royalty were descendants of the hypothesized children of Jesus and Mary Magdalene, and his secondary thesis being that Akhenaten and Moses were one and the same person.

Thus, for example, on page 11 of *Bloodline of the Holy Grail*, Gardner equates Moses with Akhenaten by simply referring to "Moses (Akhenaten)", a device which is repeated on page 221.

My attention was further aroused by other erroneous statements to the effect that Nefertiti was the daughter of Sitamun and Amenhotep III, and therefore the half-sister of Akhenaten, and that Tutankhamun was the son of Nefertiti and Akhenaten, all of which I intuitively knew was false.

Only then did I focus my attention on this key sentence, which I had previously overlooked, on page 10: "The Cairo-born historian and linguist Ahmed Osman has made an in-depth study of these personalities and their contemporary environment and his findings are of great significance."

Upon discovering that the source of Laurence Gardner's disinformation regarding Akhenaten and Moses was an unorthodox Egyptian scholar by the name of Ahmed Osman, I immediately made a point of examining Osman's first three books.

In his first book, *Stranger in the Valley of the Kings*, which was published in 1987, Osman announced his brilliant insight (based on *Genesis* 45:8 and 50:26 and supported by his interpretation of *Genesis* 15:13-16) which enabled him to identify the mummy of Yuya (who had been a minister

Item 16: Laurence Gardner

Item 17: Ahmed Osman

Item 18: Mount Shasta
bottom photo © 2002 Jane English

of Pharaoh Thutmose IV and Pharaoh Amenhotep III) as being the mummy of Joseph the Israelite.

However, in his second book (which was initially published in 1990 with the title *Moses, Pharaoh of Egypt* but then republished in 2002 with the revised title *Moses and Akhenaten: The Secret History of Egypt at the Time of the Exodus*), Osman advanced the fallacious hypothesis that Akhenaten and Moses were one and the same person and then proceeded to develop that fallacious hypothesis into a delusional theory which, for some strange and mysterious reason, promptly received the full support of Laurence Gardner.

In his third book, *The House of the Messiah*, which was published in 1992, Osman provided unmistakable evidence that he had completely lost his way in a totally insane labyrinth of delusional thinking which, in addition to the irrational hypothesis that Moses was Akhenaten, also included the insane hypotheses that King Solomon was Pharaoh Amenhotep III, and that Jesus the Christ was Pharaoh Tutankhamun.

From 1998 to 2001, I turned my attention to the task of helping my twin-flame soulmate Claire Heartsong prepare her channeled manuscript for publication in 2002 as *Anna: Grandmother of Jesus*.

Then, from May of 2002 to December of 2006, I focused my energies on the process of creating my internet website (www.planetaryascension.net) which gradually grew to well over two hundred articles.

PRELUDE

I shall now provide you with a detailed account of my experiences during the sixty days immediately preceding the channeling of my treatise in December of 2006.

Let me begin by saying that in October of 2006 I was thoroughly enjoying my golden years as I approached the age of eighty while living harmoniously by myself in a small but comfortable apartment situated near the center of a peaceful alpine village on the slopes of beautiful Mount Shasta in northern California, just 50 miles south of the Oregon border.

At six o'clock on the morning of 10 October 2006, I woke up from the following dream: I am focusing my attention on the final stage of the global contest between the dark and the light, and at this point I experience that the light is delivering and the dark is receiving devastating body blows in what seems to be a boxing match.

I interpreted this dream as a prophetic message portending an imminent conclusion to the global contest currently taking place between the civilized love-based lightworkers who had chosen peace and the uncivilized fear-based darkworkers who had chosen war during the pivotal year of 2006, which I recognized as constituting the dividing of the ways.

On 12 October 2006, I had another remarkable dream in which I was advising someone how to move out of the negative state into the positive state. Humor is the key ingredient that enables us

Item 19: Grace of Mount Shasta

to transform our negative creations into positive masterpieces, because humor is an expression of the enlightened attitude that we don't have to take our experiences in this world of illusion so seriously. Thus, lighthearted laughter constitutes the magical means of moving out of the fear-based orientation, which characterizes the negative illusion of hell, into the love-based orientation, which characterizes the positive reality of heaven.

Then, on 15 October 2006, I had the following key dream: I am working with the ascended master Saint Germain to raise the frequency of the first three chakras on Planet Earth so as to raise the light quotient of humanity.

During the last week of October, I flew to Austin, Texas with my beloved friend Grace of Mount Shasta to give a series of overlighted presentations to a group of dedicated lightworkers known as the Circle of Intention, led by our dear friend George Humphrey. Suffice it to say that Grace is an enlightened being who travels internationally as an Essene Bishop, offering satsang, darshan, and healing sessions. I treasure her as my closest friend and shall herewith provide a sample of her sublime poetry, which I regard as the finest on the planet. (See Items 19 & 20)

On 7 November 2006, when the American people signaled their desire for peace by decisively repudiating the Bush regime in our national midterm election, I was profoundly relieved to learn that my prayers had been answered. However, being acutely aware that the Dark Illuminati were in control of the Democratic Party as well as the Republican Party, I was not at all surprised when Nancy Pelosi, who was slated to become the first female Speaker of the House of Representatives, declared on 8 November 2006 that impeaching Bush was not an option and therefore was "off the table".

Shortly after the election, on 10 November 2006, I had this dream: I am one of twelve male initiates who are being taught to remember that we are immortal spirit beyond the embodied mind which incarnates through birth and death and which is symbolized by striking matches.

On the following day, I then placed on my website this apocalyptic preview dated 11 November 2006: "According to Anna (the grandmother of Jesus), channeled by Claire Heartsong and confirmed by Archangel Gabriel through his dedicated full-body channel Karen Cook during the year 2000, Moses (the older brother of Akhenaten) had direct access to Creator Source (I AM THAT I AM), whereas his older half-brother Aaron was deceived and misled by Yahweh Jehovah (a false god masquerading as Creator Source). But the split that developed between the enlightened esoteric Israelites led by Moses and the unenlightened exoteric Israelites led by Aaron, which is revealed by the episode of the golden calf (*Exodus* 32), was later concealed and covered up by Hebrew scholars around the time of the Babylonian Captivity (586 BC)."

Having recently read *The Mayan Calendar and the Transformation of Consciousness*, by Carl Johan Calleman, Ph.D., I next sent one of several email messages to my list of friends around the world, encouraging them to read his comprehensive interpretation of the divine plan for planetary ascension as prophesied by the Mayan calendar and especially calling their attention to his momentous prediction that humanity was destined to experience a worldwide collective awakening to Christ Consciousness during the twelve-month period from 24 November 2006 to

Item 20
Resurrection

You touched once more the Earth;
now you can embrace it -
that which once you cried upon
and struggled to be free of...
Now you bless
with gratitude and tenderness
the rocks and thorns that tore your flesh
and the icy winds that chilled you.

You touch once more the Earth;
with loving eyes you look upon
that which once you turned from
in anguish and despair,
and you know why you were here,
and you know that you will go...

It is the time now, it is the dawn,
and like the fading stars,
you too will soon be gone.
And the rising sun
never seemed so brilliant before,
nor the birdsong so sweet,
nor the wind so pure,
nor your heart so very sure
that you ever loved this fully before...

Come, child of the stars;
you have walked a long, long way
in worlds of form,
and yet you never left the Father's Home...
It was His dream, you see,
and the wisdom gained
through aeons of Earth experience
is now distilled
into one crystalline drop of light
that rests like a jewel upon your heart.

And this is the gift
that you bear home to your Father,
this is the gift for which you have come...
the love, the wisdom, and the precious knowing
of yourself and all that is, as One...
One that is All, becoming many...
to dream, to see,
to feel, to know, to be...
like rays of One Sun,
radiating out as many,
yet never separate from the One.

I am full now,
for I have touched the Earth,
and I have worn her robes.
I have known what it is to be limited,
and I have known what it is to be free...
and the fullness of life
overflows this soul,
for I have known myself to Be...

I, the Father,
I, the Son,
I, the Light, the Source, the One...
Love's becoming, I am,
and love's fulfillment...
Life I am,
and the wisdom of experience.

For I have touched the Earth,
and the tears have turned to jewels,
and the heavy stones
that once did block my path
now form a golden stairway,
and the ropes that bound me tight
have now become my wings...
And in this ancient heart
there sweetly sings
the familiar, angelic songs from afar,
for I have touched the Earth,
and now I return to the stars...

©1989 Grace

19 November 2007 (called "The Fifth Day of the Galactic Underworld" in Calleman's system).

Several days later, after reading Paul Levy's new book, *The Madness of George W. Bush: A Reflection of Our Collective Psychosis*, I woke up around three o'clock on the morning of 16 November 2006 to find myself immersed in a tidal wave of love for my Creator Source that culminated in a blissful state of unity consciousness.

Then, at five o'clock that same morning, I was awakened by my higher self to channel the following email message, which I sent to my list of 65 friends around the world:

Beloved Friends:

To arrive at a deeper understanding of the key role which George W. Bush plays in regard to the rest of humanity . . . the key thing for us to understand is that George W. Bush constitutes the quintessential archetype of who we are as human beings in the third dimension of consciousness.

From this it follows that to be in judgment of George W. Bush (as he engages in global war and endless battle with his projected shadow) is to be in judgment of ourselves.

Consequently, if we wish to love ourselves free from the illusory dream-world of separation consciousness, we must make the empowering choice to release our judgments of George W. Bush by practicing unconditional forgiving love even as we call for the impeachment of both Bush and Cheney.

Once we have learned this crucial lesson by passing this extremely challenging test, which constitutes our final examination prior to graduation, we will then be in a position to graduate from the third dimension of consciousness (characterized by separation consciousness) to the fourth dimension of consciousness (characterized by unity consciousness) by means of the planetary ascension process that began in 1987 with Harmonic Convergence and will be completed by 2012 in accordance with the divine plan prophesied by the Mayan calendar.

Thus, forgiving Bush is the quintessential key to liberating ourselves from this dream-world of illusion.

In Love's pure Light,
All-is-one Heartsong

Three days later, on 19 November 2006, I wrote the following note in my personal journal: "The magical comforting presence of the Holy Spirit is palpable this evening."

Then, from three to seven o'clock on the morning of 22 November 2006, my higher self channeled through my consecrated mind an article titled *Psychoanalyzing the Apocalypse*, which I placed on my website later that same day. (See Item 21)

Around six o'clock on the morning of 23 November 2006, my higher self next channeled the following message through my embodied mind to be transmitted by email to my list of 65 treasured friends around the world, together with a link to the article on my website titled *Psychoanalyzing the Apocalypse*:

Item 21
Psychoanalyzing the Apocalypse
by
Allisone Heartsong
© 22 November 2006 In God We Trust

Like all unenlightened human beings who lose their way in the third dimension of consciousness, George W. Bush has disowned his subconscious shadow by projecting it onto other people so as to externalize the internal superego conflict, thereby directing his aggressive impulses outward against the world in an endless battle to avoid the alternative of punishing himself for his unconscious feelings of guilt which he has repressed and denied.

Having thus chosen the homicidal path of the sadist to escape from the suicidal path of the masochist, he now derives conscious pleasure from deceiving, subjugating, and destroying other human beings.

In other words, having lost his way in the labyrinth, he has sold his soul to the devil and, in the very process of trying to avoid being devoured by the Minotaur, has become the Minotaur.

Consequently, like all psychopaths who run protection rackets, George W. Bush is a destroyer disguised as a protector.

Because of his unique position as the fraudulent president of the fraudulent United States government, however, he is able to provide us with a clear reflection of humanity's collective insanity, which is the ultimate consequence of separation consciousness in the third dimension.

We may even go so far as to say that George W. Bush constitutes the quintessential personification and prototype of what happens to human beings who choose the negative downward spiral of the uncivilized darkworker rather than the positive upward spiral of the civilized lightworker, who has renounced the use of deception and coercion in human relationships.

Having failed to open their heart chakra by first making the empowering choice to place their minds in the service of their hearts and then releasing all judgmental emotions through the healing power of forgiving love, they stay imprisoned in their minds and remain stuck in the first three dimensions of consciousness instead of loving themselves free and graduating into the higher dimensions of consciousness.

In short, they become the educational dropouts who are left behind during our planetary ascension process as a result of the dividing of the ways, which is a natural consequence of our final examination prior to graduation.

Having condemned themselves to another round of hell in the outer darkness known as the third grade (unless they have made the insane choice to pursue the segregated dead-end path of the black magician adept in the fourth dimension), they are deserving of our heartfelt compassion.

For those who wish to awaken from the current transmogrification of the American dream into the American nightmare, which was contrived by the Dark Illuminati and induced through the unconstitutional presidency of George W. Bush, I wholeheartedly recommend that you read and contemplate "The Madness of George W. Bush: A Reflection of Our Collective Psychosis" by Paul Levy, beginning with the following quotations from pages 88-90.

"The entire Bush administration is suffering from a form of criminal insanity which we are all complicit in by allowing it to happen."

"Contemplated symbolically, as a dreaming process, the archtype of the terrible father that is playing itself out through George Bush is provoking and prodding us to step into our true authority, or else."

"This means that the figure of the dark father is initiatory, in that it either destroys us or propels us to have an expansion of consciousness."

"Whether we are destroyed by the negative father or empowered is up to no one but ourselves. We collectively bear the responsibility for our current situation, and we also have within us the power to change it. The responsibility is ours. Someone's gotta do it. Might as well be us."

My treasured friends:

When our collective dream becomes transformed into an insane Alice-in-Wonderland nightmare, what this means is simply that it is now time for us to wake up.

The awakening of humanity from our insane nightmare in the third dimension of separation consciousness is the apocalyptic process of revealing the concealed psychodynamics of the superego-shadow within the human psyche, which is simply the psychoanalytic process of making conscious what was previously unconscious.

In Love's pure Light,
All-is-one Heartsong.

Later that morning, I recorded the following note in my personal journal: "I am acutely aware on this Thanksgiving Day (23 November 2006) that in composing and transmitting this particular article and its introductory message, I am carrying out my assignment and fulfilling my mission for which I volunteered to incarnate on Planet Earth, namely to facilitate the awakening and enlightenment of humanity as an integral part of the planetary ascension process."

After enjoying a free Thanksgiving dinner with well over one hundred grateful people at the Mount Shasta Community Center that afternoon, I was next inspired to gift my friends with this timely reminder:

Beloved Friends:

For a truly inspirational reminder of what happens in this world when a genuinely enlightened political leader arrives on the scene to lead his people, I refer you to GANDHI (1986) starring Ben Kingsley, which is unquestionably one of the greatest cinematic masterpieces of all time.

In Love's pure Light,
All-is-one Heartsong

That very same day, I also sent the following email message to my brother Robert H. Jones, in the Hawaiian Islands, and to my brother-in-spirit Erich W. Thomas, in Germany, both of whom had been my loyal supporters for years:

On this particular Thanksgiving Day, I want to express to you my deepest heartfelt appreciation and gratitude for your steadfast support during the last several years, without which my dedicated service to the awakening and enlightenment of humanity by means of the articles on my website and my daily email messages to sixty-five treasured friends around the world would not have been possible.

On 25 November 2006, I then sent the following email message to my list of sixty-five lightworkers around the world:

Dear Friends:

It is time to be alert, awake, and aware. As I have repeatedly stated, humanity is currently passing through our final examination prior to graduation, and this year of 2006 constitutes the dividing of the ways, during which every human being is compelled by current events to make the pivotal choice between fear-based war and love-based peace.

What is more, we are now very close to the culmination of the global contest between enlightened civilized lightworkers and unenlightened uncivilized darkworkers, which has been gradually intensifying during the past century and which has become blatantly obvious during these past few years.

To be more specific, the Dark Illuminati, who constitute the psychopathic core of the global elite and their so-called New World Order agenda based on the diabolic *Protocols of Zion*, are about to make their final moves prior to checkmate.

And the long-awaited benevolent intervention by the fifth-dimensional emissaries of the Galactic Federation will then usher in a period of peace and prosperity in accordance with the divine plan for Planet Earth that will allow humanity to prepare for graduation from the third dimension of separation consciousness to the fourth dimension of unity consciousness by means of our planetary ascension process, which began with Harmonic Convergence in 1987 and will be completed by 2012.

While I encourage us to keep our attention focused on the glorious future which is now about to unfold during the next few years for all those who have made the empowering choice to align to the source of their being, rather than dwelling on the negative current events such as the collapse of the housing bubble, the depreciation of the dollar, and the fascist violations of our Constitution by the blatantly illegitimate United States government, I have received inner guidance from my higher self to disseminate this particular message as a means of alerting you to the prospect of a 'final showdown' event, which could happen before the end of this year and could actually take place at any moment.

No matter what happens, remember that life is always a choice between love and fear, and that how we experience the events in our lives is determined, not so much by what happens, as by how we choose to respond to what happens.

In Love's pure Light
All-is-one Heartsong

On the following morning, my embodied mind was next guided by my higher self to compose this extraordinary apocalyptic message, which I transmitted by email to my list of friends on the afternoon of 26 November 2006 and later posted on my website:

My Beloved Friends:

"These things says the First and the Last, who was dead and came to life: 'I know your works, tribulation, and poverty (but you are rich), and I know the blasphemy of those who say they are Jews and are not, but are a synagogue of Satan'." (Revelation 2:8-9)

Let all that was concealed now be revealed. For these are truly the Last Days of the End of Time, and this is indeed the Apocalypse.

Know therefore that the Zionist Movement of the Dark Illuminati is the Synagogue of Satan, composed of non-Israelite Khazarian Jews "who say they are

Jews and are not" and whose intention it is to divide the Israelites against the Ishmaelites, the Israelite Jews against the Israelite Gentiles, and the Israelite Sephardic Jews against the Israelite Ashkenazi Jews for the ultimate purpose of dividing and conquering all of humanity by means of the Dark Illuminati agenda known as *The Protocols of the Learned Elders of Zion*.

For a convincing confirmation of these apocalyptic facts, see the message dated 13 October 2006 from the higher consciousness of Matthew Ward recently channeled by Suzanne Ward. (See Appendix B)

It only remains to note that the scholarly revelation of the illuminating information regarding the collective conversion of the Turkish Khazars to Judaism around 744 AD occurred in 1976 with the controversial publication of *The Thirteenth Tribe* by Arthur Koestler, who died with his wife at their London home under mysterious circumstances in 1983.

In Love's pure Light
All-is-one Heartsong

Even more remarkable is the fact that I then wrote the following words in my personal journal that very evening: "Once again, I am acutely aware that in composing and transmitting the apocalyptic message on 25 November 2006 and this apocalyptic revelation on 26 November 2006, I am carrying out my assignment and fulfilling the mission for which I volunteered to incarnate on Planet Earth: to facilitate the awakening and enlightenment of humanity as an integral part of the planetary ascension process. So help me, God."

When my beloved friend Ana Holub of Mount Shasta responded to my apocalyptic messages with a passionate challenge that included a description of her recent work, I replied as follows on 27 November 2006:

Beloved Ana:

Thank you for your beautiful, profound, and deeply moving article describing your courageous peace education work with Peter among the prisoners of San Quentin.

Your passionate response to my most recent article seems to suggest that you have somehow formed the mistaken impression that I am what is known as a WASP.

Please understand that, because of my previous incarnations in the Israelite lineage as well as my present incarnation as an Israelite Gentile of predominantly Welsh, Irish, and Scottish extraction, I have never made the mistake of identifying myself as a White Anglo-Saxon Protestant, but have instead come to think of myself as being "psychosemitic".

As my name implies, I start from the position of seeing the oneness and equality of every human being and focus on the task of helping people understand the polarized global contest between uncivilized darkworkers and civilized lightworkers, which is currently manifesting as an insane Alice-in-Wonderland nightmare of Hell on Earth in the third dimension of consciousness, which is an integral part of our final examination prior to graduation via the planetary ascension process, and which has the ultimate purpose of motivating humanity to wake up.

To help you avoid the mistake of projectively misperceiving me, let me say further that my communications are intentionally designed to put people to the test of choosing between emotional judgment and forgiving love, which is precisely what life in this wondrous labyrinthine world of polarized illusion is all about.

Next, let me say that I agree with you wholeheartedly regarding the false equation that Jews equal Zionists in the defectively formulated article titled "Israel False Flag Attacks on US Carriers to Spark War on Iran."

As I am sure you understand, my article titled "The Synagogue of Satan" is designed to expose and correct that false equation.

In any case, I agree that there is a lot of mud in the water of human consciousness, which is crying out for us to clear it up.

Far from coming straight off a neo-Nazi hate site, the words "synagogue of Satan" come straight off Chapter 2, Verse 9 of the last book of The New Testament, which is titled "The Revelation of Jesus Christ" and which is rightly referred to as "The Apocalypse", not only because "apocalypse" is the Greek word for "revelation" but also because it reveals the apocalyptic fact that the Zionist Movement of the Dark Illuminati is composed of non-Israelite Khazarian Jews "who say they are Jews and are not, but are a synagogue of Satan", a crucially important fact which was unquestionably and irrefutably foreseen, predicted, and precisely prophesied two thousand years ago by an enlightened Jew who became an ascended master and whom the world now knows as Jesus.

Can you see now why I regard this amazing revelation (which certainly does not in any way imply that all Khazarian Jews are Dark Illuminati Zionists) as being worthy of our top-priority attention?...

With my love and blessings always,
All-is-one

Eleven days later, on the afternoon of 8 December 2006, I recorded the following thoughts in my personal journal: "I am All-is-one Heartsong, the enlightened mental body of the physical embodiment known as Arthur. I have been living from the outside in rather than from the inside out. I have become dependent on the channeled messages of Mike Quinsey and Sheldan Nidle rather than on the intuitive inspirations from my own higher self. It is time for me to make myself available as a direct channel of the Holy Spirit. It is simply a matter of choice, and I therefore choose to refine and purify my instruments of body and mind in whole-hearted dedication to Spirit."

I then made the empowering choice to immediately undertake a spontaneous experiment in automatic writing, which allowed my higher self to communicate directly through my mind by writing the following words without any hesitation whatever: "Peace be with you. I am Kumara Zora Torith, your sixth-dimensional higher self, come this day in response to your welcome invitation. There is no need for you to doubt that you can receive messages from me. You do it all the time, and the only difference here is that you are writing down your thoughts as I inspire them in your mind. That you may know the validity of this communication, I will give you a blessing in the form, not of a prediction, but of an insight."

As it turned out, the insight with which I was blessed by my higher self was nothing less than the miraculous gift of absolute knowing. It soon became clear to me, however, that this absolute knowing was confined to the events of the Eighteenth Dynasty in ancient Egypt, which I was being invited to explore and illuminate with the powerful searchlight of enlightened sixth-dimensional consciousness.

As I have revealed in the autobiographical account of my spiritual journey during this lifetime (which I wrote in 1999 and published initially in 2001), I had been blessed with momentary experiences of absolute knowing approximately a dozen times during the course of my life prior to this time. On this particular occasion, however, it is no exaggeration to say that I was living in the Eighteenth Dynasty of ancient Egypt most of the time between 8 December 2006 and 3 January 2007.

Why the insight took this particular form was itself a mystery that I myself did not understand until later. For now, I shall simply say that one of my previous incarnations occurred during the latter half of the glorious Eighteenth Dynasty and that my illustrated historical treatise provides subtle clues as to the supporting role which I played in that grand drama.

CHANNELING

The process of channeling the text for my treatise began with the extremely concise Introduction, which was composed of these three extraordinary sentences that were written on the evening of 8 December 2006:
"The time has now come when hidden truths which have long been concealed may finally be revealed to an awakening humanity. We may even go so far as to say that the time for thinking is over and the time for knowing is here. There are three cover-stories in the Old Testament of the Bible, the uncovering of which will provide an appropriate way to begin this apocalyptic process."
Six months later, after the initial publication of my treatise in May of 2007 (known as version 6), I received guidance from my higher self to add six parenthetic sentences to the text (thereby creating version 7), including the following parenthetic clarification after the second sentence of the Introduction: "(Whereas third-dimensional consciousness thinks, sixth-dimensional consciousness knows.)"

It is worth noting that there are almost no entries in my personal journal for the ten days from 9 December until 19 December 2006, which constitutes convincing evidence that something extraordinary was happening in my life at that time.

That this was indeed the case is confirmed by the following entry, dated 9:30 p.m. on 19 December 2006, and titled "Revelation":
"During the past two weeks since 7 December 2006, I have been inspired to devote all of my time and energy to writing the first two sections of an article titled *The Bible's Cover-Stories*

Revealed, the first section being devoted to the covert Hebrew-Egyptian lineage derived from Sarai and Pharaoh Thutmose II, and the second section being devoted to the overt Hebrew-Egyptian lineage derived from Joseph the Israelite and his Egyptian wife Asenath, whose daughter Queen Tiye was the mother of Moses and Akhenaten. This evening, I was guided to watch *The Ten Commandments* for the first time, and to thank the Source of my being that I was never brainwashed with this fraudulent disinformation."

On 20 December 2006, I finally managed to find the time to transmit to my list of friends around the world a message from the ascended master Saint Germain which had been channeled on 18 December 2006 by my spiritually gifted friend Mike Quinsey in England and which, by a remarkable synchronicity, just happened to contain the following key passages: "You will also find that with the expansion of your consciousness, you are more able to keep in tune with your Higher Self... In time you will merge more closely to your Higher Self until you become as One. (See Item 22: Surfing the Ascension Wave with Germain.)

It was not until this point that I began to explore the Internet to see what scholars other than Laurence Gardner and Ahmed Osman had to say about Akhenaten and Queen Tiye.

Thus, my first attempt to connect with the professional community of Egyptian scholars took the form of this email message (dated 21 December 2006) to Marianne Luban, who chose not to respond.

Dear Marianne Luban:

I am currently in the process of writing an article that revolves around the Eighteenth Dynasty of ancient Egypt, and I have recently read the articles on your website as part of my ongoing research.

I was favorably impressed with the thoughtfulness and sensitivity of your work (especially the articles on Thutmose IV and Queen Tiye), and I received clear inner guidance in the form of a strong intuitive feeling that I should contact you for the purpose of cultivating a friendly exchange.

Suffice it to say that I am a retired psychologist approaching my eightieth year and that the name that I use for my non-professional articles is not the same as the name that I was born with.

With kindest regards and good wishes on this winter solstice of 2006,
Arthur Earl Jones, Ph. D.

Note: Prior to sending this email message to Marianne Luban, I had also read her 1999 website article titled "Do We Have the Mummy of Nefertiti?"

On 22 December 2006, I then added the following entry in my journal, which provides a brief but vivid description of the extraordinary experience that I was going through at that time: "During the two-week period from December 8 to December 22 of 2006, I channeled the first two sections of *The Bible's Cover-Stories Revealed* by means of intense mental concentration and focused attention that was emotionally nourishing at the same time that it was physically exhausting."

Item 22

SURFING THE ASCENSION WAVE WITH GERMAIN

Channeled by Mike Quinsey in England, the ascended master Saint Germain, who is in charge of orchestrating humanity's ascension, blesses us with divine guidance on how to allow ourselves to be carried by the ascension wave into the Golden Era of God.

St. Germain 18 December 2006

There is an enormous amount of merging taking place that involves the new energies that are being directed to Earth. They affect individuals and the Earth itself, and this is indeed the intention as part of the plans for upliftment. Even where there is no knowledge of them or intent to take them in, they will nevertheless still raise the level of consciousness. To what extent depends on whether an individual wishes it to so happen. If you find yourself acting in harmony with them, they will become an essential part of your consciousness that will carry you forward.

You have in fact been merging with the new energies for quite a long time, and as you have already experienced, there are people on Earth who foresee such events and make them known. It will always benefit you to prepare for such occasions, which enables a smooth transition of the energies. With your developing higher levels of consciousness, it is now possible for you to actively participate and have the awareness of exactly how they impinge upon you. You will certainly notice the subtle changes within yourself, and they strengthen your ability to remain firmly and calmly in your own space.

Another benefit is your ability to place a strong protective light barrier around yourself. You will as a result become less affected by the negative energies around you. You link with others who become One with your level of consciousness, and this is the Law of Attraction at work. In fact, many of you will unknowingly become part of a group consciousness. Through this growth, you become a prime bearer of the Light, whilst still remaining as ever an individual part of the whole.

As you are beginning to understand, you cannot rise above the level of your vibrations except that you increase them first. It then becomes an automatic attraction that allows you to enter higher and higher dimensions. Your destiny, as souls who seek to take this opportunity for Ascension, is to venture into the Fifth Dimension. Already you walk between the Third and Fourth Dimensions, as energies do not have a clearly marked line that divides them. You move in and out of them depending on your level of consciousness.

You will also find that with the expansion of your consciousness, you are more able to keep in tune with your Higher Self. This has the benefit of allowing the higher guidance to help you along your path, and your perception will also be very much enhanced. In reality everything you need to know is already within, and if you carefully listen to those promptings, sometimes referred to as your intuition, you will need little outside help. Remember that each soul has a personal life plan, even if they may be aiming to reach the same goals. What seems to work for one is not necessarily going to work for others.

Finding your path is what you are engaged in at present, although many of you already have a clear vision and understanding of it. In that event, do not be diverted from it by others who have a different one to follow, no matter how attractive it may appear. The fact is that all complement each other and are equally important. Humans have a tendency to jump from one thing to another, chasing after the pot of gold at the end of the rainbow. Settle into that which is in harmony with your vibrations and you will find what you seek.

The Universe is a living force that is continually changing, but subject to the result of incoming energies from the Central Sun. It is also subject to all manner of changes brought about by the way in which they are used. It results in a continual ebbing and flowing that affects the whole. The Earth, although a small speck amongst the millions of planets involved, also has its own input that contributes to the overall effect. The Earth is a microcosm of the macrocosm, albeit at the lower end of the scale of vibrations.

The Creator has envisioned the perfection in which life can evolve, and you and every other soul are experiencing it as made manifest. In serving the Creator, those of the highest vibrations who are the Light Beings of expansive consciousness that hold the power of creation, have carried out the Creator's bidding. Consequently, at their level, all is in absolute perfection, and only loses that perfection as the vibration is lowered through the various dimensions. Yet, as you rise up, you would be forgiven for thinking that you had already found the highest levels.

The magnificence of the Creator's vision is beyond mortal words and in your finite lives, is beyond your comprehension. What awaits you with the birth of the Golden Age, is your first glimpse of the dimensions of Light, held together by the glue of the Universe that is God's Consciousness. All is in the energy of Light and Love; there is no other. As you ascend, so that which has no place in the higher vibrations must be transmuted, and the higher you go the more refining takes place.

So we come back to you on Earth, lifting your heads up out of the sands of time and beginning to see once more the beauty and harmony that beckons. Suddenly, earthly matters will seem of little consequence, as your thoughts dwell in the higher dimensions. In so doing, you are helping manifest those very thoughts, and the new Earth is slowly being imprinted over the old one. When the optimum level of vibration is reached, in the twinkling of an eye it will be manifest, and the old one shall be gone from your sight. You are therefore the co-creators of Ascension, and have far exceeded our expectations in your ability to use your creative powers in this way.

Now, a most wonderful year is about to start, and before long it will truly be said of you that you are indeed not just Gods in the making, but have commenced the manifestation of your true Self. In time, you will merge more closely to your Higher Self until you become as One. The remaining years will present you with the chance to freely express your highest concepts, in the fullest expression of yourself.

I am St. Germain, coming to you in the joy of your successful awakening to the truth. Let Love be your guide to the goal that is now within your grasp.

Thank you St. Germain
Mike Quinsey.

Item 23: Mike Quinsey

On 24 December 2007, I spent Christmas eve at Morningstar on the slopes of Mount Shasta with my beloved friends Grace, Shalomar, Mike and Erik, during the course of which I shared the essence of what I had been experiencing while channeling what I was beginning to recognize as not just another article for my website, but rather a treatise to be published.

During the week between December 23 and December 30, I channeled the third section of *The Bible's Cover-Stories Revealed*, after which I channeled the Prologue.

On 30 December 2006, however, I wrote the following entry in my personal journal: "Yesterday, I thought I had completed the second part of my article titled *The Bible's Cover-Stories Revealed*, but last night at one o'clock in the morning, my higher self suddenly gave me insight into the sixth and seventh components of the cover story #2, which allowed me to bring the second section of my article to a fuller and much more satisfying conclusion today. I have been in an extremely focused state of mental concentration continuously since my work on this article began 8 December 2006."

It is that entry, dated 30 December 2006, which reminds me to mention that the channeling of this extraordinary treatise usually took place in the middle of the night between one and four o'clock, when my body and mind were completely relaxed, as a consequence of which the only conscious effort involved was that of getting out of bed to scribble down the thoughts which were flowing spontaneously through my mind, and then transcribing my scribbled notes during the following day.

On 31 December 2006, I celebrated the end of the old year and the beginning of a new year by sending the following email message to approximately seventy friends around the world:

> Beloved Friends: The year 2007 is going to be the happiest new year ever because it is destined to be the year of miracles, and if only we will realize that we are creators rather than merely creatures, we can create our lives any way we choose from this time onward. In Love's pure Light, All-is-one Heartsong.

On 1 January 2007, I received a telephone call from my good friend Bruce Schiltz, who had recently retired from his tourist business at Mount Rushmore, where he had personally flown the helicopters for many years. Two days later, on 3 January 2007, I sent him the following email:

> My dear friend Bruce:
>
> I have finally completed the writing (*The Bible's Cover-Stories Revealed*) which has required my focused attention during the past month and am now ready to shift the focus of my attention to the question of how spirit wants me to facilitate its publication in addition to posting it on my website.
>
> I very much appreciate your offer to assist me with the task of publishing these truly radical revelations...
>
> This morning, I received a clear message from my higher self (Kumara Zora Torith), reminding me of your offer and your suggestion which you communicated to me during our telephone conversation on 1 January 2007, and strongly encouraging me to consider accepting your offer...
>
> I intend to give this matter my careful attention during the next several days and will communicate with you again after I have had time to contemplate and

meditate further...
With my love and gratitude, Arthur ➡ All-is-one ➡ Kumara Zora Torith

On the morning of 6 January 2007, I was awakened by a most unusual dream, which I recorded and interpreted by writing the following words in my private journal:

"Dream: Align to change from Autumn Equinox to Winter Solstice. Interpretation: This remarkable dream seems to be a message from my higher self predicting radical change from September 23 to December 22 during the latter part of 2007."

ILLUSTRATIONS

On 6 January 2007, I wrote the following report in my personal journal: "Having completed the preliminary version of my treatise *The Bible's Cover-Stories Revealed*, which my higher self has channeled through my consecrated mind, I am now engaged in the process of selecting the illustrations and searching the Internet for possible publishers."

From the very outset, I knew that the sculptured head of Queen Tiye would be on the front cover, together with a bold announcement that she was the mother of Moses as well as Akhenaten, the two illustrious founders of monotheistic religion.

I had brought back a photograph of that sculptured head of Queen Tiye from my trip to Egypt in November of 1996, and had placed it in a gold frame on the living-room wall of my tiny Mount Shasta apartment without really knowing why. All that I knew at that time was that I loved her and her beloved son Akhenaten with a love that seemed incomprehensible, yet was comparable to the love that I felt for Mary and her beloved son Yeshua ben Joseph, whom the world knows as Jesus the Christ.

I also knew from the very outset that the illustrations for my treatise would include full-page photographs of the beautifully-preserved mummies of Yuya and Thuya, whom I recognized as Joseph the Israelite and Asenath, beloved daughter of Poti-Pherah, the Egyptian priest of On.

Although unbecoming portraits of the heretic Pharaoh Akhenaten were in abundant supply on the Internet, a determined search was required to locate a photograph of his sculptured head which was worthy of this enlightened being.

During the course of this search on the Internet, I was guided by spirit to encounter a sculptured portrait of the young Akhenaten which was of extremely poor quality. However, with the help of a friendly librarian at our local library, I was able to track down the source of that image in the 1936 edition of Helen Gardner's encyclopedic masterpiece, *Art Through the Ages*.

At that point, although my third-dimensional mind was thoroughly imprisoned by the mental set that a valid portrait of Moses was simply out of the question, my sixth-dimensional higher self provided me with yet another miraculous demonstration of its superhuman abilities by guiding me to the sudden realization that figure 43 on page 50 of Dorothea Arnold's masterpiece *The Royal Women of Amarna*, which was incorrectly identified as Akhenaten, was actually the sculptured self-portrait of Moses, aka Thutmose the Sculptor.

I next made the decision to use three other photographs, which I had acquired in 1996 during my visit to the Egyptian Museum in Cairo: 1) the sculptured head of Pharaoh Thutmose III, which demonstrated his unmistakably Semitic nose; 2) the sculptor's model of Ay, whom I recognized as Ephraim; and 3) the classic Egyptian wall painting of Pharaoh Tutankhamun being immortalized by Pharaoh Ay.

When I then found the spectacular color photograph of Pharaoh Tutankhamun's funerary mask during a trip to the library of the nearby town of Yreka, I experienced clear guidance that it had to be included in my list of illustrations.

On 14 January 2007, I sent the following email message to my list of seventy friends around the world:
> Beloved Friends: This is the year when we shall see our beloved Planet Earth transformed from Hell on Earth to Peace on Earth, which is the essential prerequisite prior to experiencing Heaven on Earth by 2012. In Love's pure Light, All-is-one Heartsong.

After locating a sculptured portrait of Pharaoh Amenhotep III which reveals his simplicity, and selecting an unfinished sculpture of Nefertiti that confirms her beauty, I then decided to include the shrine stele and the chariot, which provide intimate glimpses of Akhenaten's family life.

Among the very last additions were the sculptured representations of Maya, the High Priest of Amun; Paramessu, the recruited assassin; and Horemheb, the Pharaoh of the Oppression.

On 20 January 2007, after completing the process of selecting the illustrations for my treatise (including a map of ancient Egypt and the Sinai Peninsula, a photograph of the Dream Stele between the paws of the Sphinx at Giza, and a symbolic portrait of the ascended master Thoth, represented as a man with the head of an ibis) I then wrote the following words in my personal journal:
"Around three o'clock this morning, I received guidance from my higher self to reverse the sequence of the last two figures so as to place the Funerary Mask of Pharaoh Tutankhamun on the back cover of the treatise.

"I then received from my higher self the following message to accompany that figure: 'How appropriate that Ephraim, the son of Joseph the Israelite, in his final role as Pharaoh Ay, chose to use the attractive power of gold to create a time capsule which would eventually reveal the hidden truth regarding the assassinations of Pharaoh Akhenaten and his family to an awakening humanity approximately 3,351 years later.

'The priceless treasure that was buried in the tomb of Pharaoh Tutankhamun circa 1344 BC (which was discovered by the archeologist Howard Carter in 1922 AD) consists in the hidden truths that now stand revealed in the unequivocal words of this humble treatise.

'It only remains to be seen which publishing company will exemplify the courage that is required to reveal these long-hidden truths to an awakening humanity.'"

Then, on the evening of 21 January 2007, I made the following entry in my journal:

"I spent the morning formulating questions to ask Archangel Gabriel (Benu) through his dedicated full-body channel Karen Cook during my next telephone session which is scheduled for 30 January 2007.

"This afternoon, I received a telephone call from Bruce Schiltz, who obviously was not able to comprehend the significance of the gift copy of my text for *The Bible's Cover-Stories Revealed*.

"I then realized that I was experiencing a state of exhaustion which caused me to take a nap from 4:30 to 8:30 p.m.

"When I woke up from my nap at 8:30 p.m., my higher self then gave me the subtitle for this amazing treatise: THE GOLDEN KEYS THAT UNLOCK HISTORY.

"At 9:00 p.m., I then received clear guidance from my higher self to contact Dr. Joann Fletcher, the English archeologist who was treated disrespectfully by Dr. Zahi Hawass in June of 2003 and again in June of 2005 after she declared on the basis of her research in February of 2003 that mummy 61072 ('the Younger Lady') is Nefertiti. (Reported in The New York Times on 13 June 2005.)"

CONTROVERSIES

Before we proceed, let us now pause for a moment to consider this particular issue in greater detail.

Around the middle of January, during the course of researching Akhenaten and Nefertiti on the Internet, I learned first about Joann Fletcher's recent controversy with Marianne Luban, an independent scholar who resided in the United States, and only then about Joann Fletcher's recent controversy with Zahi Hawass, who was Secretary-General of Egypt's Supreme Council of Antiquities.

In 1999, Marianne Luban had posted on her Internet website an article titled "Do We Have the Mummy of Nefertiti?", in which she set forth the original hypothesis that mummy 61072, known as "the Younger Lady" in King's Valley tomb number 35, might be the mummy of Queen Nefertiti.

After personally examining that mummy in June of 2002 and again in February of 2003 (as field director of a team of Egyptologists from the University of York, financed by the Discovery Channel), Dr. Joann Fletcher then issued a public announcement, dated 9 June 2003, providing strong evidence that "the Younger Lady" was indeed the mummy of Nefertiti.

Thus, for example, on 10 June 2003, the following quote was carried by BBC News: "'There is a very, very strong possibility that . . . this in fact is the great female Pharaoh Nefertiti herself', said British mummification expert Dr. Joann Fletcher, who led the expedition, which was sponsored by the Discovery Channel."

Two weeks later, the specific evidence was clearly described in the 26 June 2003 issue of the *Al-Ahram Weekly* as follows: "Apart from the similarity in physiognomy and the swan-like neck of the mummy that bears a resemblance to Nefertiti's beautiful face as immortalized in the limestone bust in Berlin, Fletcher pointed to other clues to support her hypothesis: a double-pierced earlobe, which she claims was a rare fashion statement in ancient Egypt; a shaven head, and the clear impression of the tight-fitting brow-band worn by royalty. 'Think of the tight-fitting, tall blue crown worn by Nefertiti, something that would have required a shaven head to fit properly', said Fletcher."

Further evidence consisted in a Nubian-style wig, such as was worn by royal women during Akhenaten's reign, which had been found in the tomb near mummy 61072, known as "the Younger Lady". And it only remains to note that all of this evidence which was used by Fletcher to support her announcement had already been used by Luban to generate her original hypothesis in 1999.

Because Dr. Fletcher had failed to give scholarly credit to the original hypothesis previously posted on the Internet by Marianne Luban, she soon became the target of a lawsuit that was eventually withdrawn.

However, because Dr. Fletcher had also neglected to obtain permission from the Secretary-General of Egypt's Supreme Council of Antiquities before making her public announcement on 9 June 2003, Dr. Zahi Hawass responded by first dismissing her claim on 12 June 2003, next making a variety of attempts to invalidate her evidence on 26 July 2003, then officially banning her from Egypt for failing to follow his rules, and finally questioning her sanity in a New York Times article dated 13 June 2005.

Thus, after describing the evidence with which Fletcher supported her hypothesis, the 26 June 2003 issue of the *Al-Ahram Weekly* continued: "For his part, Secretary-General of the Supreme Council of Antiquities Zahi Hawass totally refutes the idea and describes it as 'pure fiction'. He accuses Fletcher of lacking in experience as 'a new Ph. D. recipient' and told *Al-Ahram Weekly* that Fletcher's theory was not based on facts or solid evidence. Elaborating on his scepticism about the mummy being that of Nefertiti, Hawass told the *Weekly* that X-ray analysis carried out previously by himself and Egyptologist Kent Weeks indicated that it was the body of a 16-year-old girl, whereas Nefertiti is thought to have died in her 30s. He explained that 'Nefertiti was involved in the assassination of her husband's successor Smenkhkare, and was later in conflict with King Horemheb, who overthrew the monotheistic cult of his predecessor and erased all traces of it. Horemheb would never have allowed Queen Nefertiti to be buried in the Valley of the Kings', he concluded." [Note: Is Hawass projecting his guilt onto Nefertiti while confirming Smenkhkare's assassination?]

In an article titled "No Discrimination", posted on his website, Dr. Zahi Hawass wrote:
"Questions resulting from the identification by Dr. Joann Fletcher of the so-called mummy of Queen Nefertiti in the tomb of Amenhotep II in the Valley of the Kings has caused repercussions in the British press, including unjustified faultfinding with the Supreme Council of Antiquities (SCA). On 22 August 2003, The Times published an article claiming that Dr. Fletcher was a 'victim' of a sensitive issue. It continued: 'The dispute has thrown British Egyptology into turmoil, with British archeologists accusing the Egyptian government of taking revenge on Britain for occupying Egypt in the 19th century, for invading Iraq, and for refusing to give back the Rosetta Stone.'

Item 24: Dr. Joann Fletcher

Item 25: The three controversial mummies in King's Valley tomb 35.
On the left, the mummy of Queen Tiye, labeled the "Elder Lady".
In the middle, the mummy of Smenkhkare, the pubescent youth.
On the right, the mummy of Queen Nefertiti, labeled the "Younger Lady".

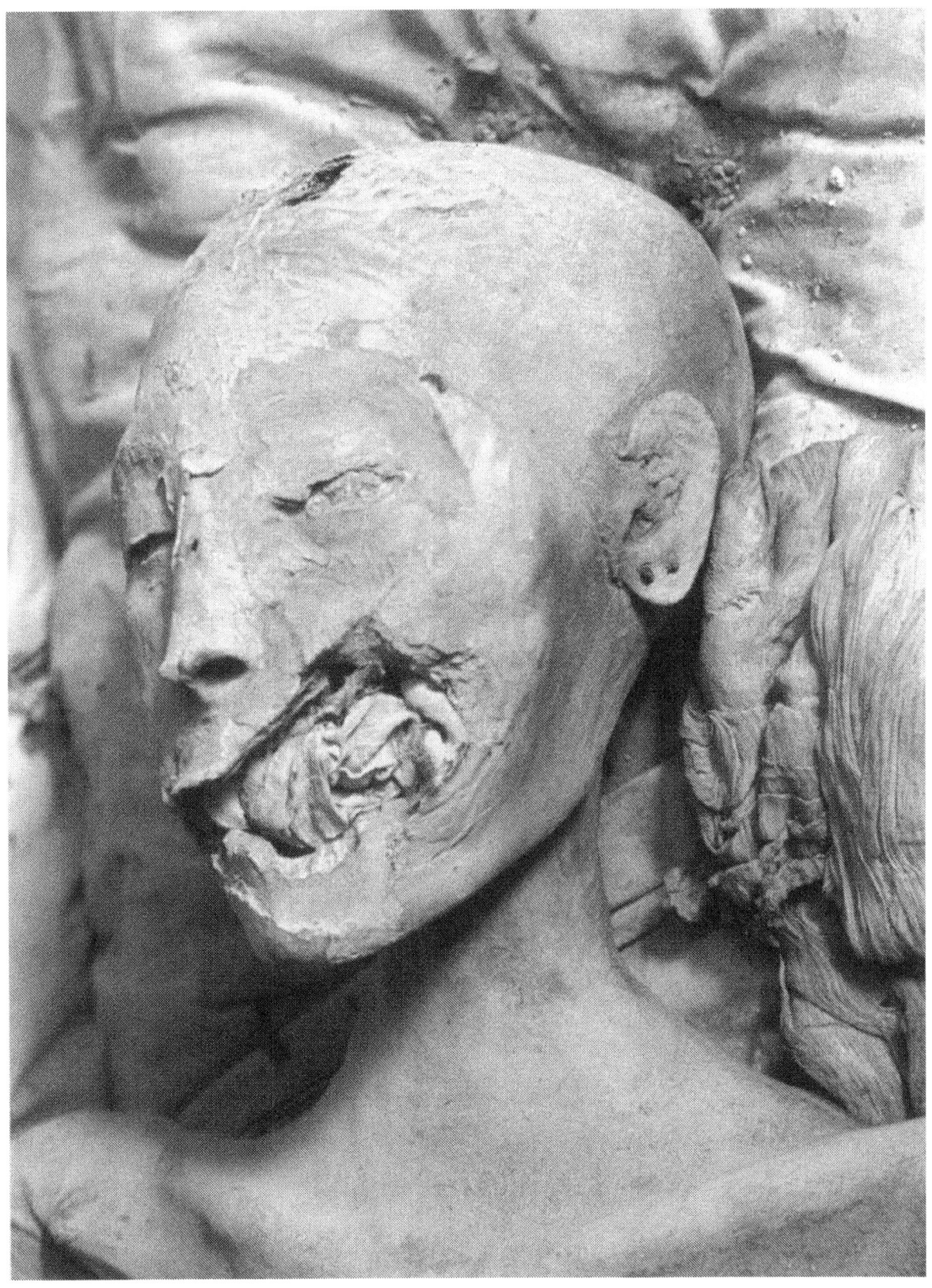

Item 26: Head of the mummy of Queen Nefertiti, revealing postmortem wound.

Item 27: Dr. Zahi Hawass

"A British Egyptologist who requested anonymity complained to The Times that the new guidelines issued by the SCA had laid restrictions which mean some people were not getting permits.

"This suggestion of discrimination is totally unjustified. There are more than 300 foreign expeditions currently working in Egypt, and they all follow the same guidelines. We grant concessions to any scholar affiliated to a scientific or educational institution, and it has long been the accepted code of ethics that any discovery made during excavations should first be reported to the SCA.

"By going first to the press with what might be considered a great discovery, Dr. Fletcher broke the bond made by York University with the Egyptian authorities. And by putting out in the popular media what is considered by most scholars to be an unsound theory, Dr. Fletcher has broken the rules and therefore, at least until we have reviewed the situation with her university, she must be banned from working in Egypt." I have written to York University asking them to clarify their position, and am waiting for a response. . .

"Joann Fletcher did not discover anything. She tried to sell herself to the world as an expert in something she knows little about. Last week I went to Luxor and entered the tomb of Amenhotep II once again, and I am now more certain than ever that this mummy cannot be Nefertiti."

It was around this time that CBC News carried the following explanation by Dr. Hawass: "I think there is no chance for Joann Fletcher to continue her research in Egypt since she did not follow the rules. She deceived the world by saying that she discovered something, and she discovered nothing."

On 14 September 2003, Dr. Hawass openly acknowledged his punitive attitude toward Dr. Fletcher by stating on the CBS program *Sixty Minutes*: "If you break a rule, you should be punished. You cannot forgive people. If you forgive people like this, it will be like a curse . . . I'm an Egyptologist for 34 years. I can smell history. I have been seeing this mummy nine times. I could not find any evidence, one single evidence to prove that she is Nefertiti."

In response to this, Dr. Fletcher stated on that same *Sixty Minutes* program: "The establishment reacted pretty much as I thought they would, as they always have done. If you're not in it, then you're not fit to have an opinion. But I've done all the hard slog, and I've got the evidence to back up my hypothesis."

Almost two years later, an article in the New York Times, dated 13 June 2005, revealed that the punitive attitude which Dr. Hawass had previously developed toward Dr. Fletcher had subsequently evolved into an insane obsession: "Dr. Hawass denounced as 'nuts' English archeologist Joann Fletcher. 'She is an amateur . . . I am now more certain than ever that this mummy cannot be Nefertiti. The mummy was not even female.'"

A careful review of the constantly changing statements by Dr. Zahi Hawass regarding the identity of mummy 61072 (commonly referred to as 'the Younger Lady') reveals that in 2002 he misidentified it as the mummy of Merytra, the primary wife of Pharaoh Thutmose III (*Hidden Treasures of the Egyptian Museum*, Zahi Hawass, American University in Cairo Press, 2002).

As we have seen, however, in the 26 June 2003 issue of the *Al-Ahram Weekly*, "Hawass told the Weekly that X-ray analysis carried out previously by himself and Egyptologist Kent Weeks indicated that it was the body of a 16-year-old-girl."

When the digital imaging which had been carried out by Dr. Fletcher's team of scientific experts in February of 2003 revealed that the "Younger Lady" mummy had been a woman between the ages of 18 and 30, Dr. Hawass then arranged for Dr. Mohamed S. Salama, a professor of molecular biology, to perform a DNA test, which purported to prove that the "Younger Lady" mummy was a male!

Fortunately, however, a professor of anatomy by the name of Sir Grafton Elliot Smith had already published conclusive proof that the "Younger Lady" mummy 61072 is female: "Both in this mummy and in the other woman (mummy 61070), the *rima pudendi* (female genitals) was widely open and plugged from the inside with linen. It takes no great knowledge of anatomy to decide that the excellently preserved naked body ... is a young woman's." (*The Royal Mummies* by G. Elliot Smith, first published in 1912 by Duckworth of London and reprinted in 2000.)

Let us now summarize the essence of what we have learned from this careful review of the controversies which have arisen between Dr. Joann Fletcher and Marianne Luban on the one hand, and between Dr. Joann Fletcher and Dr. Zahi Hawass on the other hand.

There is no mystery to the conflict that arose between Marianne Luban and Joann Fletcher, which was obviously a product of two highly gifted egos competing with one another for scholarly credit.

However, there is definitely a mystery to the conflict which arose between Dr. Zahi Hawass and Dr. Joann Fletcher, where the extreme intensity and prolonged duration of his punitive attack clearly constitutes a puzzle to be solved.

As you may recall, the Epilogue of my treatise ends with what I called my "Hide-and-go-seek Hypothesis: namely, that the souls of those darkworkers who incarnated as Paramessu, Horemheb, and Maya, the High Priest of Amun, some 3,333 years ago may quite possibly have reincarnated on Planet Earth at this particular time for the specific purpose of trying to prevent this exposé of their crimes and cover-ups by attempting to oppose the publication and dissemination of this treatise."

Because my sixth-dimensional higher self (Kumara Zora Torith) blessed my third-dimensional mind (All-is-one Heartsong) with limited access to the akashic records for one miraculous month, which began on 8 December 2006 and which took the specific form of superhuman insight into what really happened during the Eighteenth Dynasty, including the absolute knowing that the "Younger Lady" mummy 61072 is in fact the desecrated mummy of the assassinated Queen Nefertiti, I am now blessed with the absolute knowing that I have a sacred responsibility to the whole of humanity which requires me to ask myself the following unexpected question: Could it be that Dr. Zahi Hawass, the Secretary-General of Egypt's Supreme Council of

Antiquities, is a reincarnation of Maya, the High Priest of Amun, or of Paramessu, the recruited assassin, or of Horemheb, the Pharaoh of the Oppression?

Although such a question seems almost inconceivable at first glance, if Dr. Hawass were a reincarnation of one of these three accomplices in the conspiracy to cover up their crimes during the Eighteenth Dynasty, that would certainly explain his determined efforts to invalidate the documented claim of Dr. Joann Fletcher and the original hypothesis of Marianne Luban.

Once this particular question has been asked and its implications contemplated, it seems only natural to ask myself similar questions regarding Ahmed Osman and Laurence Gardner, both of whom have demonstrated a similar propensity for confusing and misleading humanity by publishing insane hypotheses that appear to have the specific purpose of covering up the truth about what really happened during the Eighteenth Dynasty.

Because of the importance of these questions and their far-reaching implications, my sixth-dimensional higher self is now asking my third-dimensional mind to record the facts that I first received guidance to prepare myself for writing this book on 15 May 2007 when I placed the initial order for printing one hundred copies of my treatise, that the guidance to begin the actual process of writing this book was received on 22 June 2007, and that the act of writing these particular questions is now taking place on 12 July 2007.

Let me say at once that my purpose in asking these questions is not to sit in judgment of these three men or to punish them for whatever transgressions they may have committed during this or previous lifetimes.

My intention is simply to discover the truth by means of which we may liberate ourselves from the vast accumulation of intentional disinformation, unintentional misinformation, and deliberate lies that have had the disastrous effect of deceiving, misleading, and subjugating humanity for thousands of years.

What is more, in discovering the truth, my intention is neither to be a hero nor to become a victim, but rather to be true to my nature as a lover of truth.

Believe it or not, my motives are as simple as that.

CONFIRMATION

My personal records reveal that, between 9 June 1997 and 30 January 2007, I had a total of sixteen one-hour telephone sessions with Archangel Gabriel Benu through his dedicated full-body channel Karen Cook, who lives in Albuquerque, New Mexico.

Perhaps I should explain that the name "Benu" is actually a nickname which means "doorway" and which is used to designate the particular portal of access to Archangel Gabriel that is available through Karen Cook.

It is also worth mentioning that the token fees which are charged by Karen Cook for this dedicated service are extremely modest, but that the waiting list is such that appointments must be made well over a year in advance of the telephone sessions.

The entries in my personal journal indicate that during the ten days between January 21 and January 30 of 2007, I was carefully preparing for my sixteenth one-hour telephone session with Gabriel by formulating a list of about fifty questions which were written out in advance on index cards.

According to one of these entries in my personal journal, I received an extraordinary message from my higher self on the morning of 22 January 2007, which took the form of the following dream: "There are twelve vast wisdom records, but the only way that access can be gained is by humbly accepting access whenever it is offered."

This extraordinary message certainly fit my experience, because it had long since become crystal-clear to me that my third-dimensional mental body is not capable of accessing the akashic records without the help of my sixth-dimensional light body and can therefore experience absolute knowing only when it occurs as a spontaneous gift from my higher self.

Needless to say, this is precisely what Jesus meant when he declared: "the Son does nothing of himself, but only what the Father shows him" (*John* 5:19).

On 23 January 2007, I received in the mail a book which I had recently ordered, titled *Akhenaten's Egypt* by Angela P. Thomas, first published by Shire Publications of England in 1988 and then reprinted in 1996.

This 60-page book, which required only three hours to read, is essentially a summary of the scholarly speculations of pioneer Egyptologists such as Arthur Weigall (1910 and 1922), Cyril Aldred (1968 and 1988), and Donald Redford (1984).

Thus, for example, whereas Aldred had argued in favor of a long co-regency between Akhenaten and his father, Pharaoh Amenhotep III, Redford had mistakenly argued against such a co-regency.

Based on a bare minimum of extremely fragmentary facts and promulgating highly speculative theories that are occasionally correct but mostly incorrect, the book ends up misrepresenting Akhenaten as "a political opportunist dogmatically and rationally imposing his will" (page 46), which "seemed to offend against the established order" (page 47).

On 24 January 2007, I researched Google for two publishing houses, Thames & Hudson of London, and W.W. Norton of New York, which previous research on the Internet had caused me to select as my prime choices.

Then, after careful consideration of the most recent scholarly books on Akhenaten, I placed orders for two books which I knew represented opposite ends of the spectrum of scholarly opinion.

At the positive end of the spectrum was *Akhenaten and the Religion of Light* (1995) by Erik Hornung, Professor Emeritus of Egyptology at the University of Basel in Switzerland, who has honored Akhenaten for his enlightened recognition that light itself constitutes the essential manifestation of the one universal creative spirit.

At the negative end of the spectrum was *Akhenaten: Egypt's False Prophet* (2001) by Nicholas Reeves, Curator of Egyptian and Classical Art at Eton College in England, who has dishonored himself by producing a classic example of pseudo-scholarship, characterized by fallacious speculations, malicious misperceptions, and slanderous defamations.

In any case, the essential point that I now wish to bring to your thoughtful attention is that not a single one of the so-called experts in the vast field of Egyptology were able to gain insight into the simple fact that what really happened toward the end of the Eighteenth Dynasty was the systematic extermination of Pharaoh Akhenaten and his extended family by a lone assassin recruited by the High Priest of Amun.

With the sole exception of the premature death of Pharaoh Tutankhamun, the typical explanation offered by Egyptologists for the mysteriously premature disappearances of Akhenaten and his numerous relatives has been a vague reference to the plagues which were supposed to have been widespread at that time.

In what follows, I will now share with you the verbatim transcript of my sixteenth session with Archangel Gabriel Benu through his dedicated channel Karen Cook, which took place between two and three o'clock on the afternoon of 30 January 2007 and which had the effect of confirming and validating all of the key facts that my higher self (Kumara Zora Torith) had channeled through my consecrated mind (All-is-one Heartsong) and that were subsequently published in my name as *The Bible's Cover Stories Revealed: The Golden Keys That Unlock History* by Arthur Earl Jones, Ph. D.

Gabriel:	Greetings
Allisone:	Greetings, Benu. This is going to be my sixteenth telephone session with you, and I have a feeling that it could turn out to be the most important session of all.
Gabriel:	Alright.
Allisone:	I again have about fifty questions to ask, which will allow us a little over a minute for each question on the average.
Gabriel:	Okay.
Allisone:	The quantum leap that you have been predicting for the past three years has finally begun to manifest in my life in a very specific and totally unexpected way during the past two months. Can you indicate whether you are aware of what I am referring to?
Gabriel:	I am very much aware of that. Yes.
Allisone:	Okay. [laughs] On 8 December 2006, I made a wholehearted decision to make myself

available as a channel for spirit, and during the next four weeks my higher self used my embodied mind to channel a very concise treatise, titled *The Bible's Cover-Stories Revealed: The Golden Keys That Unlock History.*

Gabriel: Right.

Allisone: And it's been quite an amazing and miraculous process of channeling what my outer mind would never be able to do by itself. So it's been a process of beginning to experience that I am my higher self and that my mind is just an instrument that my higher self is using.

Gabriel: Exactly.

Allisone: So it's a wonderful breakthrough, and it's the beginning of what I experience is going to become a quantum leap.

Gabriel: Good.

Allisone: Now, all three of these cover-story revelations involve radical exposés which could have far-reaching consequences, but the only parts for which I need your confirmation or clarification are the specific exposés that are contained in the second cover-story revelation. So, let me begin by assuring you that I feel so sure about the dates for the Eighteenth Dynasty of ancient Egypt that I have no need to ask you to confirm any of the dates unless you indicate that there is a particular date which needs to be revised.

Gabriel: Alright.

Allisone: In regard to the first cover-story revelation, I'll simply ask you to confirm that the ascended master Thoth arranged for Abram and Sarai to visit Egypt around 1500 BC for the specific purpose of allowing Sarai to serve as a concubine for Pharaoh Thutmose II so as to provide him with a male heir who became known as Pharaoh Thutmose III.

Gabriel: Yes, that is correct.

Allisone: Okay. I was pretty sure that was right. I just wanted to get your confirmation. It's an easy way to begin.

Gabriel: Right.

Allisone: Now, in regard to the second cover-story revelation, I'll begin by asking you to confirm that the ascended master Thoth arranged for Pharaoh Amenhotep III to marry

	Queen Tiye when they were both around seventeen, even though Amenhotep III had already married his heiress sister Sitamun in order to inherit the throne and Tiye had just given birth to an illegitimate child by the name of Aaron. Can you confirm that?
Gabriel:	Yes, I can.
Allisone:	Okay. Are you comfortable going into the details of ancient Egypt?
Gabriel:	We can. Yes.
Allisone:	Okay. [laughs] It's probably pretty easy for you.
Gabriel:	Relatively so, yes.
Allisone:	For most levels of consciousness, it would be pretty obscure. So let us now focus our attention on the second cover-story revelation, which revolves around the fact that Moses and Akhenaten were brothers, whose father was Pharaoh Amenhotep III and whose mother was Queen Tiye, the daughter of Joseph the Israelite (whose Egyptian name was Yuya) and his Egyptian wife Aseneth (whose Egyptian name was Thuya). Can you confirm that?
Gabriel:	Yes, that I can confirm.
Allisone:	Now, I seem to recall that several years ago you told me that one of my key "soul group" incarnations was Ephraim, the younger son of Joseph the Israelite, whose Egyptian name was Ay, who served as the Chief Minister of Pharaoh Akhenaten, and who eventually became the Pharaoh Ay.
Gabriel:	That's correct.
Allisone:	Can you confirm that?
Gabriel:	Yes, I can.
Allisone:	So far, so good. Now, I also seem to recall that you then told me that Pharaoh Akhenaten was assassinated and that Pharaoh Ay was also eventually assassinated, which was a subject I was not inclined to explore at that time, as I recall.
Gabriel:	That's correct.
Allisone:	Are you confirming that both were assassinated?
Gabriel:	Both were assassinated. Yes.

Allisone: That's a very important detail, because there are some sources that say Pharaoh Akhenaten was never assassinated and so forth, but I don't need to go into the alternative.

Gabriel: No. In the alternative, they are basing their idea on faulty information.

Allisone: Okay. Since all of the various sources of scholarly investigation agree that the bodies of Akhenaten and Ay were never found . . .

Gabriel: That is correct.

Allisone: . . . I would like to ask you to explain exactly what happened to their bodies after they were assassinated.

Gabriel: They were literally buried beneath another tomb. And when the archeologists were looking for them, they found the first tomb, but they did not go deeper. They were buried so deeply because it was not supposed to be known that they were assassinated.

Allisone: Yes, I understand.

Gabriel: But it was a tomb beneath a tomb.

Allisone: A tomb beneath a tomb. Okay. And that's in both cases.

Gabriel: Yes.

Allisone: Even though they were assassinated, let's see, at least ten years difference.

Gabriel: Exactly. But they are both buried within a quarter of a mile of each other.

Allisone: Do you think there's any point in you specifying under what tomb Akhenaten was buried? I don't know whether that's appropriate for me to ask.

Gabriel: Not really, but what I would tell you is that Egyptologists, whenever they are searching for things like that, they stop at the first tomb, and they never look beneath that.

Allisone: Sure.

Gabriel: And I can tell you that it is in the Valley of the Kings.

Allisone: Can you indicate whether the body of Akhenaten was left intact?

Gabriel: Yes.

Allisone: So it wasn't totally destroyed.

Gabriel: No.

Allisone: It was buried in a tomb beneath a tomb . . .

Gabriel: Exactly.

Allisone: . . . in the Valley of the Kings.

Gabriel: Right. And it was not destroyed. There was contemplation about destroying it, but they never did. They wanted to.

Allisone: Very good. Thank you very much. I appreciate.

Gabriel: You're welcome.

Allisone: When my higher self began to inform my outer mind that a whole series of assassinations were carried out for the specific purpose of exterminating every member of Akhenaten's family . . .

Gabriel: That is correct.

Allisone: . . . I didn't want to believe it at first.

Gabriel: They did, though. They really wanted to destroy any and all evidence with this one.

[Note: With these words, Archangel Gabriel has confirmed the genocidal agenda of Maya, the High Priest of Amun, and Paramessu, the recruited assassin, which decisively reversed the course of human history.]

Allisone: Yes, I understand. My higher self gradually made that very clear to me, and I . . . At first, I found it difficult to accept, but I gradually came to realize that that was . . .

Gabriel: Right.

Allisone: In fact, here is the next card that I'm going to read: Then I came to the realization that part of my mission in this lifetime is to reveal the truth about what really happened toward the end of the Eighteenth Dynasty in ancient Egypt. Can you tell me whether

	this is really part of my mission in this lifetime?
Gabriel:	This is really part of your mission. Yes. But I can also tell you the other thing that has come to light on this is that there was no embalming done whatsoever.
Allisone:	No embalming . . .
Gabriel:	No.
Allisone:	. . . on the bodies of . . .
Gabriel:	. . . of either one of them.
Allisone:	. . . of Akhenaten and . . .
Gabriel:	Right. They wanted them not to be able to enter into any kind of sanctuary at all.
Allisone:	Yes, that's obvious.
Gabriel:	And not permit them to reincarnate.
Allisone:	Right. That's clearly my understanding. Yeah.
Gabriel:	Right.
Allisone:	Now, can you confirm that Pharaoh Akhenaten's wife (Queen Nefertiti) and his mother (Queen Tiye) were both assassinated approximately three years before the assassination of Pharaoh Akhenaten himself?
Gabriel:	That is true.
Allisone:	They were both assassinated.
Gabriel:	They were both assassinated. Definitely.
Allisone:	And they were assassinated at the same time, those two?
Gabriel:	Precisely at the same time.
Allisone:	Yeah, that's what I sensed. Okay, let's go on. This is very helpful. I'm sure you realize how helpful this is to me.
Gabriel:	Yes, I do.

Allisone:	Because these are such important . . . If there's going to be a publication of this kind of information, it has to be confirmed and validated.
Gabriel:	Well, it does. Now, I will tell you that there are some Egyptologists who will argue with you on it.
Allisone:	Of course. Right. I expect that.
Gabriel:	Yeah.
Allisone:	I'm not surprised. Okay, that's not a problem. I guess I just want to pause for a moment to express how grateful I am to you for being able to confirm this kind of detailed information.
Gabriel:	Not a problem at all.
Allisone:	It's a great blessing. Can you confirm that the mummies known as "the Younger Lady" and "the Elder Lady" (which were discovered about one hundred years ago lying on the floor of King's Valley tomb number 35) are the bodies of Queen Nefertiti and Queen Tiye?
Gabriel:	That's correct.
Allisone:	I was quite sure that that was true, but having your confirmation and validation is extremely valuable.
Gabriel:	It is amazing to watch how much they wanted to discredit that.
Allisone:	Of course. I understand. I don't think we need to go into how it happened that these mummies were brought into another tomb and just left on the floor without being placed in coffins or . . .
Gabriel:	Right. Well, they were never in a sarcophagus or anything like that. But they were done deliberately like that. Even the individuals who brought them there were not told who they were.
Allisone:	Really.
Gabriel:	Yeah.
Allisone:	Okay, now can you tell me whether the severe facial wound exhibited by the mummy of Nefertiti, who is referred to by scholars as the mummy of "the Younger Lady", occurred at the time of her assassination, or whether it was something that happened

afterwards?

Gabriel: Afterwards.

Allisone: It didn't occur during the assassination.

Gabriel: No. They sought to deface the great beauty that she was so that it would make it difficult . . . If she was ever discovered, they would not know who she was.

Allisone: Mhmm. So the damage to her face was done after her death . . .

Gabriel: Yes.

Allisone: . . . and not at the time of her death.

Gabriel: No.

Allisone: Okay. Can you give me a general idea of what kind of death they suffered: whether it was, I don't know, being hit on the head or being given poison.

Gabriel: Poison.

Allisone: Poison. Okay, that seems like the more appropriate way, so to speak.

Gabriel: Well, that is how they tended to dispatch a lot of people.

Allisone: Yeah. Okay, I don't need any more details on that. Let me proceed slowly here. Can you confirm that Pharaoh Smenkhkare (who became the co-regent of Pharaoh Akhenaten after the assassination of Queen Nefertiti) was a son of Pharaoh Amenhotep III by his secondary wife Kiya and therefore a half-brother of Akhenaten?

Gabriel: That's correct.

Allisone: Okay. Now, can you tell me further whether the secondary wife Kiya of Amenhotep III, who was the mother of Smenkhkare, . . . Was Kiya Egyptian or Hebrew or foreign? Can you tell me anything about Kiya?

Gabriel: Kiya looks like she is . . . Hebrew.

Allisone: That's what I thought. I had a hunch that might be the case.

Gabriel: Hebrew. Right.

Allisone: Okay, I guess that's all I really need to know on that. Let's proceed. Can you confirm that Akhenaten's eldest daughter Queen Meritaten and her young husband Smenkhkare were assassinated just a few months after the assassination of Akhenaten?

Gabriel: That is correct.

Allisone: Okay.

Gabriel: It's actually about three months.

Allisone: That's exactly what I had in mind.

Gabriel: Right.

Allisone: It's interesting how my higher self has given me this information, which . . . I don't know . . . I trust it, but it's so helpful to have confirmation from you.

Gabriel: Good. Well, I am pleased.

Allisone: Now, let's take our time on this, and do this slowly. Can you tell me whether the mummy of the pubescent youth which was found lying on the floor between the mummies of Queen Nefertiti and Queen Tiye in King's Valley tomb number 35 is the body of the assassinated Pharaoh Smenkhkare?

Gabriel: Yes.

Allisone: Can you tell me how old he was when he was assassinated?

Gabriel: I'm looking at . . . Extremely young, actually.

Allisone: Yeah.

Gabriel: I mean I'm looking at under the age of ten.

Allisone: Really?

Gabriel: Yeah.

Allisone: Would you call that pubescent or pre-pubescent.

Gabriel: Pre.

Allisone: Prepubescent.

Gabriel: Yeah

Allisone: That's a surprise. Okay, I knew he was young.

Gabriel: Very young. But bear in thought, too, that their age was very dissimilar than what ages are nowadays.

Allisone: Yes, I sensed that.

Gabriel: And ten would be the equivalent of about eighteen years old.

Allisone: What?!

Gabriel: Yeah, aging very rapidly in those times.

Allisone: Well, that's hard to believe! [laughter]

Gabriel: Yeah, I know.

Allisone: Ten equates to . . .

Gabriel: . . . between fifteen and eighteen. Yeah.

Allisone: Well, then, how. . .

Gabriel: Now, don't forget they got married or they were promised to each other at the age of three.

Allisone: So . . . I'm glad we're taking the time to clarify this. Then, was he prepubescent or post-pubescent or fully adolescent?

Gabriel: No, not fully adolescent. He hadn't got that far.

Allisone: You said that he was prepubescent, but then you say that ten equals about eighteen.

Gabriel: Alright, but if you're looking at him and equating him to nowadays. . .

Allisone: Yeah?

Gabriel: Then, he would be pre. In his timeline, he would be pubescent.

Allisone: In his timeline, he would be pubescent.

Gabriel: Right, and moving towards being a young adult.

Allisone: I see.

Gabriel: They were required in those days to have bodies that aged very rapidly.

Allisone: I see.

Gabriel: Like your average person that nowadays would be 45 would be about the average of 65 in looks and how the body aged.

Allisone: Really.

Gabriel: Yeah. They didn't have a lot of the things that you've got nowadays.

Allisone: Oh, yeah, I understand that.

Gabriel: Yeah.

Allisone: Okay, thank you very much.

Gabriel: You're welcome.

Allisone: So, even though he was only about ten years old, he was really in the midst of adolescence.

Gabriel: Yes.

Allisone: Okay, so let me ask specifically: Could a ten-year-old produce a child?

Gabriel: Yes.

Allisone: Really!

Gabriel: Definitely. As far as the aging of that body, yes.

Allisone: Okay. That's very interesting.

Gabriel: Nowadays, could a ten-year-old produce a child? Highly unlikely.

Allisone: Of course. Right. I understand.

Gabriel: Mhmm.

Allisone: Okay, I might as well take a moment for this, which is a bit of a mystery. Can you tell me the identity of the mummy of a youth in his late adolescence, which was found (in a coffin originally made for Kiya) within King's Valley tomb number 55 (which was originally made for Queen Tiye) and which has been mistakenly identified as the body of the assassinated Pharaoh Smenkhkare? If you want me to, I can read that question again.

Gabriel: No, what I'm looking at is this mummy's identity. It was obviously not him.

Allisone: Yeah.

Gabriel: But this was actually a servant that was supposed to – how do you say this? – throw people off the track.

Allisone: It was designed to throw people off the track?

Gabriel: Yes, it was.

Allisone: So, the real Smenkhkare was the mummy between the mummies of Nefertiti and Queen Tiye?

Gabriel: That's correct.

Allisone: And this mummy, which was placed in a position that could be misperceived as Smenkhkare was designed to throw people off the track.

Gabriel: That's correct.

Allisone: Very good. That makes sense.

Gabriel: This is an individual that had some of the physical characteristics.

Allisone: Uh-huh.

Gabriel: This one was illegitimate.

Allisone: Mhmm.

Gabriel: This one was picked distinctly because of the similarity.

Allisone: Yeah. Very good. Makes sense. Thank you very much! You're so helpful.

Gabriel: Good.

Allisone: Could you tell me whether the death of Akhenaten's second daughter, Meketaten, which occurred about one year before the assassination of Queen Nefertiti, was due to natural causes rather than assassination?

Gabriel: Natural causes.

Allisone: That's what I thought. I was pretty sure that that was the case.

Gabriel: Yeah, it was natural.

Allisone: Akhenaten's second daughter died about a year before the assassinations began, and the indications were that it was somehow a natural death, and I'm glad to have your confirmation on that.

Gabriel: Yes.

Allisone: I know that there were plagues going around at that time. Do you have any indication?

Gabriel: I am looking at . . . It was one of the current . . . You would call it a plague nowadays.

Allisone: Mhmm.

Gabriel: Yeah.

Allisone: Okay. Very good. Now, let's see. Slow and sure. Tutankhamun, King Tut. . .

Gabriel: Right.

Allisone: . . . who was the younger brother of Smenkhkare, then married Akhenaten's third daughter Ankhesenamun when they were both around nine years old . . .

Gabriel: That's correct.

Allisone: . . . and reigned as Pharaoh for nine years before he died at the age of eighteen.

Gabriel: Right.

Allisone: Can you tell me whether he was assassinated?

Gabriel: Yes, he was.

Allisone: I was quite sure that that was the case, but again, it's extremely helpful to have your confirmation.

Gabriel: Yeah. No, he was definitely assassinated.

Allisone. Okay.

Gabriel: He became quite a big threat to them.

Allisone: Yeah. Okay, I'll follow through with this question: The mummy of Pharaoh Tutankhamun has a fractured first cranial vertebra and a broken leg. But a recent investigation by a group of scientists led by Dr. Zahi Hawass found no evidence of murder. Can you help me reveal the truth about how Tutankhamun died?

Gabriel: He was murdered with poison.

Allisone: He was murdered with poison.

Gabriel: But he fought them.

Allisone: Uh-huh.

Gabriel: So therefore, that's how he got the hit on the head and the broken leg.

Allisone: Mhmm.

Gabriel: Yeah. I can tell you that there is some irony in this. This Egyptologist, at the time of Tutankhamun, was one of the priests that did murder him.

Allisone: Alright.

Gabriel: He was covering up what he did.

Allisone: Yes, I understand. Okay, thank you for that. I sensed that it was something like that. Okay. Do you think he has any awareness of what he did at that time?

Gabriel: Yes. Definitely.

Allisone: He's aware of what he . . .

Gabriel: He's very much aware.

Allisone: How interesting! Okay. The plot thickens [laughter].

Gabriel:	Mhmm.
Allisone:	I regard this all as a drama, including my participation as the Pharaoh Ay. You know. It's all God at play, creating a grand drama.
Gabriel:	Right.
Allisone:	And I'm not in judgment of any of it.
Gabriel:	No, because now, you've already passed through it. You're just viewing it as odd.
Allisone:	And the real purpose of all this is to help humanity wake up . . .
Gabriel:	Right.
Allisone:	. . . by uncovering the truth.
Gabriel:	Correct.
Allisone:	The love of truth is what is my motivation.
Gabriel:	Right.
Allisone:	It's as simple as that. Okay, now, after the death of Pharaoh Tutankhamun, his Chief Minister Ay (whose Hebrew name was Ephraim and who was about 62) married Queen Ankhesenamun (who was about 18) even though she was his own granddaughter, in order to become Pharaoh Ay.
Gabriel:	Right.
Allisone:	In order to become Pharaoh, the Chief Minister Ay had to marry his own granddaughter, which is quite curious.
Gabriel:	That is correct.
Allisone:	Can you tell me what happened to Queen Ankhesenamun after Pharaoh Ay was assassinated four years later?
Gabriel:	She was also assassinated.
Allisone:	Okay, that's all I need to know. And poison was the regular pattern.
Gabriel:	Yes, definitely.

Allisone: Okay.

Gabriel: They had developed a poison that was not detectable . . .

Allisone: I see.

Gabriel: . . . and would leave the body right after death.

Allisone: Wow!

Gabriel. You have the equivalent now, in your time.

Allisone: Yeah. Okay, we're just about halfway through, and I'm right on schedule. Is it true that the systematic assassinations of Pharaoh Akhenaten and his entire family were authorized and arranged by the High Priest of the Egyptian priesthood?

Gabriel: Yes.

Allisone: It had to be. I mean, any one assassination could be explained in another way, but a systematic assassination of the whole family requires that the High Priest of the Egyptian priesthood know.

Gabriel: They knew about all of it, and they were very, very systematic on that.

Allisone: Yeah.

Gabriel: They wanted not a scrap of that family to survive.

Allisone: That was very clear to me in my consciousness, and again I thank you for confirming that. Now, I'm going to try to get more specific at this point. Is it true that the assassinations of Queen Nefertiti and Queen Tiye were carried out by a young army officer who had been recruited by the High Priest of the Egyptian priesthood for this specific purpose?

Gabriel: Yes.

Allisone: Thank you for that confirmation. Is it true that the subsequent assassination of Pharaoh Akhenaten was also ordered by the High Priest of the Egyptian priesthood and carried out by the same young army officer?

Gabriel: Yes.

Allisone: Now, is it true that the name of the assassin is Paramessu, who eventually came to

	be known as Pharaoh Ramesses?
Gabriel:	Yes.
Allisone:	Can you confirm that?
Gabriel:	Yes, I can.
Allisone:	Thank you so much. [laughs] My higher self was telling me this, but – I don't know – I just needed some confirmation.
Gabriel:	Right.
Allisone:	It's so potentially loaded as far as current scholarship goes. Especially when the current head of the Egyptian scholars is trying to cover up.
Gabriel:	Yes, well, they're trying very much to cover up, because otherwise it puts what they would call a blot on the history of Egypt.
Allisone:	Exactly. And of course I'm not in judgment, and I have no desire to stir up trouble, but my higher self has made very clear to me that it is time for the truth to be revealed.
Gabriel:	Right.
Allisone:	So, I'm so grateful to you. Okay, would you please be so kind as to tell me whether it is appropriate for me to reveal the specific name of this key assassin as a means of facilitating the awakening of humanity at this pivotal point in human history?
Gabriel:	I would say yes.
Allisone:	Thank you much. I'm just grateful, beyond all words to express, to have this confirmation.
Gabriel:	Right. But put a flak jacket on.
Allisone:	Say that again?
Gabriel:	Put a flak jacket on.
Allisone:	[laughs] In other words, be prepared for a lot of controversy.
Gabriel:	You're right.

Allisone: I'm going to write that down: "Put a flak jacket on." [laughter]

Gabriel: Because they will attempt to discredit you.

Allisone: Okay, I'll be prepared. Thank you for that. Okay, let's see. Can you tell me whether the assassination of Pharaoh Akhenaten was also authorized by General Horemheb, who authorized the assassination of Pharaoh Ay thirteen years later? I think Horemheb was a general by the time Akhenaten was assassinated.

Gabriel: Yes, he was. He had a lot of ambition, but he was not apprised of this until after the fact.

Allisone: So Horemheb was not in a position to authorize it before Akhenaten was assassinated.

Gabriel. No, no.

Allisone: But he did become informed about it afterwards.

Gabriel: Afterwards, yes.

Allisone: Yeah. In the case of Pharaoh Ay, who was immediately succeeded by Horemheb, it seems virtually certain that General Horemheb authorized the assassination of Pharaoh Ay.

Gabriel: Right.

Allisone: And was it the same High Priest of the Egyptian priesthood that had ordered it?

Gabriel: Yeah, go all the way back to the top again. Right.

Allisone: Yeah. Okay.

Gabriel: And all were intimidated by this individual.

Allisone: By which individual?

Gabriel: By the priest.

Allisone: I see. Everyone was . . .

Gabriel: Everyone was under this one's control.

Allisone:	Would there be any purpose for me to know the name of the High Priest who authorized all of this?
Gabriel:	If you dig deeper into it, you will find the name of this one.
Allisone:	Yes?
Gabriel:	I will make sure of it. Yes.
Allisone:	Okay, I know that eventually Paramessu became Pharaoh Ramesses, and at that point he was the High Priest of the Egyptian priesthood.
Gabriel:	Right. Because he had the original High Priest murdered.

[Note: My working hypothesis is that Archangel Gabriel Benu was here confusing Paramessu's act of murdering the High Priest with Horemheb's decision to murder the High Priest.]

Allisone:	Really!
Gabriel:	Yep.
Allisone:	Paramessu had the original High Priest murdered?
Gabriel:	Right.
Allisone:	Are you sure?
Gabriel:	I am positive.
Allisone:	[laughs]
Gabriel:	Now, it looked like a natural death.
Allisone:	For heaven's sake!
Gabriel:	Yeah.
Allisone:	This is . . .
Gabriel:	This is almost like an Egyptian soap opera.
Allisone:	That's exactly what I was thinking [laughs]. Oh, my God! Okay, I'm going to just pause for a moment to get this written down.

Gabriel: Alright. Now, he was not the one who ordered the murder of the High Priest.

Allisone: No?

Gabriel: So that was Horemheb.

Allisone: I see. Okay.

Gabriel: We have a lot of individuals in this drama . . .

Allisone: Of course.

Gabriel: . . . that have little or low regard for each other.

Allisone: I understand.

Gabriel: And to have somebody assassinated in those days was nothing.

Allisone: Really?

Gabriel: Yeah.

Allisone: Gosh.

Gabriel: Except self-promotion. A lot of greed.

Allisone: The implication is that the priesthood had severely degenerated morally. There was a moral degeneration. Because you would think that the priests would be reluctant to engage in assassination.

Gabriel: No, not reluctant, because they considered what they were doing was to protect the gods.

Allisone: I see. I get the picture.

Gabriel: Right.

Allisone: Okay. Oh, my God! So Horemheb ordered the death of the High Priest . . .

Gabriel: Right.

Allisone: . . . who had ordered all the other assassinations.

Gabriel: Right, because of his corruption. He felt that what he was doing was putting it back into divine balance.

Allisone: And by eliminating the High Priest, it would intimidate people and prevent the truth from coming out.

Gabriel: Exactly.

Allisone: So Horemheb was a great cover-upper! [laughs]

Gabriel: He was very good at that.

Allisone: [laughs] Okay, can you tell me whether Horemheb and Paramessu had already become friends by the time that Akhenaten was assassinated?

Gabriel: Yes.

Allisone: They knew each other.

Gabriel: Right. They didn't trust each other, but they knew each other.

Allisone: Okay. Knew but didn't trust. Eventually, of course, Horemheb invited Paramessu to become his heir apparent and successor.

Gabriel: Exactly.

Allisone: But that happened very gradually as they gradually came to trust each other.

Gabriel: Right.

Allisone: Okay. Let's see.

Gabriel: Well, actually they didn't even begin to trust each other. That was the only likely candidate!

Allisone: [laughs] Right. I understand.

Gabriel: Yeah.

Allisone: Yeah. In other words, they both knew the truth, and that brought them together.

Gabriel: Right. Partners in crime, so to speak.

Allisone: Partners in crime. That's it! I understand. Okay. So they kind of depended on each other.

Gabriel: Right. They never turned their back on each other, but they followed the philosophy of "Keep your enemies close."

Allisone: Yep. Okay. Oh, my goodness. What a plot!

Gabriel: Right.

Allisone: Amazing! It's even beyond what I had imagined. Okay. Next question. Is it true that Pharaoh Horemheb assigned Paramessu the job of chief taskmaster to subjugate and enslave the Israelites?

Gabriel: Yes.

Allisone: So, after Horemheb had Ay assassinated . . . I guess I might as well check that out. Was it Paramessu who again was the primary assassin of Pharaoh Ay?

Gabriel: Yes.

Allisone: So, Paramessu was the key.

Gabriel: He was the key in many of those things.

Allisone: Yeah. And after Ay was assassinated and Horemheb became the Pharaoh, then Horemheb assigned Paramessu the job of chief taskmaster in subjugating and enslaving the Israelites.

Gabriel: Exactly.

Allisone: Okay. Now, can you tell me whether it was Pharaoh Horemheb who arranged for Paramessu to join the Egyptian priesthood, where he eventually became the High Priest, and Primate in charge of all Egyptian temples?

Gabriel: Yes.

Allisone: Is that true?

Gabriel: That is true.

Allisone: Okay. It's amazing how I seem to know all of this from my higher self, and you're just confirming it. It's almost too good to be true.

Gabriel:	No, it's just the fact that your higher self – if you call it that – removes itself from the emotional drama.
Allisone:	Of course! Completely!
Gabriel:	And it's like looking at a video, as it were.
Allisone:	Of course. I understand. Well, actually, what I'm experiencing is . . . I'm actually experiencing awe that my sixth-dimensional higher self could transmit this information so accurately to my outer mind, so that this session is basically just you confirming again and again and again what I already knew from my higher self . . .
Gabriel:	Right.
Allisone:	. . . but hesitated to take on the scholars without having some kind of confirmation.
Gabriel:	Correct.
Allisone:	Okay. Okay. We understand. Now, let's see. Where are we? Okay, we're doing fine. Is it true that the Egyptian Pharaoh who was confronted by Moses and his half-brother Aaron at the time of the exodus of the Israelites from Egypt was the Pharaoh Ramesses who was formerly known as Paramessu?
Gabriel:	Yes.
Allisone:	Can you indicate approximately how old he was at that time?
Gabriel:	Hmm.
Allisone:	I know that Moses was eighty, and the question is how old was Paramessu (who became Pharaoh Ramesses) at the time of that encounter with Moses?
Gabriel:	There was not much of an age difference in them, but I'm looking at this one being about ten years younger.
Allisone:	Yeah, I'd say that fits. About seventy.
Gabriel:	Yeah.
Allisone:	About ten years younger. Excellent! Okay. Whew! Let's see. Okay. Next question. Did the son of Pharaoh Ramesses (whose name was Seti) lead the Egyptian army which pursued the Israelites during their exodus from Egypt?

Gabriel: Yes. Reluctantly, though. No, it's reluctantly.

Allisone: Yeah, it had to be his son Seti, because he was too old.

Gabriel: Well, he was too old. But Seti really didn't believe in it.

Allisone: I see. I can understand that.

Gabriel: Yeah, Seti was much more of a peacemaker.

Allisone: Yeah. Now, could you tell me the essence of what happened that allowed the Israelites to escape from the pursuing Egyptian army? Was there an actual parting of the Red Sea?

Gabriel: There literally was. Yes.

Allisone: It was a miraculous thing.

Gabriel: A miraculous thing.

Allisone: It wasn't just crossing the marshlands at the north end of . . .

Gabriel: No. No, it was a parting. I mean it wasn't a Cecil B. DeMille parting, but it was a parting.

Allisone: [laughs] So it was a genuine miracle.

Gabriel: Yes, it was.

Allisone: Moses was really aligned to . . .

Gabriel: . . . to Prime Source.

Allisone: . . . to Prime Source.

Gabriel: Definitely. Awesome individual!

Allisone: Yeah.

Gabriel: And his faith was that strong.

Allisone: That's wonderful. I'm deeply moved by this. I'm sure you understand how I feel about that.

Gabriel: Yes.

Allisone: Okay, now let me read this card. It is a well-established fact that Queen Tiye had a daughter whose Egyptian name was Beketaten. Can you confirm that Beketaten's Hebrew name was Miriam?

Gabriel: Yes.

Allisone: And can you indicate whether Miriam was older or younger than her brother Moses?

Gabriel: Younger.

Allisone: Younger! You're quite sure?

Gabriel: I'm quite sure.

Allisone: Because, in the cover-story, the cover-story indicated that the sister who observed Moses in the – you know – being taken into the palace . . .

Gabriel: Right.

Allisone: . . . was an older sister. And that established in my mind the idea that Moses' sister was older than him.

Gabriel: Moses had two sisters.

Allisone: Okay.

Gabriel: The older one did observe. The younger one did as well. But Miriam is the younger one.

[Note: My working hypothesis is that Archangel Gabriel Benu was here talking as if the older Miriam in the myth and the younger Miriam in history both existed, the implication being that, when viewed from Gabriel's perspective, both were creations of the human imagination.]

Allisone: Miriam was the younger.

Gabriel: Right. Exactly.

Allisone: Can you indicate roughly about how many years younger Miriam was from Moses?

Gabriel: Only about one.

Allisone: Oh, just slightly younger.

Gabriel: Yeah. It's slight. It's not big.

Allisone: Oh, okay. Miriam was about a year younger.

Gabriel: About a year younger, and very chatty.

Allisone: Very what?

Gabriel: Chatty and very nosey.

Allisone: Chatty and nosey. [laughs]

Gabriel: Right. Well, she observed these things and went around telling everybody.

Allisone: [laughs] Okay. Now this is a particularly important question, so what I'm going to do is read this card. You may already have the answer, because I've learned never to underestimate you in your level of awareness. But let me read the card and then explain the options, and then you can tell me.

Gabriel: Alright.

Allisone: Okay, here's what I put on the card. In the illustrated book *The Royal Women of Amarna*, can you tell me whether the sculptured face which is labeled "Akhenaten" in Figures 43 and 50 is actually the face of Akhenaten's brother Moses . . .?

Gabriel: Right.

Allisone: . . .who was at that time called Thutmose the Sculptor?

Gabriel: Correct.

Allisone: Are you telling me that you know that that . . .

Gabriel: I know exactly who that is. Yes, and it is not Akhenaten.

Allisone: That's what I . . .I was quite sure that . . . Intuitively, I knew that it was not Akhenaten. I'm looking at it at this moment, and this sculptured face is very similar to the face of Queen Tiye.

Gabriel: Right.

Allisone: And there were only three possibilities. It could be Akhenaten, but I intuitively felt that it wasn't.

Gabriel: No, it was not.

Allisone: So it would have to be either Huya (also known as Manasseh, the brother of Queen Tiye) or it would have to be Moses (also known as Thutmose the Sculptor).

Gabriel: No, it was the sculptor, although he did do a bust of the other one.

Allisone: He did do a bust of Huya or Manasseh?

Gabriel: Yes, Huya. Yeah. They looked very similar because they had similar features.

Allisone: This is so important historically that I have to double-check this. My understanding is that you are in a position to know what this image looks like that I'm looking at at this moment – this sculptured head.

Gabriel: Correct.

Allisone: And you can confirm that we actually have a likeness of Moses?

Gabriel: Yes. Not a perfect likeness, but a likeness of Moses, yes.

Allisone: This is a very rough sculpture.

Gabriel: It's very rough, because he didn't want to sit for it.

Allisone: [laughs] He was in charge of this workshop of sculptors.

Gabriel: Right.

Allisone: Let me ask specifically . . . He became known as Thutmose the Sculptor in history.

Gabriel: Right.

Allisone: I mean scholars refer to this sculptor as Thutmose the Sculptor. Did Moses actually do sculpting in those early years.

Gabriel: Yes, he did. He was quite good at it.

Allisone: That's my sense. Gosh, we actually have an image of Moses! . . .

Gabriel: You do.

Allisone: . . . that has been misidentified as Akhenaten in this book.

Gabriel: That's correct.

Allisone: Well, that's major! I mean, I recognize that that's really a major revelation!

Gabriel: Right.

Allisone: Wow! I mean – I don't know – I'm amazed! Again, intuitively I sensed this, but I couldn't believe it. I said: "I can't assume that this is true. . ."

Gabriel: No, but it is quite true.

Allisone: ". . . I've got to get Gabriel to confirm this." [laughs]

Gabriel: Yes.

Allisone: I'm amazed. I'm amazed and impressed and overwhelmed, actually. Okay. Well, that's quite a revelation. I mean, that's major.

Gabriel: Yes, it is.

Allisone: That's going to really get a lot of attention.

Gabriel: Yes, it will

Allisone: Okay. Is it true that Akhenaten was an incarnation of a highly evolved soul from Sirius, which required special DNA coding that was arranged by the ascended master Thoth as an experiment?

Gabriel: Yes, but he wasn't from Sirius. He was Pleiadian.

Allisone: Say that again?

Gabriel: He's not Sirian. He's Pleiadian.

Allisone: Really!

Gabriel: Yes.

Allisone: Where did I get the idea that it was Sirius? You know best.

Gabriel: Yes.

Allisone: [laughs] It's a Pleiadian soul.

Gabriel: Yes, it is. Well, it's a Pleiadian countenance, if you look at it.

Allisone: Say that again?

Gabriel: Pleiadian countenance. But souls are all from Prime Source, of course.

Allisone: Oh, of course. Pleiadian . . . How did you express that?

Gabriel: Countenance.

Allisone: Say that again. I still don't get it.

[Note: Gabriel was pronouncing "countenance" so that it sounded like "continence".]

Gabriel: Pleiadian countenance. The outer is Pleiadian.

Allisone: Oh, the countenance.

Gabriel: Yes.

Allisone: Pleiadian countenance.

Gabriel: Correct.

Allisone: Did it . . . Let me see if I can formulate a question here. I don't have this on the card. Was the unusual physiological structure of Akhenaten's body a normal Pleiadian structure?

Gabriel: No. It had to do with the Earth's atmosphere at the time . . .

Allisone: Uh-huh.

Gabriel: . . . and the fact that the body had a difficult time adjusting to that.

Allisone: Yeah, I can imagine.

Gabriel: And then, if you look throughout the Egyptian history . . .

Allisone: Uh-huh.

Gabriel: . . . that, whenever somebody went out of favor, they tended to distort features.

Allisone: I see.

Gabriel: The same way they did with Cleopatra.

Allisone: Umm.

Gabriel: Her brother was extremely jealous of her, and so he had her looking like a cow. And it wasn't to represent Hathor.

Allisone: I see. Oh, my goodness. Let's see. Are the representations of Akhenaten's body at the time a reasonably accurate portrayal? You know, very wide hips and . . .

Gabriel: But not excessively so.

Allisone: Not excessively so.

Gabriel: No.

Allisone: So, it's not that there was any abnormal illness. It wasn't a hormonal or endocrine disorder.

Gabriel: No.

Allisone: It was just the effect on the body with this special DNA coding.

Gabriel: That's correct.

Allisone: And can we say that the ascended master Thoth arranged this as an experiment?

Gabriel: Yes.

Allisone: Yeah. Okay. I guess that's enough. That's amazing. Thank you for that.

Gabriel: Because he was actually quite an attractive individual.

Allisone: Oh, the face is beautiful!

Gabriel: Oh, yes.

Allisone: When I saw the sculptured head of Akhenaten in the museum of what used to be Thebes . . . What is the name of that town in Egypt that used to be Thebes? It doesn't

	matter.
Gabriel:	Right.
Allisone:	Anyway, when I saw that sculptured head in that museum – the sculptured head of Akhenaten – without knowing, at the time, that I had any connection . . .
Gabriel:	Right.
Allisone:	. . . I fell in love with Akhenaten! I mean, it was a beautiful face!
Gabriel:	Well, the entity is extraordinary.
Allisone:	Absolutely. Yeah. I mean, I sensed it. I could see it, and I could feel it! And I guess I began to remember at that point.
Gabriel:	You did.
Allisone:	Because I . . . now I understand that . . . I wanted to ask you for confirmation. Ay was a group soul situation. In other words, it wasn't an individual incarnation.
Gabriel:	No, not with that one.
Allisone:	I was participating in a soul group . . .
Gabriel:	Right.
Allisone:	. . . in that incarnation.
Gabriel:	That's correct.
Allisone:	And that group soul served as the Chief Minister for Akhenaten, so that in that sense I, participating in the incarnation of Ay, had a very close . . . I was basically functioning like an uncle to Akhenaten, and was very close to him and able to observe his . . . whew! I feel like there was a profound love-bond.
Gabriel:	There was. Completely! Very loving and supportive, both ways.
Allisone:	Yeah. I guess I should ask for confirmation . . . Was this experiment that was carried out by the ascended master Thoth, bringing in a Pleiadian soul with special DNA coding . . Was Akhenaten basically demonstrating Christ Consciousness?
Gabriel:	Yes. That's why you're all so attracted to him.

Allisone: And that's also why most of the people could not comprehend him.

Gabriel: Right.

Allisone: They couldn't understand what he was.

Gabriel: No. He was representing the One God, which intimidated all.

Allisone: And he wasn't acting like the usual warrior-pharaoh.

Gabriel: No, not at all.

Allisone: He was . . .

Gabriel: . . . very loving and very kind.

Allisone: Yeah. So he was way ahead of his time, so to speak.

Gabriel: Well, he was! And that's what disturbed the priests, as well.

Allisone: Of course.

Gabriel: It scared them, because they would be out of jobs.

Allisone: They were very threatened, obviously.

Gabriel: Yeah.

Allisone: Okay. Next question. Okay. In regard to the third cover-story revelation, is it true that the Essenes evolved from an esoteric faction of enlightened Israelites led by Moses, who worshiped Creator-Source using the name "I AM that I AM", and that the Pharisees evolved from an exoteric faction of unenlightened Israelites led by Aaron, who worshiped an imposter god using the name "Yahweh" or "Jehovah"...

Gabriel: Correct.

Allisone: . . . who was punitive and judgmental rather than loving and forgiving?

Gabriel: Exactly!

Allisone: So there was a division of the Israelites into . . .

Gabriel: Definitely.

Allisone: ... into an esoteric faction led by Moses and an exoteric faction led by Aaron.

Gabriel: Exactly. But now you can take the Essenes all the way back to the Gnostics, and you can take it all the way back even further than that. But yes, they were warring factions.

Allisone: Mhmm.

Gabriel: But you've got Yahweh and Jehovah, that were warlords.

Allisone: Sure. Understood. Okay. Okay, thank you for the confirmation.

Gabriel: You're welcome.

Allisone: Let's proceed. Does my higher self (Kumara Zora Torith) want this treatise *(The Bible's Cover-Stories Revealed)* to be published in a way that will facilitate the global awakening of humanity?

Gabriel: Yes.

Allisone: Is it appropriate for you to assist me in finding the right publishing company for this purpose?

Gabriel: I can, once I get permission from Prime Source. Yes.

Allisone: Okay, I ask for your assistance, and I trust that you will provide it in the appropriate way . . .

Gabriel: Right.

Allisone: . . . at the appropriate time. For now, I'll just ask . . . I've done some preliminary research, so I'll ask this question. Can you tell me whether one of these two publishing companies is the right choice: one is Thames & Hudson in London, and the other is W. W. Norton in New York.

Gabriel: The one in London. There's more energy.

Allisone: Yeah. Thames & Hudson in London seems to be the top-of-the-line publishing company . . . and would be first choice.

Gabriel: Right.

Allisone: And they seem to have a working relationship with Norton in New York, which seems to be second choice.

Gabriel: Yes, they do.

Allisone: So let me ask you this question. Should I send a book proposal to both publishers simultaneously, or should I just focus on Thames & Hudson?

Gabriel: Focus on Thames & Hudson.

Allisone: And not send to both at the same time.

Gabriel: Right.

Allisone: Okay. Thank you very much for that. That's extremely helpful. Can you tell me whether there is any other publishing company that you would recommend?

Gabriel: That would be the first one. But then, when you submit it, use your doctor name.

Allisone: Yeah, that's what I'm getting to.

Gabriel: Yeah.

Allisone: Okay. Let's see. I guess . . . Wait a minute. Let's see, where is that? I'm coming to that. Okay, let me ask you this question first. Should I contact a man by the name of David Lorton, who lives in Baltimore, Maryland, and who translated a book by Professor Erik Hornung titled *Akhenaten and the Religion of Light* from German into English? Wouldn't it be helpful for me to contact this translator, who had a relationship with Professor Erik Hornung?

Gabriel: No.

Allisone: There's no point in getting his advice?

Gabriel: No.

Allisone: Okay, I'll just skip that. Now, is it appropriate for this treatise to state that the information which it contains comes from my higher self and has been confirmed by Archangel Gabriel through his dedicated full-body channel Karen Cook?

Gabriel: No, basically because you want it to be accepted by academia and you want to stir their pot. If you bring in too much metaphysics, then it becomes threatening to a lot of other individuals. So what you want is: under your name . . .

Allisone: Mhmm.

Gabriel: . . . and that it comes from deep meditation and deep contemplations with higher self.

Allisone: Yeah. Okay.

Gabriel: Since most people tend to equate me with the Catholic Church.

Allisone: [laughter] That hadn't occurred to me. [laughs]

Gabriel: Yes. And they're thinking, "He's talking to a saint", or something like that, which is . . .No.

Allisone: I guess there's a part of me that feels that if I said, "This is all confirmed by Archangel Gabriel", it would avoid a lot of unnecessary controversy. But I guess we have to go through the controversy?

Gabriel: Yep. You do.

Allisone: [laughs] And I can't depend on you to protect me. [laughs]

Gabriel: Well, I will do my utmost to do that.

Allisone: Okay. This comes down to . . .We're now down to this key question. Should the dedication of this treatise be signed:

> Kumara Zora Torith, the higher self of
> All-is-one Heartsong, the consecrated mind of
> Arthur Earl Jones, Ph. D.?

Gabriel: Yes.

Allisone: So it's referring to the multidimensional nature of the whole thing.

Gabriel: Exactly.

Allisone: But including Arthur Earl Jones, Ph. D.

Gabriel: Right.

Allisone: Okay. That was about signing the dedication on the first page. Now, closely related to that is this question. Should the treatise be published in the name of 1) All-is-one Heartsong, 2) Allisone Heartsong, Ph. D., or 3) Arthur Earl Jones, Ph. D?

Gabriel: Arthur Earl Jones, Ph. D.

Allisone: You're sure?

Gabriel: Yep.

Allisone: You understand that, from my point of view, Arthur Earl Jones, Ph. D. is [sigh] just a name for this body; and, except for signing checks, I haven't used that name Arthur Earl Jones Ph. D., for about twenty years!

Gabriel: Right, but what it does is it lends credibility to what you have written.

Allisone: Okay, I understand.

Gabriel: Yeah.

Allisone: You're the expert on this. [laughs] I bow to your wisdom.

Gabriel: No.

Allisone: You know, I stopped publishing things in the name of Arthur Earl Jones twenty years ago.

Gabriel: Right.

Allisone: And everything that I've done on my website for the past many years has been All-is-one Heartsong.

Gabriel: Right.

Allisone: But you're telling me . . .

Gabriel: I'm telling you for the people that you want to reach with this.

Allisone: Yeah? . . . that it has to be Arthur Earl Jones, Ph. D.?

Gabriel: Yep.

Allisone: Okay. I accept. [laughs]

Gabriel: Good.

Allisone: I accept your wisdom.

Gabriel:	Good.
Allisone:	I'm very grateful. Okay, let's see, we've got . . . Oh, just about one minute!
Gabriel:	Right.
Allisone:	Please rate the present condition of my physical body on a scale of one to ten, and then give me a detailed assessment of any problems that may be affecting the health of my body at this time.
Gabriel:	About an eight.
Allisone:	About an eight.
Gabriel:	That's not bad, considering the maturity of the body.
Allisone:	Mhmm. Yeah.
Gabriel:	Arthritis. The pH is much better than it was last time.
Allisone:	Yeah, I'm drinking lemon and lime every day.
Gabriel:	Good.
Allisone:	And I notice the kind of stiffness in the neck and the spine occasionally.
Gabriel:	Right.
Allisone:	Let me ask you this: Is it okay for me to include honey in my diet?
Gabriel:	Yes, it is. As long as it's from the area in which you reside, yes.
Allisone:	Yeah, okay. And I'll try to keep the honey minimal rather than maximal.
Gabriel:	There you go.
Allisone:	And the prostate and kidneys and liver are okay?
Gabriel:	They're all okay. Prostate is a little enlarged but not a big problem.

[Note: At this point, I asked one question for a friend regarding his health-related condition.]

Allisone:	Okay. During my last session, you predicted that I will meet my fourth twin-flame

soulmate in the spring of 2007, which is . . .

Gabriel: Right . . . which is coming up.

Allisone: Can you tell me what the purpose of this encounter is, when viewed from the perspective of my life plan?

Gabriel: Further growth.

Allisone: Further growth.

Gabriel: Right. And we're out of time.

Allisone: Okay, we're out of time. I have one more question, but I will release it and express my heartfelt gratitude for your wonderful assistance in this project.

Gabriel: I always enjoy helping you.

Allisone: My love and blessings.

Gabriel: To you as well.

Allisone: Namaste.

REFINEMENT

Suffice it to say that on the evening of 30 January 2007, I felt a combination of profound gratitude to Archangel Gabriel for confirming virtually all of the information that my higher self had channeled through my consecrated mind, plus profound relief as I gradually came to the realization that I could now publish this apocalyptic revelation with total confidence in its validity.

On 31 January 2007, while reading *Akhenaten and the Religion of Light* by Erik Hornung, whose scholarly book is a challenging mixture of valid insights and invalid misperceptions which I welcomed as a useful exercise in discernment, I experienced momentary confusion when I read the following words on page 118: ". . .the high priest Parennefer presided over the renewal of the cult of Amun at Karnak."

I knew that "Parennefer" was the name of Akhenaten's loyal pedagogue and butler, and I also knew that "Maya" was the name of the High Priest of Amun who had been disciplined when he dared to challenge Akhenaten's revolutionary decree that henceforth the unenlightened polytheistic worship of anthropomorphic gods was to be replaced with the enlightened worship of One Universal Creator.

During the next few days, as I contemplated the idea that Maya might have been replaced as High Priest of Amun by another man with the name of Parennefer, it became increasingly clear to me in my feelings that this was not the case, and I gradually arrived at the realization that Maya had simply adopted the name "Parennefer" as an alias at some point in an attempt to disguise his identity.

On the afternoon of the first day of February, I formulated the diagram of Hebrew-Egyptian lineages, during the course of which I received clear guidance to use red ink for Egyptians, blue ink for Hebrews, and green ink for Hebrew-Egyptian hybrids.

Then, in the middle of the night, between two and four o'clock on the morning of 2 February 2007, I received specific guidance from my higher self to conclude the treatise with an epilogue containing what I call my "Hide-and-go-seek Hypothesis": namely, that the souls of Paramessu, Horemheb, and Maya, alias "Parennefer", the High Priest of Amun, may quite possibly have reincarnated as darkworkers during this current pivotal point in human history for the specific purpose of attempting to prevent the revelation of their crimes and coverups during that previous pivotal point in human history.

At the very same time, I also experienced the absolute knowing that Kiya, the secondary wife of Pharaoh Amenhotep III and the mother of Smenkhkare and Tutankhamun, was the daughter of Manasseh (Huya), the elder son of Joseph the Israelite (Yuya).

When I then made the decision to trust this intuitive revelation, my higher self responded by inviting my consecrated mind to celebrate the occasion with a tea party in the middle of the night.

On 3 February 2007, as a direct consequence of the clarifications that I had received during my recent telephone session with Archangel Gabriel Benu, I received further guidance from my higher self in the specific form of over a dozen refinements for the text of my treatise; and I spent the whole day carrying out these miraculous instructions with an attitude of gratitude that involved the total surrender of my outer mind to my inner being, which was now coming forth to demonstrate its presence in my life as my true self.

Here is the report that I wrote in my personal journal on the evening of 7 February 2007:
"I have been working continuously since my session with Archangel Gabriel through Karen Cook on 30 January 2007 to bring the channeled treatise (*The Bible's Cover-Stories Revealed: The Golden Keys That Unlock History*) to completion.
"My humble mind is in absolute awe regarding the miraculous way in which my higher self is using it to add the final refinements that embellish and polish the whole.
"This morning after getting the semifinal version from my friend Zepp (an expert word processor and political commentator whose website is zeppscommentaries.com), I worked very intensively all day to do the final proofreading and to make the final corrections.
"I then got into bed to rest this evening, and celebrated by listening to my CD of David Oistrakh's performance of Prokofiev's First Violin Concerto, which is a perfect musical reflection of my experience of my higher self, Kumara Zora Torith.

"Suffice it to say that listening to this inspiring music on this particular occasion was a profound spiritual experience of recognition, accompanied by overwhelming feelings of love and gratitude.

"I realize that my outer mind and my inner being are now in the process of becoming one through the process of ascension that is now under way."

On the morning of 10 February 2007, I had the following dream: I am standing on the edge of an old elevator shaft, observing a broken wooden bar which is part of its primitive mechanical system. My inner being then says to my outer mind: 'Having overcome the fear of falling, you are now master of the elevator, and are no longer required to use the old system. The new man is being born!' To which my outer mind responds, 'So be it!'

After recording this extraordinary dream in my journal, I then added the following interpretation: "This is an extremely important dream, which confirms that I am now in the process of merging and becoming one with my sixth-dimensional higher self, Kumara Zora Torith."

On 11 February 2007, I received inner guidance to add the last paragraph to the commentary which I had recently written as an accompaniment for the illustration of Paramessu, so as to include in my treatise a specific reference to Dr. Zahi Hawass, the Secretary-General of Egypt's Supreme Council of Antiquities. (The names of Ahmed Osman and Laurence Gardner had already been included in the Prologue of my treatise, which as I have previously indicated, was channeled in 2006 during the last week of December.)

It is also worth noting that, during my morning walk on 11 February 2007, I received the following joyful message from my higher self: "Be lighthearted."

During the middle of the night, between the hours of two and four o'clock on the morning of 12 February 2007, I received specific guidance from my higher self regarding the precise wording to be used in describing Pharaoh Akhenaten's command to the Egyptian priesthood and the firm yet benevolent manner in which the defiant High Priest of Amun was disciplined.

Upon awakening around seven o'clock on the morning of 12 February 2007, I experienced a profound expansion of my consciousness which I recorded in my journal as follows:
"I deeply desire to put an end to the illusion that I am this limited mind receiving enlightening messages from unlimited spirit.
"I realize that I am not my limited mind, for I know that I am that unlimited spirit which is aware of having this limited mind as a divine instrument of self-limitation.
"I am the light of unlimited spirit peering into the darkness of limited mind and seeing wonderful things, like Howard Carter when he peered into the darkness of the newly discovered tomb of Pharaoh Tutankhamun in 1922 and said to his sponsor, Lord Carnarvon: "I see wonderful things!"
"I am Howard Carter and I am Lord Carnarvon and I am Paramessu and I am all of it because I am All-is-one!

"I am learning to release the illusion of being one limited sunbeam so as to realize that I am the sun, with potential access to all of the sunbeams that I am.

"Today is a great day of God-Realization."

On the afternoon of 12 February 2007, I sent a brief email message to Dr. Anneke Bart (a gifted mathematician and artist, for whom Egyptology is an avocation) expressing my appreciation for her assistance in locating information on the Internet regarding the tomb of Parennefer / Wennefer, High Priest of Amun during the reign of Pharaoh Horemheb, which was discovered north of Dra Abu el-Naga in 1989 AD.

At this point, I felt ready to prepare for publication.

REJECTION

On 13 February 2007, I composed the following book proposal, which I then sent to Thames & Hudson via email on 14 February 2007.

BOOK PROPOSAL
Thames & Hudson, Ltd.
Attention: Editorial Staff

Let me say at once that the 32-page illustrated minibook which I am here proposing for your thoughtful consideration is not an ordinary book by a conventional scholar.

Before I explain what I mean by this, let me first state that the immediate objective of this very concise treatise is to solve the puzzle of the Eighteenth Dynasty in ancient Egypt, which constitutes the essential prerequisite to resolving the riddle of Judeo-Christian religion.

I shall state further that the ultimate purpose of this project is to facilitate the awakening of humanity at this pivotal point in human history by locating and revealing three key cover-stories in the Old Testament of the Bible.

The title of this historical treatise is: THE BIBLE'S COVER-STORIES REVEALED, and the subtitle is: THE GOLDEN KEYS THAT UNLOCK HISTORY.

To further prepare you for what I am about to say, let me now explain that, whereas the first half of my life was devoted to the process of developing an educated mind, the second half of my life has been devoted to the process of placing my educated mind in humble and consecrated service to my higher self, which is now able to use my mind as a channel for the purpose of transmitting information from my higher consciousness.

As a consequence, what we have here is a remarkably concise treatise which was transmitted by my higher self (whose name is Kumara Zora Torith) through the channel of my consecrated mind (whose name is All•is•one Heartsong) and was then independently confirmed by an impeccable full-body channel for higher consciousness who prefers to remain incognito because of the controversial nature of the subject matter.

Believe it or not, this is the truth, the whole truth, and nothing but the truth.

The dedication on page 1 states, "This apocalyptic revelation of truths which have long been concealed is humbly dedicated to the enlightenment of an awakening humanity."

A brief prologue then declares that "humanity has lost its way in a labyrinth of illusions and delusions composed of intentional disinformation as well as unintentional misinformation, and the simple truth of the matter is that only the truth can set us free."

This is followed by a succinct introduction which announces: "The time has now come when hidden truths which have long been concealed may finally be revealed to an awakening humanity . . . There are three cover-stories in the Old Testament of the Bible, the uncovering of which will provide an appropriate way to begin this apocalyptic process."

The first revelation exposes the cover-story contained in the twelfth chapter of Genesis by revealing how the ascended master Thoth made secret arrangements to covertly inaugurate a royal Hebrew-Egyptian lineage that began with Pharaoh Thutmose III (circa 1494-1440 BC) early in the Eighteenth Dynasty.

The second revelation exposes the famous cover-story contained in the first two chapters of Exodus by revealing how the ascended master Thoth arranged for the young Pharaoh Amenhotep III (circa 1395-1358 BC) to overtly inaugurate a further compounding of this royal Hebrew-Egyptian lineage by marrying Queen Tiye, whose illustrious sons Moses and Akhenaten were in fact brothers (contrary to the incorrect hypothesis recently advanced by the unorthodox Egyptian scholar, Ahmed Osman).

The third revelation exposes the cover-story surrounding Chapter 32 of Exodus by revealing that, far from being a temporary issue with no lasting consequences, the altercation which occurred when Aaron molded a golden calf for the Israelites to worship while Moses was receiving the Ten Commandments on Mount Horeb was in fact the beginning of a permanent division between an esoteric faction of enlightened Israelites led by Moses, and an exoteric faction of unenlightened Israelites led by Aaron, which culminated in the conflict that occurred between the Pharisees and the Essenes during the ministry of Jesus 1,333 years later.

While it is clear that this remarkable series of apocalyptic revelations is intended primarily for biblical scholars (the essential focus being on the books of Genesis and Exodus in the Old Testament of the Bible and, more specifically, on Hebrew-Egyptian relations during the Eighteenth Dynasty), it is also obvious that these extraordinary revelations will be of great interest to everyone who wishes to arrive at a deeper understanding of what really happened at the pivotal point in human history known as the Eighteenth Dynasty.

Consequently, there is reason to believe that this humble proposal for a 32-page illustrated minibook (using an 8.5" by 11" format, and combining 16 pages of text with 18 full-page color illustrations, including the front and back covers) is

worthy of your top-priority attention.
   If you are interested in pursuing this opportunity further, I will be happy to send you a simplified version of my curriculum vitae for your consideration.
Sincerely,
Arthur Earl Jones, Ph.D.

Knowing that I was searching for a love-based publisher in a fear-based world, I was not surprised when I received the following reply from Helen Farr on behalf of the editorial staff at Thames & Hudson, Ltd.:

"I'm afraid that your book proposal doesn't quite fit our publishing programme."

If you have read the Epilogue of my treatise or are familiar with *The Book of Choices* by Allisone Heartsong, then you will know that my philosophy of life revolves around the fundamental axiom: **How we experience the events in our lives is determined, not so much by what happens, as by how we choose to respond to what happens**.

On the morning of 17 February 2007, during my regular two-and-one-half-mile walk under a clear blue sky between eleven and twelve o'clock, I then received clear guidance from my higher self in the form of absolute knowing, which answered my prayers by showing me how to proceed with the publication and distribution of my illustrated historical treatise as a print-on-demand minibook.

   PUBLISHER: In God We Trust, c/o Arthur Earl Jones
   PRINTER: Lulu.com
   DISTRIBUTOR: Liberty Rising Productions, c/o Leah Lewis.

Since her website (www.fearorlove.com) and her company (Liberty Rising Productions) were already serving as distributor for *The Book of Choices*, which I had self-published in the year 2000, it seemed perfectly natural for me to invite my dear friend, Leah Lewis, to also serve as the distributor for my treatise.

And so it was that on 18 February 2007, I joyfully celebrated my 79th birthday, which marked the beginning of my 80th year, by going to the website of www.bowker.com and becoming a publisher by the simple act of applying for an ISBN in the name of In God We Trust.

On 20 February 2007, I then wrote the following letter to my friend Bruce Schiltz:
My dear friend Bruce:
   When Thames & Hudson, Ltd., of London (a top-of-the-line publisher) declined my invitation with a brief reply which stated 'I'm afraid that your book proposal doesn't quite fit our publishing programme', I decided to stop wasting my time looking for a love-based publisher in a fear-based world and to celebrate my 79th birthday on February 18 by applying for my own ISBN and becoming a publisher

myself so that I can self-publish this treatise within a few weeks.

Archangel Gabriel through Karen Cook assured me that my humble treatise is going to stir up considerable controversy amongst Egyptian scholars as well as Biblical scholars, and advised me to wear a flak jacket.

If you would now be willing to loan me one thousand dollars to cover the start-up costs of publishing via Lulu.com, which is the most reliable yet least expensive of the print-on-demand publishers, I promise that I will pay you back in full within one year.

With my love and gratitude, Arthur.

On 22 February 2007, I sent this email message to my list of friends around the world:

To experience and contemplate Paddy Chayefsky's brilliant and perceptive insights into the negative impact which the Illuminati-controlled media in general and commercial television in particular have had on the brainwashed and contracted consciousness of humanity during the past fifty years, see the film NETWORK (1976) starring Peter Finch, Faye Dunaway, William Holden, and Robert Duvall.

In my whole life, I have spent only a few hours watching television, which is clearly one of the wisest choices I have ever made.

On the morning of 24 February 2007, I was inspired to write the following entry in my personal journal: "Declaration of Identity. I am a multidimensional sunbeam of the One Universal Being that I Am, stepping down through the twelve dimensions of consciousness and manifesting as ZoRaMuEL on the ninth dimension, Kumara Zora Torith on the sixth dimension, All-is-one Heartsong on the third dimension, and Arthur Earl Jones, Ph. D. on the first dimension. I can no longer live in separation consciousness."

On the afternoon of 24 February 2007, I then proceeded to send the following email message to seventy friends around the world:

Dear Friends:

In case you haven't yet realized it, there is one specific fact of life that needs to be recognized and acknowledged at this particular point in human history: thanks to the fascist 'new world order' agenda of the psychopathic Dark Illuminati core of the global elite, which has systematically corrupted and subverted the United States of America during the past two centuries, our beloved nation is now experiencing the terminal stage of decadence.

The good news is that this insane Alice-in-Wonderland nightmare which we are currently witnessing is having the positive effect of gradually awakening the American people from their brainwashed and hypnotized state of somnambulistic sleep, with the salutary result that We The People are beginning to withdraw our consent from this criminal government which has degenerated into a fraudulent protection racket that seeks to enslave us in the guise of protecting us.

In Love's pure Light,

All-is-one Heartsong

Shortly thereafter, my sixth-dimensional higher self inspired my third-dimensional mind to transmit this email message to my friends:

Dear Friends:

Did you ever see the cinematic masterpiece M*A*S*H, which was released in 1979 as Robert Altman's radically courageous response to the Vietnam War, and which I still regard as the most politically significant film that has ever been made?

An appropriate subtitle for this brilliantly subversive and irreverent anti-authoritarian movie would be: "How to maintain your sanity when the whole world has been turned into an insane asylum by the Dark Illuminati."

In Love's pure Light,
All-is-one Heartsong

PUBLICATION

At this point, I knew that it was time for me to act on the inner guidance which I had received at nine o'clock on the evening of 21 January 2007.

On 28 February 2007, I sent the following email message to Dr. Joann Fletcher at the University of York in England, to which she responded by immediately sending me an email message containing her postal address:

Dear Dr. Joann Fletcher:

I am currently in the process of completing a concise historical treatise which constitutes my humble contribution toward solving the puzzle of the Eighteenth Dynasty in ancient Egypt and resolving the riddle of Judeo-Christian religion.

If you would be so kind as to provide me with the appropriate postal address, I will be happy to send you a gift copy when it is published next month as an expression of my appreciation for the results of your investigation in 2003 which are confirmed by my findings.

With kindest regards and good wishes,
Arthur Earl Jones, Ph. D.

On 4 March 2007, after receiving a friendly response from Dr. Fletcher containing her postal address, I then sent the following acknowledgment, clarification, and offering:

Dear Joann Fletcher:

Thank you for your positive response to my invitation.

The title of my treatise is *The Bible's Cover-Stories Revealed: The Golden Keys That Unlock History*, and I hope to be able to send you a gift copy before the end of this month.

In the meantime, I would like to clarify that this treatise was not influenced by your investigation, which did not come to my attention until after I completed the text in January and was searching the Internet in February for possible illustrations.

If you would like to learn more about my life after you have read my contribution, I would be happy to send you a gift copy of a 61-page autobiographical

Item 28

PRESS RELEASE

FOR
The Bible's Cover-Stories Revealed:
The Golden Keys That Unlock History
by
Arthur Earl Jones, Ph. D.

The ultimate aim of this humble contribution is to facilitate the awakening of humanity at our present pivotal point in human history.

That imperative purpose is accomplished by first solving the puzzle of the Eighteenth Dynasty in ancient Egypt (which, until now, has been an impenetrable mystery, intentionally designed to conceal a whole series of sensational secrets) and then finally resolving the perplexing riddle of Judeo-Christian religion.

This apocalyptic revelation of the akashic records by enlightened consciousness will be of great interest, not only to Biblical and Egyptian scholars, but also to everyone who wants to understand the truth of what really happened at that pivotal point in human history.

Eye-openers include: 1) uncovering three cover-stories in the Bible which constitute "the golden keys that unlock history"; 2) identifying the progenitor of the covert Hebrew-Egyptian lineage that Abraham's wife Sarah secretly birthed prior to the birth of Isaac; 3) revealing the momentous fact that Moses and Akhenaten, the illustrious founders of monotheistic religion, were brothers; 4) confirming with photographic evidence that Joseph the Israelite was their maternal grandfather; 5) discovering a photograph of the sculptured self-portrait which Moses bequeathed to us; 6) exposing the assassinations of Pharaohs Akhenaten, Smenkhkare, Tutankhamun, and Ay, which decisively altered the subsequent course of human history; and 7) elucidating the origin of the contest between the Pharisees and the Essenes which culminated in the crucifixion of Jesus.

Review Apéritif: "A spectacular bolt of lightning that brilliantly illuminates the dark landscape of human history."

This remarkably concise historical treatise (with 21 magnificent color illustrations in an 8.5" by 11" format of 36 pages) is now available at the special introductory price of just US$19.95 plus shipping until 30 September 2007, after which the regular price will be US$24.95 plus shipping.

Published by In God We Trust and distributed by Liberty Rising Productions, it may be ordered by email at

fearorloveorders@austin.rr.com

account of my spiritual journey during this lifetime, titled *Illustration of Spiritual Awakening*.
    Sincerely,
    Arthur Earl Jones, Ph. D.

On 5 March 2007, a treasured friend of mine whose first name is Rebekah had a personal telephone session with Archangel Gabriel Benu through his dedicated channel Karen Cook, during the course of which she asked three questions for me, the answers to which provided me with additional confirmation regarding the validity and reliability of this unconventional source of information.

Question 1: Did Dr. Zahi Hawass have a previous incarnation as Paramessu (the assassin) or Maya (the recruiter of the assassin) or Horemheb (the Pharaoh of the Oppression)?
Answer: Dr. Zahi Hawass had a previous incarnation as Maya (the recruiter of the assassin).

Question 2: Did Pharaoh Akhenaten become the ascended master Serapis Bey?
Answer: No.

Question 3: Did Horemheb help Maya to disguise his identity as the High Priest of Amun by assigning him the role of Overseer of the Treasury during the reign of Pharaoh Tutankhamun?
Answer: Yes.

During the month of March, a series of totally unexpected technical problems brought the work on my treatise to a virtual standstill, and on 23 March 2007, I wrote the following report in my journal: "The month of March has been characterized by a major breakdown in the computer system of my friend Zepp, who has become extremely frustrated over his inability to complete the word processing and graphic layout of my treatise, which I had hoped to complete around the middle of March. However, I have been able to release my expectations and maintain my patience because I trust the process and know that this delay allows further refinements to be made.

As a consequence of these technical problems, virtually the only thing that I was able to accomplish during the month of March was the formulation of a press release for my treatise, which was finalized on 26 March 2007. (See Item 28)

On 26 March 2007, I sent the following email message to my good friend George Humphrey, with copies to over eighty people around the world:
Dear George:
    Thank you for reporting the recent changes that you have observed in your state of being.
    During the past several weeks, the gradually escalating planetary ascension energies have intensified to the point where life-as-usual is no longer tenable because our old patterns of thinking, feeling, and acting have been rendered obsolete and are no longer workable.

We are now entering an extremely challenging time of radical change (physically and emotionally as well as mentally and spiritually), which calls for the radical choice to align to our Creator-Source manifesting through our higher selves and to release our materialistic attachments to our third-dimensional lives and identities as we have known them, which are now beginning to disintegrate or dissolve.

In Love's pure Light,
All-is-one Heartsong

On the morning of 30 March 2007, I wrote the following report in my journal:

"Before falling asleep, I asked my higher self to show me why Zepp and I had encountered total blocking of our work on my project due to computer malfunctioning.

"In the middle of the night, at two o'clock this morning, my higher self gave me an answer that took the form of three distinct messages.

"In the first message, my higher self revealed to my outer mind that Zepp prefers to work alone following written instructions rather than as a team using spoken interactions.

"In the second message, my sixth-dimensional higher self invited my third-dimensional mind to explain to Zepp what happened two weeks ago, around March 15, when Zepp decided to eliminate double spacing between the paragraphs of my text and to insert page numbers for my illustrations, which caused me to feel like he was sabotaging my project, but to instead regard this unexpected development as an opportunity to make further refinements, which inspired me to introduce a dozen additional details before completion.

"The third message consisted in a suggestion from my higher self to my outer mind that I arrange with Zepp to pay the remainder of what I owe after the project is completed and published by Lulu within a few more days.

"This combination of three messages from my higher self was experienced as a tremendous relief, not only by me last night but also by Zepp when I told him this morning.

"Before meeting with Zepp at ten o'clock this morning, I first wrote out a set of 21 instructions on how to complete the diagram of Hebrew-Egyptian lineages, and then wrote out another set of instructions on how to complete the Chariot Illustration designated as Figure 20 on page 35.

"As a consequence, my meeting with Zepp was very brief and very harmonious.

"I am profoundly grateful to my higher self for answering my request by showing me how to relate to Zepp harmoniously.

"The files for my illustrated treatise will soon by ready to send to Lulu for publication."

Those of you who have read the autobiographical account of my spiritual journey during this lifetime (*Illustration of Spiritual Awakening* by Arthur Earl Jones, Ph. D.) will understand why I have a special feeling for the following entry in my personal journal, which is dated 31 March 2007:

"This morning, I woke up at six o'clock with an inspiration from my higher self to add the following sentence to the commentary for Figure 5: Thoth.

"'Just as the creation of the United States of America in modern times was secretly inspired by the ascended master Saint Germain, so the creation of the Hebrew-Egyptian lineages in ancient times was secretly inspired by the ascended master Thoth.'

"I then received further guidance from my higher self to place the Egyptian icon symbolizing ascended masters (using a violet-blue color) at the top of the last page (page 36) which contains the ISBN and information for ordering the illustrated treatise.

"When I expressed my desire for these refinements to be the last additions prior to publication, my higher self responded with the message: 'Let this ascended master icon be the seal of completion.'"

Little did I anticipate at this point in the creative process that, after versions 4 and 5 of my treatise were printed and corrected around the end of April, and after version 6 was published around the middle of May, my higher self would then inspire me to add several parenthetic sentences between June 7 and July 3, which were published as version 7 around the middle of July.

On 3 April 2007, I began mailing out copies of the press release for my treatise, the first two copies going to Dr. Joann Fletcher and Dr. Anneke Bart.

On 5 April 2007, Zepp and I began making final adjustments in the layout of the text and illustrations for my treatise.

On 10 April 2007, I became aware that I was experiencing signs of physical exhaustion as a consequence of my nonstop focused attention and intense concentration during the past four months.

On 11 April 2007, after automatically applying some black salve to a very small red spot at the base of my right thumb, I was surprised and shocked when it produced a severe lesion that rendered my right hand completely nonfunctional for approximately three weeks.

On 21 April 2007, my treasured friend whose first name is Rebekah made special arrangements for me to have an emergency session with Archangel Gabriel Benu through his dedicated full-body channel Karen Cook, which was scheduled for the earliest available opening on 8 May 2007.

Rather than waiting for the emergency consultation with Gabriel, however, I instead made the empowering choice to take full responsibility for solving this problem by first regarding it as an integral part of my final examination prior to graduation (by which I mean the planetary ascension of humanity that is scheduled to culminate in 2012 according to the ascended master Saint Germain) and by then recognizing that I had unwittingly given my power away by mistakenly thinking that the power to heal my hand was outside of myself in the form of the black salve rather than within myself in the form of my spiritual being.

Of particular significance is the fact that, as soon as I realized my mistake and reoriented my mind to the truth, I immediately experienced the absolute knowing that my hand was going to be healed.

Then, at three o'clock on the morning of 30 April 2007, I woke up from what I shall call MY PLANETARY ASCENSION DREAM, which I recorded in my journal as follows: "I am with a group of unidentified friends who are going through the planetary ascension process, which begins with a series of huge ocean waves that appear to be on the verge of engulfing us, but which then involves passing through a series of empty rooms that require an act of faith, from which we emerge joyfully empowered and transformed from black-and-white consciousness to technicolor consciousness. I am left with the impression that the act of faith is the key element in the ascension process."

At four o'clock on the morning of 30 April 2007, after recording my planetary ascension dream, I then wrote the following DECLARATION in my journal: "I am Kumara Zora Torith taking conscious command of this consecrated body temple of the God I AM. So be it."

In retrospect, it is clear to me that the events of 30 April 2007 marked a major milestone in my journey into wholeness.

My emergency session with Archangel Gabriel took place on the afternoon of 8 May 2007 and can be summed up in a few sentences:
During the first part of the session, Gabriel confirmed that the temporary incapacitation of my right hand was an important part of my final examination prior to graduation, that faith and trust were the essential issue, and that I had solved the problem by reorienting from "black salve is the healer" to "God I AM is the healer".
During the second part of the session, Gabriel confirmed that the task of channeling my treatise for the purpose of facilitating the enlightenment of humanity during my eightieth year was chosen before I was born, and that, while serving as my humble contribution during this incarnation, it also served to facilitate the merging of my third-dimensional mental body with my sixth-dimensional light body.
In addition to confirming my knowing that Kiya, the secondary wife of Amenhotep III, and the mother of Smenkhkare and Tutankhamun, was the Hebrew-Egyptian daughter of Manasseh, whose Egyptian name was Huya, Gabriel also confirmed that Pharaoh Ay and his son Nakhtmin were assassinated simultaneously.
However, when I asked Gabriel to confirm the report that Moses had murdered an Egyptian prior to escaping from Egypt to the land of Midian on the Sinai Peninsula, he revealed that the report contained in *Exodus* 2:11-15 is actually fallacious disinformation concocted by Jewish scribes during the Babylonian captivity (circa 597-538 BC).
It only remains to add that I also asked Gabriel three questions for my treasured friend Rebekah, in reciprocation for the questions that she had asked for me during her session on 5 March 2007.

Of all the many things that happened in my life during the next few days while I was on the verge of publishing my treatise, the most important thing by far was my channeling of the following article, titled *It's Your Choice*, for my website on 12 May 2007:
"If you choose not to accept the fact that you are responsible for creating your own

experiences with every choice that you make as an empowered creator–every thought, every desire, and every action that you choose–then you are choosing to accept the illusion that you are a disempowered creature who is a helpless victim of circumstance.

"So whatever it is that your outer mind or your inner being have chosen to experience during this particular lifetime, always remember that it's your choice."

On 13 May 2007, I decided to use one of the test copies of Version 5 of my treatise as a review copy, which I mailed to John Miglio, Editor/Publisher of *Online Review of Books*.

On 14 May 2007, I mailed the following letter to Dorothea Arnold, together with another test copy of Version 5:

Dorothea Arnold, Curator
Department of Egyptian Art
Metropolitan Museum of Art.
1000 Fifth Avenue at 82nd Street
New York, NY 10028-0198
Dear Dorothea Arnold:

As a courtesy to you, I am enclosing a gift copy of my illustrated treatise, *The Bible's Cover-Stories Revealed: The Golden Keys That Unlock History,* which has just been published.

I particularly want to call your attention to the caption for Figure 9, which reads: "Moses, a.k.a. Thutmose V and Thutmose the Sculptor (Agyptishes Museum, Berlin). Image source: Figure 43 on page 50 of Dorothea Arnold's masterpiece, *The Royal Women of Amarna*, where it is incorrectly identified as Akhenaten."

For further information, please see page 17.
With kindest regards and good wishes,
Arthur Earl Jones, Ph.D.
In God We Trust
P.O. Box 450
Mt. Shasta, CA 96067

On the evening of 14 May 2007, I ordered fifty copies of Version 6 to be distributed by myself to professional reviewers and personal friends.

On the morning of 15 May 2007, I ordered fifty copies of Version 6 to be sold by Leah Lewis through her website www.fearorlove.com

Immediately after I placed this order with Lulu.com on 15 May 2007, I received clear guidance from my higher self to begin preparing for the publication of a sequel that would include a record of peoples's responses to my illustrated historical treatise.

It was around this time that I gifted my friends with the following message:
Dear Friends:

Have you seen the film PRETTY WOMAN (1990) starring Julia Roberts and Richard Gere?

This modern-day version of the classic Cinderella fairy tale provides a beautiful illustration of how love can transform a fearful and heartless man into a courageous and caring person at the same time that kindness and generosity transform a lowly prostitute into a self-respecting lady.

The moral of the story is that loving kindness constitutes the royal road to enlightenment and mastery.

In Love's pure Light,
All-is-one Heartsong

On 19 May 2007, I was inspired by my higher self to send the following email message to Professor Noam Chomsky, with whom I had corresponded on several previous occasions:

Dear Professor Chomsky:

I predict further that your lifelong efforts to awaken, educate, and enlighten humanity are going to be rewarded with a successful positive outcome during the next six months and that the global chess game between lightworkers and darkworkers will culminate miraculously in a dramatic checkmate before the end of this pivotal year of 2007.

With my heartfelt appreciation and gratitude as well as my kindest regards and good wishes,

Arthur Earl Jones, Ph.D.

Two days later, on 21 May 2007, I composed the following email message, titled HOW TO LIVE YOUR LIFE AS A MASTER, which I transmitted to my list of eighty friends around the world:

Dear Friends:

Up until this point in the history of humanity, we human beings have had to go through our lives without the benefit of a genuine and truly effective operator's manual.

Needless to say, there have been a number of attempts to provide such a manual throughout the course of history, and several enlightened teachers of mankind have provided us with valuable hints and clues which have been extremely helpful.

It is not until now, however, that humanity has been provided with a genuine and truly effective operator's manual which reveals the universal laws that govern our lives and which shows us exactly how to live our lives joyfully and harmoniously as master creators.

The title of this book is: *The Law of Attraction: The Basics of the Teachings of Abraham* by Esther and Jerry Hicks.

Channeled by Esther Hicks, it is a product of the enlightened consciousness known as Abraham responding to the questions posed by Jerry Hicks.

This priceless book is easy to read and easy to understand.

I sincerely recommend that you obtain a copy, read it, and begin to apply its

easily-understood teachings in your life.
>In Love's pure Light,
>All-is-one Heartsong

On the morning of 22 May 2007, I sent the following email message to my elder daughter (Lisa), who had been taking care of her mother (Antonella) during the final months of her terminal illness.

Beloved Lisa:
>This is to confirm that Karen Cinnamon has kept me informed regarding the most recent developments in Nella's condition, and that I will continue to be with all of you in spirit as Nella makes her transition and discovers that she is far more than her physical body.
>Your father who loves you.

Antonella had been my wife from 1959 until 1982, at which point an amicable parting of the ways occurred by mutual agreement when her orientation as a medical doctor made it impossible for her to comprehend the increasingly miraculous experiences that I was having on my spiritual path.

On the morning of 23 May 2007, my younger daughter (Karen Cinnamon) called to inform me that Antonella had made a peaceful transition on the previous evening in the loving presence of her daughters and their husbands.

Thus it was that, on the afternoon of 23 May 2007, I composed the following tribute titled IN CELEBRATION OF ANTONELLA, which I transmitted to my daughters (Lisa and Karen Cinnamon) and my granddaughter (Tess):

Beloved Karen Cinnamon, Lisa, and Tess:
>On the occasion of our celebration of Antonella's life and her welcome liberation from the limitations of her physical body, I would like to affirm that she was unquestionably one of the finest human beings I have ever met in my entire life — exceptionally beautiful, exceptionally intelligent, and exceptionally gifted as an artist as well as a physician.
>Several months ago, I asked Nella to tell me what she regarded as the high points of her life, and without hesitation she declared that the birthings of her two magnificent daughters were unquestionably the most precious and memorable experiences of her entire life.
>She particularly remembered how, after Lisa's birth, the anesthesiologist placed the stem of a red rose between her teeth with the words: "and now make your exit like Carmen", and how, just before Karen's birth, the nurses were shouting, "Dr. Zakin, Dr. Zakin, come quickly!"
>I will never forget the early years of our relationship, from the day that I met her at the party of a mutual friend on 25 May 1957 and experienced the absolute knowing that she was the woman with whom I was destined to have children, until the fulfillment of that premonition.

Those were truly magical years, incredibly rich and characterized by an enormous expansion of consciousness.

With all my love to my magnificent daughters and my magnificent granddaughter,

Arthur.

On the morning of 24 May 2007, I woke up with the following dream: I am complimenting a community on its civilized orientation, which allows loving debate that puts the loving principle before the fighting principle.

On the afternoon of 24 May 2007, I began the process of mailing fifty gift copies to a list of friends and reviewers that included the following list of professional reviewers:

1) The London Review of Books
2) The Times Literary Supplement (London)
3) New York Review of Books
4) New York Times Book Review
5) Boston Book Review
6) Los Angeles Times Book Review
7) Midwest Book Review
8) Online Review of Books
9) Publishers Weekly
10) American Library Association Book List
11) Ancient Egypt Magazine
12) KMT Magazine

Then, on 25 May 2007, I placed the following ANNOUNCEMENT on my website, together with the press release for my treatise.

Dear Friends:

I am happy to announce the publication of a major message from my sixth-dimensional higher self, whose name is Kumara Zora Torith.

Channeled by my outer mind, whose name is All•is•one Heartsong, this message is nothing less than an apocalyptic revelation.

It has just been published in the form of an illustrated historical treatise titled THE BIBLE'S COVER-STORIES REVEALED: THE GOLDEN KEYS THAT UNLOCK HISTORY by Arthur Earl Jones, Ph. D.

The purpose of this apocalyptic revelation is to facilitate the enlightenment of an awakening humanity by demonstrating how spiritual access to the akashic records can reveal hidden truths which were intentionally concealed over three thousand years ago.

To be more specific, this demonstration is accomplished by first solving the mysterious puzzle of the Eighteenth Dynasty prior to the exodus of the twelve tribes of Israel from ancient Egypt and then resolving the perplexing riddle of Judeo-Christian religion.

In the process of uncovering three key cover-stories in the Old Testament of the Bible, it not only reveals that Moses and Akhenaten, the two illustrious founders of monotheistic religion, were in fact brothers, but also provides us with an actual picture of Moses in the form of a photograph of his sculptured self-portrait.

For information about how to obtain a copy of this illustrated historical treatise, please see the following press release.

On the morning of 29 May 2007, my third-dimensional mind received clear guidance from my sixth-dimensional higher self advising me to make the most of my next regular session with Archangel Gabriel Benu, which was scheduled for 5 June 2007, by asking how many Israelites participated in the exodus from Egypt.

I already knew that *Exodus* 12:37 was false because *Exodus* 12:40 was false, the former verse stating that the number of Israelites who participated in the exodus from Egypt was "600,000 men on foot, besides children", and the latter verse stating that "the sojourn of the children of Israel who lived in Egypt was four hundred and thirty years".

Knowing that the time frame for the Egyptian sojourn of the Israelites was actually four generations rather than four centuries (*Genesis* 15:13-16) and lasted for approximately ninety-four years (circa 1404 BC to 1310 BC) rather than four hundred and thirty years, it was a relatively simple matter for me to calculate that the actual number of Israelites who participated in the exodus was somewhere around 4,000, as follows:

100	original group	
250	first generation	
625	second generation	estimating five children per couple
1560	third generation	
3900	fourth generation	

On 30 May 2007, I mailed the following letter to Jamie Camplin, the managing director of Thames & Hudson, Ltd.

Jamie Camplin, Managing Director
Thames & Hudson, Ltd.
181 A High Holborn
London, WC1V-7QX
UK

Dear Jamie Camplin:

Last February, when I saw your photograph on the Thames & Hudson website while

I was looking for an appropriate publisher for my illustrated historical treatise, I experienced an intuitive feeling that we might eventually become treasured friends.

It was for this reason that I submitted a book proposal to the Editorial Staff of Thames & Hudson on 14 February 2007.

Knowing that I was searching for a love-based publisher in a fear-based world, I was not at all surprised by Helen Farr's response: "I'm afraid that your book proposal doesn't quite fit our publishing programme."

Please find enclosed a gift copy of my illustrated historical treatise, which I have published myself.

If, after you have completed the process of confirming its validity, you would like to consider the possibility of publishing a hardcover version that might eventually include foreign languages, please let me hear from you.

With kindest regards and good wishes,

Arthur Earl Jones, Ph.D.
In God We Trust
P.O. Box 450
Mt. Shasta, CA 96067

Here is the first response to my illustrated historical treatise, which I received from Leah Lewis of Austin, Texas on 31 May 2007:
> Your book is absolutely beautiful and even more inviting to read than I had imagined it would be. Congratulations on a marvelously done project brought to completion. Thank you for including me in this great energy.

Dear Leah:
> I would like to offer a suggestion as to how you might best incorporate my treatise into the catalogue on your website at www.fearorlove.com
> Just as you made a distinction between two different aspects of the second awakening (spiritual alignment and physical health), I recommend that we also make a distinction between two different aspects of the first awakening: POLITICAL INSIGHT and RELIGIOUS INSIGHT.
> The key thing to understand in this regard is that the first awakening involves gaining insight, not only into the way that darkworkers use politics (and economics) to deceive and subjugate humanity, but also into the way that darkworkers use religion (and history) to deceive and subjugate humanity.
> My treatise is essentially an exposé of the way that darkworkers have used religion (and history) to keep humanity unenlightened and disempowered.

To be specific, my treatise is designed to facilitate the awakening and enlightenment of humanity by revealing that, far from being the true Word of God, the Old Testament of the Bible contains disinformation in the form of cover-stories which are intentionally designed to keep humanity in an unenlightened and disempowered state of being.

The most important part of my treatise consists in the third revelation that, whereas the esoteric faction of enlightened Israelites (who followed Moses and became known as the Essenes) were worshiping our Creator (whose name is I AM THAT I AM and who is by nature loving and forgiving), the exoteric faction of unenlightened Israelites (who followed Aaron and became known as the Pharisees) were worshiping a fifth-dimensional warlord (whose name was Yahweh or Jehovah and who was by nature a wrathful and punitive impostor).

I hope that you will find this information helpful.

With my love and blessings,

All-is-one

Here is the second response to my treatise, which I received from Dr. Carl Johan Calleman of Sweden on 1 June 2007:

Dear Arthur,

I have received your booklet on Moses and Echnaton and would like to thank you for this fine piece. I find your hypotheses very plausible and what is more they have been presented in a very nice form with the pictures of personages from ancient Egypt. It may well become an esoteric classic. Your thesis that Echnaton was of a semi-Jewish lineage may also be supported by the suggestion that the name Aton may be related to the Hebrew word Adonai.

From the perspective of the Mayan calendar, the 18th dynasty and the New Kingdom of Egypt are products of the Third day of the National Underworld (1538-1144 BC) one that anchored the particular left brain mentality that this Underworld was carrying. This left brain consciousness was manifested in a surge of Palace Cultures from the Shang dynasty in China to the palaces of Mychene, Knossos and Thebe. This meant a great step forward in terms of construction works, but also to the emergence of alphabetic writing and the monotheistic faith. In my view, these advances came at the price of separation from oneness, evident especially among Jewish farisees that were immersed in the written word, but also from nature which at the time was the controversial aspect of the belief in the One God beyond our physical existence. An interesting question to be asked here is why the monotheistic faith survived among the Jews and not among the Egyptians, especially if, as you are asserting, this monotheism had an origin in the Echnaton-Moses brethren. My own answer would be that the Jews, as a result of the pulse of the Third Day, invented the alphabet which is a much more powerful and abstract system of writing than the Egyptian hieroglyphs. Hence, the Jewish mentality became more conducive to the abstract notion of One God.

There is one point where I diverge from your ideas. This is in the qualification of the ancient Egyptian deities as anthropomorphic. I would instead say that they are remains of the kind of shamanic consciousness people were living in in the Regional Underworld. I feel the Egyptian animal-man gods really do have an existence in the spirit world, but as the Third day of the National Underworld started these contacts were superseded by its dualist consciousness, one aspect of which was the emphasis on monotheism.

    Thank you for a beautiful work.
    All the best
    Carl Johan

Dear Carl Johan:

    Thank you for your feedback, which is the second response to my treatise that I have thus far received.

    Let me say at once that I have great respect for your wisdom and for the outstanding contributions that you have made to the task of awakening and enlightening humanity at this pivotal point in human history.

    What I want you to understand is that my third-dimensional mind (whose name is All-is-one Heartsong) is not the author of my treatise but merely the humble channel for the absolute knowing of my sixth-dimensional higher self (whose name is Kumara Zora Torith and who is the true author of this revelation based on access to the akashic records).

    Thus, although it may appear to readers who have not yet gained conscious access to the absolute knowing of their sixth-dimensional higher selves, that my treatise is composed of speculative hypotheses which are the product of my third-dimensional mind, the fact of the matter is that what we have here constitutes a genuine revelation of akashic truth.

    It has also become unmistakably clear to me that my third-dimensional intellect does not have direct access to the akashic records, but is provided with access to the absolute knowing of akashic truth only when my sixth-dimensional higher self chooses to provide such access, which has the inevitable effect of keeping my third-dimensional mind in its proper place as a humble servant of what is commonly referred to as the Holy Spirit.

    With kindest regards and good wishes,
    Sincerely,
    Arthur

Here is the third response to my treatise, which I received from Barbara Stamp of Eden Prairie, Minnesota on 3 June 2007:

Dear All-is-one:

    Thank you so much for the copy of your latest writing! It looks like it involved a lot of research and hard work. Impressive!

    Barbara Stamp

Dear Barbara Stamp:

    Thank you for your feedback. While it is true that the process of bringing forth my illustrated historical treatise required my focused attention for the past six months, the truth is that the process of channeling this akashic information from the absolute knowing of my sixth-dimensional higher self was spontaneous and effortless----something that no amount of research, speculation, and hard work on the part of my third-dimensional mind could ever have accomplished. My outer mind is humbled by this miraculous apocalyptic revelation from my inner being.

    Sincerely,
    All-is-one

RECONFIRMATION

My eighteenth telephone session with Archangel Gabriel Benu took place at noon on 5 June 2007, during the course of which I asked the following questions for Gabriel to answer.

Allisone: Is the unorthodox Egyptian scholar Ahmed Osman (who has recently published the erroneous theory that Moses and Akhenaten were one and the same person) a reincarnation of either Paramessu or Horemheb?

Gabriel: Paramessu.

Allisone: Wow. You're sure about that?

Gabriel: Yes.

Allisone: [laughs] I know you usually are speaking from absolute knowing.

Gabriel: Definitely.

Allisone: Okay. I had a feeling that that might be the case, because the theory that Moses and Akhenaten were the same disrupts the discovery of the truth of what really happened.

Gabriel: Correct.

Allisone: It's understandable that Paramessu would come back to prevent the revelation of what really happened.

Gabriel: Exactly! He would be terrified of that!

Allisone: Yeah. Okay.

Gabriel: Because then people would find out what kind of individual he really was.

Allisone: Yeah. So it's actually quite ingenious that he reincarnated and then created an erroneous theory that would mislead and confuse people.

Gabriel: Exactly.

Allisone: Okay. That makes a lot of sense to me.

Gabriel: Good.

Allisone: Is the unorthodox Biblical scholar Laurence Gardner (who recently published *Bloodline of the Holy Grail*, containing disinformation about Akhenaten and Moses as well as about Jesus and Mary Magdalene) a reincarnation of Horemheb by any chance?

Gabriel: Yes.

Allisone: Really?

Gabriel: Yeah.

Allisone: My God! My intuition is . . .

Gabriel: . . . is very good!

Allisone: . . . phenomenal! [laughs] Okay, that's all I need to know.

Gabriel: Good.

Allisone: I'll go on to the next one. That's amazing! I mean, that's major revelation we've got here. I'm very grateful.

Gabriel: Mhmm.

Allisone: The next question is particularly important to me, so I'll take this slowly. In accordance with the disinformation contained in *Genesis* 15:13, which states incorrectly that the Israelites were in Egypt for four centuries rather than for four generations, *Exodus* 12:37 states incorrectly that the exodus from Egypt involved 600,000 Israelites, not including their children. That would be understandable if it were actually four hundred years rather than four generations.

Gabriel: Correct.

Allisone: So, please tell me how many Israelites were actually involved in the exodus.

Gabriel: How many do you think?

Allisone: I did a simple calculation starting with 90 to 100 Israelites that came from Canaan to northeastern Egypt.

Gabriel: 103

Allisone: Okay, starting with 103.

Gabriel: Right.

Allisone: And figuring five or six children per couple over four generations would give an answer of something like four thousand to eight thousand.

Gabriel: That's right.

Allisone: Now, would it be possible for you to be even more specific about the precise number of Israelites who actually participated in the exodus? I realize that's asking a lot, but knowing your skill with numbers, I don't consider anything impossible.

Gabriel: No. Let me look. The actual ones that made the exodus without panic or fear and literally did what they said they were going to do was four thousand and four.

Allisone: Four thousand and four.

Gabriel: Yep.

Allisone: That's not very many!

Gabriel: No, it wasn't very many.

Allisone: So it's not even close to the eight thousand that I thought would be possible.

Gabriel: No.

Allisone: I'm not surprised.

Gabriel: You had a lot of individuals that wanted to go, but they were fearful.

Allisone: I see.

Gabriel: Eight thousand and six started out but didn't finish.

Allisone: Eight thousand and six started out . . .

Gabriel: Right.

Allisone: . . . were originally intending to join the exodus?

Gabriel: Exactly. Some were disinformed.

Allisone: Mhmm.

Gabriel: Some of them actually panicked and would not go.

Allisone: Sure. I understand.

Gabriel: Some went a different route and were lost.

Allisone: Okay. So the actual number that made the exodus with Moses and Aaron was four thousand and four people.

Gabriel: Correct.

Allisone: That's so important that I think I'm going to find a way of including that in a final version of my treatise.

Gabriel: Good.

Allisone: Okay. Next question. During the exodus of the Israelites from Egypt, did the miraculous parting of the sea occur at a place known as the Reed Sea ("yam suph" in the Hebrew language) rather than at the Red Sea?

Gabriel: Correct.

Allisone: Now, I'm going to try to locate where that was. Let's see. If the exodus began with a march southward from the supply city of Rameses (now known as Qantir) to the city of Succoth, which is located halfway between the Mediterranean Sea and the Red Sea (a total distance of about eighty miles), how much further south of Succoth was the Reed Sea?

Gabriel: Hmm. It looks like a journey of about a day and a half. It's not far.

Allisone: If it's only eighty miles all the way from the Mediterranean to the Red Sea . . .

Gabriel: Right. I say a day and a half because you had not just men, women, and children...

Allisone: Okay, a day and a half.

Gabriel: Right.

Allisone: Let's see now. It would be something less than forty miles, because forty miles would take them all the way to the Red Sea.

Gabriel: Right. No, it's less than that.

Allisone: So, a day and a half . . . well, with several thousand people . . .

Gabriel: Right. It was a day and a half, but not walking all at the same time. Remember the time of year.

Allisone: What time of year was it?

Gabriel: In the heat.

Allisone: In the heat.

Gabriel: Right.

Allisone: So it was a pretty minimal amount of miles.

Gabriel: Right.

Allisone: It couldn't be more than forty miles, so maybe it was something like twenty miles.

Gabriel: Actually, twenty-two.

Allisone: Twenty-two. [laughs] Okay.

Gabriel: But bear in thought, you know, to move that many people . . .

Allisone: Yeah.

Gabriel: And not everybody walks at the same pace.

Allisone: Sure.

Gabriel: And you've got little children. You've got babies.

Allisone: So they moved slowly.

Gabriel: Exactly.

[Note: At this point, our telephone line was disconnected by the effects of a storm somewhere between Mount Shasta, California, and Albuquerque, New Mexico, so it took me about thirty seconds to reestablish the connection.]

Gabriel: Hello.

Allisone: Hello. We got cut off somehow.

Gabriel: Yes, it's a storm . . .

Allisone: A storm!

Gabriel: . . . between Mount Shasta and New Mexico.

Allisone: I see. Okay.

Gabriel: But any way, next question.

[Note: At this point, I asked a series of questions which elicited answers from Gabriel revealing that Moses was the author of key portions of the first five books of the Old Testament, but that ninety percent of *Exodus*, and seventy percent of *Leviticus*, *Numbers*, and *Deuteronomy* were composed by Jewish scribes during the Babylonian captivity (circa 597-538 BC).]

Allisone: Okay, I'll go on to the next question. Am I correct that my higher self wants me to publish a record of the various responses to my treatise . . .?

Gabriel: Correct.

As I have already indicated, the initial guidance to prepare myself for writing this book was received from my higher self on 15 May 2007, three weeks prior to this confirmation by Archangel Gabriel; and the subsequent guidance to actually begin writing this book was received on 22 June 2007, just seventeen days after this confirmation by Gabriel on 5 June 2007.

REVIEWERS

Here is the fourth response to my treatise, which I received from Matthias Chang of Malaysia on 6 June 2007:
Dear Mr. Jones,
It was such a pleasant surprise to receive your excellent book, "*The Bible's Cover Story Revealed*" today.
You are indeed an erudite scholar and I shall always treasure this wonderful

gift. Thank you so very much.
God bless you always.
As ever,
Matthias

Dear Matthias Chang:
Many thanks for your email message indicating that you have just received your gift copy of my humble treatise today (6 June 2007).

I want you to know that I did not read the intellectual speculations, projective misperceptions, and deliberate disinformation of erudite scholars such as Erik Hornung, Nicholas Reeves, and Ahmed Osman until after my third-dimensional mind had completed the process of channeling this apocalyptic revelation of the akashic records from my sixth-dimensional higher self.

Truly I am blessed, as are you.
Arthur

And here is the fifth response to my treatise, which I received from Mary Mageau (Sestriel) of Australia on 6 June 2007:

Dear All Is One,
Today a copy of your new publication reached my mailbox and I extend a heartfelt thank you for posting this forward to me. It's been beautifully presented, and I look forward to reading it in the next few days.

I've always been drawn to ascended master Akhenaten, as a wonderful channel and friend (Soltec, Sydney) frequently channels him.

I believe that he and Nefertiti (through their Sirian connection) were fully conscious humans with all 12 DNA strands functional and that the Reptilians tried and succeeded in removing their last link to humanity, - hence our corrupted DNA of today. It will be of great interest for me to read your new publication to learn more about this event.

With love and blessings.
Mary (Sestriel)

Dear Mary (Sestriel):
Thank you for letting me know that you have received your gift copy of my humble treatise today (6 June 2007).

When I visited Egypt with my twin-flame soulmate Claire Heartsong in November of 1996, I knew nothing about the Eighteenth Dynasty in general or Akhenaten in particular; however, when I saw the sculptured head of Akhenaten in the Luxor Museum, I experienced a profound feeling of love and soul recognition.

I had no intention of writing this treatise prior to 8 December 2006, when my sixth-dimensional higher self unexpectedly invited my third-dimensional mind to channel this apocalyptic revelation for the purpose of facilitating the awakening and enlightenment of humanity at this pivotal point in human history.

What is more, I did not read the intellectual speculations, projective misperceptions, and deliberate disinformation of scholars such as Erik Hornung, Nicholas Reeves, and Ahmed Osman until after I had completed the channeling process on 3 January 2007.
With my love and blessings to you,
All-is-one

The sixth response to my treatise, which I received from Patricia Cota-Robles of Tucson, Arizona on 11 June 2007 is as follows:
Dear All*is*one
Thank you so much for sending me a copy of your new book. Congratulations! I look forward to reading it. I appreciate all of your Loving support and the Light you are adding to the world.
Lots of Love,
Patricia Cota-Robles

Dear Patti:
Thank you for your note confirming that you have received the gift copy of my illustrated historical treatise which I sent to you recently.
If you (or any people that you know) have sixth-dimensional access to the akashic records and are able to validate the information that I have published in this treatise, please let me know.
With my love and blessings,
All-is-one
formerly known as
Arthur Earl Jones, Ph.D.

Then, at one o'clock on the morning of 15 June 2007, I was awakened by this truly extraordinary and completely unexpected dream:
There is an important choice to be made, so the mind makes a request to meet with the spirit to discuss the current situation before making that choice, but the spirit replies that ascension is now the only choice that really matters because at this point any other choice is clearly nothing more than a distraction, so there is actually nothing to discuss.

Before proceeding further, I invite you to pause for a moment to contemplate the profound significance of that extraordinary dream.

The seventh response to my treatise, which I received from Mike Quinsey of England on 18 June 2007, is as follows:
Hi Allisone,
Thank you once again for sending me a copy of your wonderfully presented book, in which the coloured plates are bold and very striking. The detail is excellent, and as one who has always had an interest in this period of Egyptian history, it is very

enlightening to read a chronology of life lines that make sense, and the stories behind them.

As to who you were in that time, my logic or is it really my intuition (is it reliable) connects you with Thutmose III. However, I did initially feel quite strongly that you were Moses, but that was before I read the book.

I must also thank you for your Email of yesterday, and although I read Sheldan's weekly messages, I must admit to not having made the connection that you have, although I felt today's message was strongly indicating some kind of major development in July.

Also thanks for the articles you send out.

In Love and Light. Mike.

As you may know, my treasured friend Mike Quinsey is an authentic and highly reliable channel for higher consciousness, who has been rendering great service to humanity by channeling the ascended master Saint Germain and six fifth-dimensional emissaries of the Galactic Federation for several years, and whose email messages I have been forwarding to my email list of friends around the world since October of 2005.

Since it was clear to me that Mike had not asked Germain to reveal the identity of my incarnation during the Eighteenth Dynasty, at my earliest opportunity I found an appropriate way to satisfy his curiosity.

The eighth response to my treatise occurred during a personal conversation that I had with my treasured friend Ana Holub of Mount Shasta, California on 20 June 2007, during the course of which I was guided to reveal more about my incarnation during the Eighteenth Dynasty than I had ever shared with anyone before.

Beloved Ana:

After our unusual sharing this afternoon, I returned home and took a nap, as I often do these days.

Upon awakening from my nap, I realized that I had shared more with you than I usually do and had gone far beyond what you were in a position to process, which may have been a stretch for you.

I therefore encourage you to regard what I shared with you today about myself and my experiences as being nothing more than a working hypothesis, the truth of which can only be confirmed by future developments.

Eventually we will understand what our soul connection is that causes me to want to share with you far more than I can with others.

In Love's pure Light,

All-is-one

Beloved Allisone,

Thank you for honoring me with your sharing. I regard everything in this amazing life as a gift from God placed here for my awakening (except when I don't, and then I pray to be reminded...and I am...of the wondrousness of this life). So, no problem. My focus is on the unfolding of what this experience is for you, and what its blessings may be for humankind and the Earth right now. The details of what you shared are not nearly as important, for me, as the essence of you and your enlightening enlightenment.

    I hope you have a wonderful day.
    Love, Ana

In the June 2007 issue of *Online Review of Books and Current Affairs*, which was the first professional reviewer to announce *The Bible's Cover-Stories Revealed*, Editor and Publisher John F. Miglio contributed an essay titled "Religious Fundamentalists, Militant Atheists: Both are Misguided and Dangerous".

The first paragraph of Miglio's essay reads as follows: "Famed mythologist Joseph Campbell once remarked that being a member of an organized religion is a sure-fire way for a person not to have a spiritual experience. In other words, many people get so hung up on the rituals and traditions of their religion (or their rejection of it, as with atheists), they miss the most important aspect of the religion itself: a chance to achieve a higher level of consciousness and commune with the source of life."

Miglio then went on to summarize his message with the following advice: "It's time to move on from the limitations and dogma of traditional religion and evolve to a higher level of consciousness as practiced in pantheism and Buddhism."

Dear J. F. Miglio:
    Congratulations on your enlightened essay, and thank you for being the first to promote the dissemination of my illustrated historical treatise, *The Bible's Cover-Stories Revealed: The Golden Keys That Unlock History*.
    May your Online Review of Books thrive and prosper.
    Sincerely,
    Arthur Earl Jones, Ph. D.

Here is the tenth response to my treatise, which I received from Chantale Gratton of New Brunswick, Canada on 1 July 2007:

Hi Allisone,
    I enjoy what you have put together...thank you.
    I just wanted to point out the work by Roger and Messod Sabbah, "Secrets of the Exodus". They propose that Moses and Akhenaten are actually the same person and make a very good case of it.
    Akhenaten would be the creator of Judaism. They analyse and highlight the parallels between the story of Moses and Akhenaten's departure from the official Egyptian capital, to build a city in the desert...and which for forty years was populated by Akhenaten's followers.... And the lack of any Egyptian record mentioning an exodus the size of what is described in the bible...other than Akhenaten's departure...are all pretty convincing.
    Anyways, great book and to me, makes perfect sense.

Keep up the good work,
Blessed be,
C.

Dear Chantale Gratton:
    Thank you for your email dated 1 July 2007, which implies that you have discovered and explored my website.
    The hypothesis that Moses and Akhenaten were one and the same person was first advanced by the unorthodox Egyptian scholar Ahmed Osman in his book titled *Moses, Pharaoh of Egypt*, which was first published in 1990 and then retitled *Moses and Akhenaten: The Secret History of Egypt at the Time of the Exodus* in 2002.
    This hypothesis was then supported by Laurence Gardner in his book *Bloodline of the Holy Grail*, which was published in 1996.
    If you want to know the truth regarding the actual relationship between Moses and Akhenaten and the actual size of the Israelite exodus from Egypt, simply go to www.fearorlove.com and order *The Bible's Cover-Stories Revealed: The Golden Keys That Unlock History* while it is still being offered at the special introductory price.
    With kindest regards and good wishes,
    All-is-one Heartsong

On 1 July 2007, my higher self inspired me to send a copy of the press release for my treatise to John Anthony West, together with the following email message:

Dear John Anthony West:
    In November of 1996, I participated in one of your memorable group tours of Egypt, accompanied by my twin-flame soulmate Claire Heartsong, who subsequently channeled the extraordinary book titled *"Anna: Grandmother of Jesus"*.
    At that time, I knew nothing about ancient Egypt and never dreamed that I would channel an illustrated historical treatise titled *"The Bible's Cover-Stories Revealed: The Golden Keys That Unlock History"*, which is nothing less than an apocalyptic revelation of what really happened during the Eighteenth Dynasty prior to the exodus of the Israelites.
    If you will provide me with a postal address, I will be happy to send you a gift copy of my treatise, which has just been published, and which could provide a spectacular stimulus for your future group tours.
    With kindest regards and good wishes,
    All-is-one Heartsong

Thanks Allisone,
    But I do not remember you under that name. What name did you use on the trip?
    My address is below. Sure, send me your book, but you'll know from being on my trip that I am, you might say, a mystic-in-skeptic's clothing. I am very open

to channeled information, but playing in the scholarly arena as I do, I can only 'use' what I can demonstrate, or, at any rate, support with a plausible scenario.
    Best,
    John

Dear John:
    Thank you for responding to my email message dated 1 July 2007 by sending me your postal address.
    I have today sent you a gift copy of my illustrated historical treatise (*The Bible's Cover-Stories Revealed: The Golden Keys That Unlock History*) as an expression of my heartfelt gratitude for that memorable group tour during November of 1996, which I am now able to appreciate much more fully as a superb introduction to ancient Egypt.
    Let me first clear up the mystery of my names by explaining that my professional name is Arthur Earl Jones, Ph. D., which must have been the name that I used during the trip to Egypt, even though I had been using my spiritual name (All-is-one Heartsong) ever since I received it from the ascended master Saint Germain in 1991.
    Similarly, my twin-flame soulmate, who received her spiritual name (Claire Heartsong) from Saint Germain at that same time must have used her given name (Laura Gipson) on the trip to Egypt.
    Let me next assure you that I honor your orientation as a mystic-in-skeptic's-clothing, especially in regard to the reputed age of the sphinx at Giza; and far from regarding you as a rogue Egyptologist, I regard you as an authentic nonconformist who is quite capable of thinking for himself, by which I mean to imply that we have a great deal in common.
    Finally, I want you to know that I do not expect you or anyone else to accept my treatise upon first reading, so please feel free to use or not use my apocalyptic revelation as your choose.
    Sincerely,
    Arthur Earl Jones, Ph. D.

    On 2 July 2007, I wrote the following entry in my personal journal: "Yesterday evening, I was guided to watch the film JOSHUA again, about opening closed hearts, healing the blind, and resurrecting the dead. Early this morning, I had a dream about investors in oil money at Rockefeller Center, who became lost in the darkness when they drove out on a highway to La Cienega, which means 'the filthy swamp'. Upon contemplating this dream, I gained insight into the fact that the La Cienega swamp of darkworkers who worship oil money is the modern equivalent of the Egyptian priesthood at Karnak, who worshiped the 'hidden god' called Amun. Thus, the current war crime of invading Afghanistan and Iraq is the modern equivalent of the ancient crime of assassinating the extended family of Akhenaten. And the rejection of Tesla by J.P. Morgan was the modern equivalent of the rejection of Akhenaten by Maya, the High Priest of Amun."

I almost forgot to mention that, shortly after I woke up from the foregoing dream and recorded it in my journal very early in the morning of 2 July 2007, my ninth-dimensional highest self, whose name is ZoRaMuEL, transmitted the following announcement to my third-dimensional mind: "I AM ZoRaMuEL, coming into this embodied mind. There is no problem that spirit cannot solve." As I reported to my treasured friend Rebekah on the following day: "The impact of the accompanying energies was so powerful that I felt dizzy and disoriented for the rest of that day."

At one o'clock on the morning of 3 July 2007, my ninth-dimensional self ZoRaMuEL contributed the following parenthetic sentence at the end of the first paragraph of the Epilogue on page 33 of my treatise, to be included in the Seventh Version: "(And choosing to open one's heart chakra is the only way to become enlightened.)"

The entry in my personal journal for 4 July 2007 reads as follows: "This afternoon, I watched my DVD of the cinematic masterpiece JOSEPH (1995), starring Paul Mercurio, Martin Landau, and Ben Kingsley; and directed by Roger Young. Although this was about the seventh time I have watched this film, I was overcome by tears as I contemplated my profound connection with Joseph the Israelite. This evening, I participated in a prayer group at the home of my dear friend Ana Holub. Before the gathering, I informed Ana about the announcement I received from ZoRaMuEL on the morning of 2 July 2007. During the gathering, I prophesied that the United States of America was destined to be resurrected and restored during the next two years. After the gathering, I told Ana that I experienced her expanding consciousness as being like an enlightened Buddha."

Having begun writing this book on 22 June 2007 and having completed the channeling section on 28 June 2007, I received guidance on 5 July 2007 to write the background section, which will be inserted before the channeling section.

Up until this point, my tentative title for this new book had been *Apocalyptic Epilogue: Responses to 'The Bible's Cover-Stories Revealed'*; however, on 7 July 2007, my higher self guided me to the clear realization that the title of this book was going to be *Channeling the Apocalypse*.

Having watched the film NETWORK for about the fifth time on the previous evening, I then proceeded to send another email message to my list of friends around the world:
Dear Friends:
    Have you ever seen the film NETWORK (1976), starring Peter Finch, Faye Dunaway, William Holden, Robert Duvall; directed by Sidney Lumet; screenplay by Paddy Chayefsky?
    This brilliant exposé by Paddy Chayefsky deserves to be subtitled: "How the American people were subverted through television."
    It documents the point at which the American people were on the verge of declaring: "I'm mad as hell, and I'm not going to take it any more!!!"
    All-is-one Heartsong

Then, at nine o'clock on the evening of 7 July 2007, I received further guidance from my higher self, which took the form of this preliminary formulation of the dedication for this book:

"This book is humbly dedicated to the love of truth. Long ago, the German philosopher Arthur Shöpenhauer observed that 'All truth passes through three stages: first, it is ridiculed; next, it is violently attacked; finally, it is held to be self-evident.'"

On the morning of 8 July 2007, I sent the following email message to my growing list of over eighty friends around the world:
"Dear Friends
On 7 July 2007, I received a solicitation from the Republican National Committee in Washington, DC, and in accordance with a dream that I had on the following morning, I mailed the postage-free return envelope, together with a white index card bearing the following momentous message:
NOW THAT WE ARE ON THE ROAD TO PEACE,
WE NO LONGER NEED A WAR PARTY.
In Love's pure Light,
All-is-one Heartsong
www.planetaryascension.net

On the evening of 8 July 2007, I watched the first half of the full version of Shirley MacLaine's film, *Out On A Limb* (1986), about reincarnation and higher consciousness.

I next spent most of the day on 9 July 2007 writing the first part of an insert to be called Controversies, which is all about the conflicts that developed between Dr. Joann Fletcher and Dr. Zahi Hawass and also between Joann Fletcher and Marianne Luban, who had posted on her Internet website in 1999 her hypothesis that the "Younger Lady" mummy might be Nefertiti, four years before Fletcher announced it as her own.

On the evening of 9 July 2007, I watched the second half of Shirley MacLaine's New Age masterpiece, which seemed to have the effect of nourishing and facilitating the connection between my third-dimensional mind and my sixth-dimensional higher self.

Then, between the hours of two and three o'clock on the morning of 10 July 2007, my higher self channeled through my consecrated mind the last part of the insert called Controversies, which raises the questions as to whether Zahi Hawass, Ahmed Osman, and Laurence Gardner might be reincarnations of Maya (the High Priest of Amun), Paramessu (the assassin of Akhenaten and his family), and Horemheb (the Pharaoh of the Oppression of the twelve tribes of Israel).

On the afternoon of 10 July 2007, during the course of responding to a telephone call from my treasured friend Rebekah, my higher self suddenly gave my conscious mind a profound insight into the solution of a problem that she was encountering in regard to the dynamics which were operating between the various members of her family.

My journal entry for 13 July 2007 includes the following passages:
"Yesterday and today, my higher self applied extraordinary pressure on my mind while I was writing the questions regarding Dr. Zahi Hawass, Ahmed Osman, and Laurence Gardner to make certain that my mind did not allow its inclination to resist or avoid the issue to prevent the writing.

"The subjective pressure was so great that it made any interruption of my writing seem intolerable so that, for example, this morning I did not even attempt to take my usual morning walk, but instead wrote about *Akhenaten: Egypt's False Prophet* by Nicholas Reeves . . .

"This afternoon, I placed an order with Lulu for ten copies of the seventh version, which contains six additional parenthetic sentences, plus the correction of the spelling of Zaphnath Paaneah on page 14, plus the addition on the last page 36: "Seventh Version: July 2007."

And my journal entry for 14 July 2007 is as follows:
"This morning, at the request of my treasured friend Leah, who is one of my spiritual daughters, I facilitated her wedding to Wayne La Chapelle by telephone connection between Mount Shasta (California) and Austin (Texas), the script for which I received from my higher self on 1 July 2007.

"This afternoon, I transcribed the verbatim record of my telephone session with Archangel Gabriel Benu on 30 January 2007 which completely confirmed and validated the channeled information that I received from my higher self between 8 December 2006 and 3 January 2007 regarding what really happened during the Eighteenth Dynasty in ancient Egypt and what really happened to the Israelites after their exodus from Egypt.

"As a consequence of being true to myself, I felt very fulfilled at the end of the day."

On 15 July 2007, I wrote the following note in my journal: "This afternoon, I attended a presentation by Grace at Shalomar's Heart of the Awakened gathering at College of the Siskiyous instead of proofreading the manuscript of my book, which left me feeling that I had **not** been true to myself."

Then, on 16 July 2007, I wrote the following report in my journal: "After the presentation by Grace on the theme of learning to transmute fear by loving it, I found myself contemplating the question of how to communicate the essence of this truth in a way that people will be able to understand more fully, and I came up with this formulation: The power to make choices is the power to create our experiences. Every moment in life is an opportunity to make choices. The art of archery is analogous to the art of choosing. There are a million ways to miss the bullseye, but there is only one way to hit the bullseye. We spend a thousand lifetimes missing the bullseye with disempowering choices. Finally, we learn how to hit the bullseye by making the empowering choice to be a lover who is one with God: first, the choice to be a lover of truth; next, the choice to be a lover of fear; then the choice to be a lover of humanity."

My journal entry for 17 July 2007 is as follows: "I set my alarm clock and woke up at four o'clock this morning to participate consciously in the FIRE THE GRID planetary meditation initiated by Shelly Yates, which was scheduled for 4:10 to 5:10 Pacific Daylight Time. Unexpectedly, I received guidance from my sixth-dimensional higher self (Kumara Zora Torith) in the form of this message which was channeled through my third-dimensional consecrated mind (All-is-one Heartsong) and then transmitted to my email list of 85 friends on the Internet at 5:11 a.m.: 'We, the Lightworkers who constitute the cutting edge of humanity on Planet Earth do hereby make the empowering choice to join together as One for the sacred purpose of firing the grid of our collective planetary consciousness on this seventeenth day of July in the year 2007 so as to create a decisive turning point from the fear-based orientation of war manifesting as Hell on Earth to the love-based orientation of peace manifesting as Heaven on Earth. We call forth the God I AM that we are to witness our collective choice. So be it, and so it is.'"

That same day, I received the following announcement from James A. Cox, Editor-in-Chief of the Midwest Book Review:

I'm very pleased to announce that the July 2007 issue of our online book review magazine *Small Press Bookwatch* features *The Bible's Cover-Stories Revealed*. A review script is enclosed for your files.

Beautifully illustrated with twenty-one photographs and illustrations, *The Bible's Cover-Stories Revealed: The Golden Keys That Unlock History* by Arthur Earl Jones was written and published for the purpose of providing contemporary non-specialist general readers with a series of reasoned explanations resolving some of the central mysteries of the Abrahamic religions of Judaism and Christianity based on an examination of the events of the Eighteenth Dynasty of Egypt. *The Bible's Cover-Stories Revealed* identifies the progenitor of the covert Hebrew-Egyptian lineage that Abraham's wife secretly birthed prior to the birth of Isaac; reveals that Moses and the radical Egyptian Pharoah Akhenaten who promoted the concept of monotheism during his reign were actually brothers; provides photographic evidence that Joseph the Israelite was the maternal grandfather of both Moses and Akhenaten; includes a photograph of a sculptured self-portrait of Moses; exposes the assassinations of four Egyptian Pharaohs (Akhenaten, Smenkhkare, Tutankhamun, and Ay) which dramatically affected the subsequent course of human history; and examines the origin of the conflict between the Pharisees and the Essenes -- a conflict that had a direct bearing on the crucifixion of Jesus. Iconoclastic, articulate, thoughtful and thought provoking, "*The Bible's Cover-Stories Revealed*" is strongly recommended reading for students of history, the Judeo-Christian religion, and Egyptology.

This review also appears in the Thomson-Gale interactive CD-ROM series "Book Review Index" (published four times yearly for academic, corporate, and public library systems); as well as such book review databases as Lexus-Nexus and Goliath; and will be archived on the Midwest Book Review website for five years at www.midwestbookreview.com

Assuming your book is registered with Amazon.com, I've also instructed our webmaster to post the review there as well.

I look forward to your next title!
Sincerely,
James A. Cox
Editor-in-Chief

Although I very much appreciated the strong recommendation which accompanied this detailed review of my treatise, my consecrated mind had no choice but to allow my higher self to dictate the following response.

    Salutations to Editor-in-Chief James Cox:

        I sincerely appreciate your choice to feature my illustrated historical treatise titled *The Bible's Cover-Stories Revealed* in the July 2007 issue of your online book review magazine Small Press Bookwatch, and to promote it as "strongly recommended reading for students of history, the Judeo-Christian religion, and Egyptology."

        Please allow me to respectfully call your attention to several misperceptions in the review script which you sent to me on 7 July 2007.

        This treatise was written and published for the general purpose of facilitating the enlightenment of an awakening humanity, but also for the more specific purpose of informing professional scholars as well as general readers regarding 1) what really happened during the Eighteenth Dynasty in ancient Egypt (when the entire family of Pharaoh Akhenaten was systematically exterminated by a lone assassin recruited by the High Priest of Amun and then covered up by Pharaoh Horemheb), and 2) what really happened to the Israelites after their exodus from Egypt (when they divided into an enlightened esoteric faction of Essenes who followed Moses and an unenlightened exoteric faction of Pharisees who followed Aaron, the crucifixion of Jesus being the ultimate outcome of this division.)

        What particularly needs to be understood and communicated is the fact that, far from consisting in "a series of reasoned explanations" (which constitutes the path of intellectual speculation followed by conventional scholars), this radical treatise consists in a series of apocalyptic revelations (based on the absolute knowing that results from spiritual access to the akashic records).

        If you will review the Dedication of my treatise, you will note that my mind is not its source, but merely the humble channel for the enlightened consciousness of my inner being.

        Thus, far from being an iconoclast who is motivated to attack humanity's cherished beliefs and traditional institutions, I am simply a humble lover of truth who is motivated to lovingly and nonjudgmentally reveal the truth for the purpose of facilitating our liberation from the deliberate lies of intentional disinformation and the perpetuated falsehoods of unintentional misinformation, which have been used for thousands of years to deceive, mislead, and subjugate humanity.

    With kindest regards and good wishes,
    Arthur Earl Jones, Ph. D.

    Shortly after I sent this letter to James A. Cox, the Editor-in-Chief at Midwest Book Review, his positive review of my treatise showed up on The Free Library website around the same time that it disappeared from his website on the Internet.

    On 19 July 2007, I sent the following email message to my growing list of over ninety friends around the world:

Dear Friends:
Please give this message your top-priority attention. The illusion is that we are on the Titanic that is about to hit the iceberg and begin to sink. The reality is that we are now passing through our final examination prior to graduation. Remember that life in third-dimensional consciousness is always a choice between fear and love. Darkworkers who choose fear will experience the illusion of the sinking Titanic. Lightworkers who choose love will experience the reality of planetary ascension. We have now reached the dividing of the ways and it is time to make your choice.
    In Love's pure Light,
    All-is-one Heartsong

During my morning walk at 11:30 on 19 July 2007, my higher self informed my consecrated mind that, by including email messages such as the above in my book, *Channeling the Apocalypse*, I will establish the connection between the ancient apocalyptic turning point which occurred in Egypt during the Eighteenth Dynasty and the modern apocalyptic turning point which is now in the process of occurring on Planet Earth.

On 21 July 2007, I transmitted the following email invitation to Dr. Joann Fletcher:
Dear Dr. Joann Fletcher:
    It has now been over six weeks since I sent you a gift copy of my illustrated historical treatise (*The Bible's Cover-Stories Revealed: The Golden Keys That Unlock History*).
    This seems to imply that you are reluctant to respond to my apocalyptic revelation without knowing more about me, which is very understandable.
    I am therefore writing to offer you a gift copy of a 61-page autobiographical account of my spiritual journey during this lifetime *(Illustration of Spiritual Awakening)*, which I wrote several years ago, and which provides a convenient way to satisfy your desire for further information.
    With kindest regards and good wishes,
    Sincerely,
    Arthur Earl Jones, Ph.D.

On the evening of 23 July 2007, I went to the local theater to see "SiCKO", the recently-released exposé by Michael Moore, which documents the totally corrupt health-care system that the Dark Illuminati have used to subjugate the American people, and which has the potential capacity to motivate the American people to decisively repudiate the entire New World Order agenda of the Dark Illuminati.

On the morning of 24 July 2007, I sent the following email to my list of over 90 friends around the world:
Dear Friends:
    Have you seen the film ERIN BROCKOVICH (2000), starring Julia Roberts and Albert Finney?

This cinematic masterpiece tells the true story of a down-and-out twice-divorced mother of three young children who, because she was unintimidatable, succeeds in exposing a multibillion dollar corporation that attempted to deceive the local community which it had poisoned with contaminated groundwater.

I regard Erin Brockovich as the heroine of our time, whose extraordinary accomplishment has set an inspiring example for all of humanity.

In Love's pure Light,
All-is-one Heartsong
www.planetaryascension.net

Then, in the middle of the night on the early morning of 26 July 2007, my higher self channeled through my consecrated mind a supplemental press release titled: Did You Know...? (See Item 29)

Consequently, on 27 July 2007, I mailed the following letter to the twelve prospective reviewers, together with the original press release and the "Did You Know?" supplement:

"Dear Prospective Reviewer:

It has now been two months since I sent you a review copy of my illustrated historical treatise, *The Bible's Cover-Stories Revealed: The Golden Keys That Unlock History*. Because this revelation is a product of the absolute knowing of sixth-dimensional consciousness rather than the speculative thinking of third-dimensional consciousness, I realize that conventional reviewers may have some qualms about accepting my unconventional contribution; however, I can assure you that it is true, and I am happy to report that is has received two courageous reviews thus far, both of which are positive.

Please find enclosed an additional press release which is designed to supplement my original press release by revealing more fully the historical significance of this revolutionary revelation.

With kindest regards and good wishes,
Sincerely,
Arthur Earl Jones, Ph. D.
In God We Trust

On 29 July 2007, I sent out the following email message to my list of over ninety friends around the world:

Dear Friends:

Have you seen the film JOSHUA, starring Tony Goldwyn and F. Murray Abraham ?

This cinematic masterpiece invites us to imagine what it would be like if Jesus (Yeshua ben Joseph), disguised as an ordinary woodcarver, came to a small town in contemporary America and began to perform healing miracles.

Item 29

Did You Know...?

1) Did you know that an enlightened Christ was born in Egypt and rejected by the Egyptian priesthood over thirteen centuries before Jesus (Yeshua ben Joseph) was born in Judea and rejected by the Judean priesthood?

2) Did you know that the name of this enlightened Egyptian Christ was Pharaoh Akhenaten and that Moses was his brother?

3) Did you know that the truth about Moses as well as Akhenaten has been intentionally concealed and completely hidden from you until now?

4) Did you know that these enlightening truths (THE BIBLE'S COVER-STORIES REVEALED : THE GOLDEN KEYS THAT UNLOCK HISTORY by Arthur Earl Jones, Ph.D.) are now available to you for a few dollars?

5) Did you know that there are still those who will try to prevent these truths from being revealed to you?

6) Did you know that the global contest between lightworkers who love the truth and darkworkers who fear the truth is what humanity is really all about?

7) Did you know that you now have a priceless opportunity to become an enlightened ascended master of Christ Consciousness within the next five years by means of what is known as the planetary ascension process?

For further information, see the spiritual catalogue at
www.fearorlove.com

This beautiful message is directed to all of humanity, inviting all of us to open our hearts to love.
In Love's pure Light,
All-is-one Heartsong
www.planetaryascension.net

Between one and two o'clock on the morning of 30 July 2007, my higher self inspired me to write the following introduction to an email transmission by Hal Turner of a top-secret document which was sent to him around 17 July 2007 and which revealed secret plans by the United States federal government to use its military forces against any attempt by the American people to oppose the government's agenda:

"Let history record that, in its desperate attempts to criminalize the American people, the fraudulent and hijacked United States federal government of George W. Bush has criminalized itself and was exposed on 24 July 2007 by the courageous actions of internet and radio talk-show host Hal Turner, an outspoken, hate-mongering white supremacist, who may eventually be regarded as the Paul Revere of our twenty-first century America."

On that same morning of 30 July 2007, Mike Quinsey channeled a top-priority message from the ascended master Saint Germain, which I transmitted to my email list of over ninety friends around the world, using the following heading: Saint Germain Prepares Us For Ascension.

Then, at seven o'clock on the evening of 30 July 2007, my higher self revealed to my consecrated mind that the full title of this book was going to be: CHANNELING THE APOCALYPSE: FROM THE EIGHTEENTH DYNASTY TO THE CURRENT INCARNATIONS.

On the morning of 31 July 2007, I woke up with the following dream: I am a naked sadhu (a Hindu ascetic or holy man) reclining on the banks of a river and then on the crowded street of a large city, looking deeply into the eyes of everyone that I meet, experiencing ecstatic states of bliss, declining intellectual conversation, and preferring to be in communion with my beloved friend Grace. (Note: This dream may be a reflection of one of my previous incarnations in India.)

At three o'clock on the morning of 1 August 2007, my consecrated mind received the following channeled message from my higher self with the understanding that it was to be included in this book titled *Channeling the Apocalypse: From the Eighteenth Dynasty to the Current Incarnations*.

"It is clear to me that Dr. Zahi Hawass has done an enormous amount of good work to compensate and make restitution for the genocidal crimes which he committed during his previous lifetime as Maya, the High Priest of Amun; but it is also clear to me that he has used his exalted position and reputation as Secretary-General of Egypt's Supreme Council of Antiquities to continue his cover-up of those crimes."

At six o'clock on the morning of 1 August 2007, I woke up with the following dream: I am a student in the Palm Springs High School physics class of my favorite teacher Paul Summers, whose lecture I suddenly interrupt by saying to the class: "Don't ever depend on the human mind to figure out what life is all about, because the third-dimensional mind simply does not know the answer."

I now invite you to see Appendix B for an exceptionally enlightening message from the God of this Universe, which was channeled through Suzanne Ward, the devoted mother of Matthew Ward, on 1 August 2007 and which I immediately placed on my website after transmitting it to my list of friends around the world.

On the afternoon of 1 August 2007, I mailed this letter to John Anthony West, together with a gift copy of *Illustration of Spiritual Awakening* by Arthur Earl Jones, Ph. D.

Dear John:

It has now been one month since I sent you a gift copy of my illustrated historical treatise, *The Bible's Cover-Stories Revealed: The Golden Keys That Unlock History*.

Although I didn't expect you to accept it on first reading, I am now inclined to interpret the fact that I have not heard from you for a whole month as meaning you are reluctant to believe the exposé of what really happened toward the end of the Eighteenth Dynasty because this might jeopardize your position in regard to the Egyptian government in general and Dr. Zahi Hawass in particular.

I therefore recommend that we keep our future correspondence completely confidential, with the understanding that I have released any expectation that you might be a means of facilitating the awakening of humanity through the dissemination of my apocalyptic revelation.

Nevertheless, because I have the highest regard for the courage that you have demonstrated in the past regarding such matters as the true age of the Sphinx, I would like to continue the process of cultivating our personal friendship by enclosing a gift copy of the 61-page autobiographical account of my spiritual journey during this lifetime, which I wrote several years ago and which is titled *Illustration of Spiritual Awakening*.

If, after reading the story of my life, you prefer not to cultivate our friendship further, I will of course honor your choice.

Sincerely,
Arthur

On the evening of 1 August 2007, I transmitted the current update by Sheldan Nidle for 31 July 2007, together with the following message in capital letters: PLEASE GIVE THIS MESSAGE YOUR TOP-PRIORITY ATTENTION. WE ARE NOW ON THE VERGE OF PLANETARY TRANSFORMATION. PREPARE YOURSELF FOR RADICAL CHANGES OVER THE NEXT FEW MONTHS

Having already been invited by my beloved friend Grace to participate in her annual Mount Shasta retreat from August 2 to August 6, I then made the most of this welcome opportunity to take a refreshing vacation from my eight-month focus on channeling the apocalypse, beginning with an invigorating swim across Cliff Lake on August 3 and ending with a baptismal ceremony at Upper Panther Meadow on August 6.

Although a global financial crisis had gradually been developing for many months, it was precisely during this time frame from August 2 to August 6 that plunging financial markets throughout the world began to register a loss of confidence that briefly escalated into panic.

It was also right at this time that the youngest of my spiritual daughters, a twenty-seven- year-old Canadian by the name of Katie Anna brightened my apartment with her annual Mount Shasta visit during the month of August.

At nine o'clock on the morning of 7 August 2007, I then sent the following email message to my list of over ninety friends around the world:

Beloved Friends:
> As you know, the old world of third-dimensional separation consciousness is now in the process of dying, and the new world of fourth-dimensional unity consciousness is now in the process of being born.
> To be more specific, the darkworkers' downward spiral which has manifested as Hell on Earth is now ending, and the lightworkers' upward spiral which is destined to create Heaven on Earth has now begun.
> According to my inner guidance, the pivotal point was finally reached by humanity on Planet Earth during this past week from 30 July to 5 August 2007.
> In Love's pure Light,
> All-is-one Heartsong
> www.planetaryascension.net

At 9:52 on the morning of 7 August 2007, I received the following response from Sue Lie (also known as Suzan Caroll):
> That is very interesting. How did you come to that conclusion? I am not disputing that statement, but I would like to know how you came to it. The shift is definitely here. Sue.

Knowing that Sue Lie (aka Suzan Caroll) is a dedicated lightworker to whom I had already sent gift copies of my autobiography as well as my treatise on 13 June 2007, I replied to her question as follows:

Dear Sue Lie (also known as Suzan Caroll);
> My inner guidance comes from my highest self on the ninth dimension of consciousness (whose name is ZoRaMuEL) through my higher self on the sixth dimension of consciousness (whose name is Kumara Zora Torith) to my consecrated mind on the third dimension of consciousness (whose name is All-is-one Heartsong.)
> In Love's pure Light,
> All-is-one

In response to my reply, Sue Lie's next message stated: "I also have quite a few higher names on different dimensions. I agree. The time is NOW. Sue."

I then concluded our email conversation as follows: "Dear Sue: I acknowledge you as a spiritual sister and a dedicated lightworker. I am deeply grateful for your confirmation of my inner knowing that we have now reached the pivotal point of our planetary ascension process. Blessings on your path, All-is-one."

On the morning of 8 August 2007, I received an email message from the ascended master Saint Germain through his dedicated channel Mike Quinsey, which I then transmitted to my list of over ninety friends around the world after carefully noting that it contained the following key words: "You have now become an enlightened being."

I also sent the following email message to my brother in the Hawaiian Islands on the morning of 8 August 2007:
My beloved brother companion:
 No one else knows me as you do. For we have been together in this lifetime from our very humble beginnings in Glendale and San Clemente through our wondrous experience of growing up in Palm Springs and Lake Arrowhead, with a devoted mother who rejected our father as a failure because she hated men, a paternal grandmother who was the personification of nonjudgmental love, and a very capable maternal grandfather who made a fortune building houses.
 Although the process of getting an education, choosing a vocation, getting married, and having children caused us to go our seemingly separate ways during the middle years of our lives, we somehow managed to survive all of the trials and tribulations of our extremely limited human condition and then made the empowering choice to come back together as devoted brothers and dedicated lightworkers for the purpose of completing our journey into the grand finale known as planetary ascension.
 As I wish you a happy birthday at this pivotal point in human history on Planet Earth, and congratulate you on your perseverance along the path that leads to wisdom, I want you to know that I am deeply and sincerely grateful for your presence in my life.
  In Love's pure Light
  Arthur ➜ All-is-One ➜ Kumara Zora Torith ➜ ZoRaMuEL

Here is the email message that I transmitted to my list of friends around the world on the morning of 9 August 2007:
Dear Friends:
 Have you ever seen THE BIG BLUE (1980), starring Jean-Marc Barr, Jean Reno, and Rosanna Arquette; written and directed by Luc Besson; with the incomparable music of Eric Serra?
 One of the great films of all time, this cinematic masterpiece is outwardly about competition for the world free-diving championship and inwardly about the

angelic nature of dolphin consciousness.
>In Love's pure Light,
>All-is-one Heartsong

On the afternoon of 9 August 2007, I met with a lightworker from Germany by the name of Christiane Rauch and immediately received inner guidance to present her with a gift copy of my autobiography, *Illustration of Spiritual Awakening*.

On the evening of 10 August 2007, after Christiane and Katie Anna returned from a hike to Squaw Meadow, high on the south side of Mount Shasta, I invited Christiane to watch first my Eye on Humanity video of the ascended master Saint Germain through his full-body channel Azena, and then my Birthing the Era of God video of the Divine Mother channeled by Claire Heartsong.

On 11 August 2007, I spent approximately ten hours of focused attention on the task of refining and expanding my manuscript for *Channeling the Apocalypse*. The first thing that I did was to write the Preface, which will precede the Prologue. After adding several items from my journal to the section titled Prelude, I then received clear guidance to revise the sequence of sections by placing the section titled Background before rather than after the section titled Prelude.

On 12 August 2007, I spent another eight hours of focused attention on the process of refining my manuscript.

Also on 12 August 2007, I placed the following prediction on my website, based on a rumor which was currently circulating on the Internet.
>DEAR FRIENDS:
>>HYPOTHESIS: Target date for shift from old Federal Reserve System to new Treasury system is 19 September 2007.
>>Transition time is 5 ½ weeks or next 38 days: 12 August 2007 to 19 September 2007.
>>BE ALERT AND READY FOR RAPID DEVELOPMENTS.
>>ALL-IS-ONE

On the evening of 12 August 2007, I discovered the extraordinary website of Lyara (www.OperationTerra.com) and immediately subscribed, but was so immersed in the process of writing this book that I had to postpone my desire to explore it for two whole weeks.

On 13 August 2007, Karl Rove, who was commonly referred to by the media as "Bush's Brain", but who had been branded by George W. Bush with the nickname "Turd Blossom", signaled the imminent collapse of the illegitimate Bush Administration by announcing his resignation.

On the morning of 14 August 2007, I wrote the following note in my journal: "The darkworkers are continuing to circulate rumors that: 1) another terrorist attack similar to that of 11 September 2001 is about to occur; 2) the Bush administration is about to declare martial law in the

United States; and 3) the United States government is about to launch a military attack against Iran."

On the evening of 14 August 2007, I sent forth the following email message, together with the current update by Sheldan Nidle:
Dear Friends:
Please give this information your top-priority attention. We have now reached the pivotal point of our planetary ascension process. Be prepared for rapid developments from this point onward. Be alert, awake, and aware at the still center of the hurricane. Know that all is well, regardless of appearances to the contrary.
In Love's pure Light,
All-is-one Heartsong.

On 15 August 2007, I wrote the following entry in my private journal: "At four o'clock this morning, I received guidance to send a gift copy of my treatise to my friend Tom Kenyon. I also received guidance to consider using the Egyptian icon of ascended masters on a gold and indigo cover for my book, to include a map of the dimensions plus *What Is a Lightworker?* and *What Is a Darkworker?*, and to order a Bowker bar code for the book."

On 17 August 2007, I mailed the following letter to my friend Tom Kenyon in accordance with the guidance that I had received two days earlier.
Dear Tom:
My sixth-dimensional higher self has recently channeled through my third-dimensional consecrated mind an illustrated historical treatise titled *The Bible's Cover-Stories Revealed: The Golden Keys That Unlock History*.
Please find enclosed a gift copy which my higher self has requested that I send to you as an expression of my heartfelt appreciation and gratitude for all that you are doing to facilitate the awakening and enlightenment of humanity at this pivotal point in human history.
I am currently working on a follow-up book that will contain a verbatim transcript of a telephone session that I had with Archangel Gabriel through his dedicated full-body channel Karen Cook on 30 January 2007 which completely validates everything that my higher self transmitted in this treatise.
Blessings on your path.
In Love's pure Light,
All-is-one Heartsong
aka Arthur Earl Jones, Ph. D.

Then, on the evening of 17 August 2007, I wrote the following report in my journal:
"When I woke up from a nap that I took between two and four o'clock this afternoon, I felt like I was in the wrong place.
"More specifically, I felt like I should be in a high council laying down God's Law to the recalcitrant darkworkers who are trying to hold on to their old system instead of facing the fact that their time is over.

"I definitely felt like I should not be in the third dimension having to focus my attention on doing my laundry.

"The implication is that, while my body was in a deep sleep during my nap, my consciousness was experiencing an entirely different aspect of my multidimensional being, with the result that, when my body woke up, I felt momentarily disoriented and extremely reluctant to shift my attention from the intense contest between lightworkers and darkworkers at this pivotal point in human history to the mundane task of going to the laundromat to do my laundry."

Here is the entry that I wrote in my journal on the evening of 18 August 2007:

"I drove up to Morningstar at ten o'clock this morning and invited Grace to come to my apartment this evening at five o'clock to read the message from Archangel Michael through Celia Finn, titled 'The Energies for August 2007: Crossing the Threshold – Activating the Infinity Codes.'

"I then pointed out the second paragraph referring to this present pivotal point as a window of opportunity for lightworkers who have completed their assignment to leave Planet Earth at this time.

"Grace confirmed that she has been feeling the invitation to leave Planet Earth at this time but has also been experiencing the activation of the Infinity Codes.

"I invited Grace to think of me every morning saying to her: 'What may I do for you today, beloved?'"

Around two o'clock on the morning of 19 August 2007, my higher self channeled through my consecrated mind this sentence for possible use on the back cover of my book:

"In this spectacular exposé, Archangel Gabriel, speaking through his dedicated full-body channel Karen Cook of Albuquerque, New Mexico, validates *The Bible's Cover-Stories Revealed: The Golden Keys That Unlock History* by providing incontrovertible confirmation of the absolute knowing of akashic truths that the sixth-dimensional higher self of Dr. Arthur Earl Jones revealed through the consecrated channel of his third-dimensional mind, thereby solving the mysterious puzzle of Egypt's Eighteenth Dynasty and the perplexing riddle of Judeo-Christian religion."

Later that same morning, I completed proofreading the manuscript for this book up to 8 August 2007.

Around noon on 19 August 2007, I transmitted the following email message to my growing list of friends around the world:

Dear Friends:

    Have you ever seen the film DANGEROUS BEAUTY (1997) starring Catherine McCormack and Rufus Sewell?

    This cinematic masterpiece is based on the true story of Veronica Franco, a Venetian courtesan whose exceptional integrity, beauty, and intelligence were more than equal to the challenge of being condemned as a witch by the Roman Catholic Inquisition during the 16th century.

    In Love's pure Light,
    All-is-one Heartsong

It is worth mentioning that, when I shared this true story of Veronica Franco with my spiritual daughter Katie Anna during her annual August visit to Mount Shasta, she was so inspired by the film that she watched it, not just once, but four times.

On 20 August 2007, I received an unexpected contribution to the cause from my brother, who lives in the Hawaiian Islands, to which I responded by sending the following message:
Dear Bob:
   I have just received your very unexpected but very welcome gift, and I want you to know that it could not have arrived at a better time, by which I mean that it must have been inspired by spirit.
   I have done a good job of living within my means during the past several years, using every spare dollar to pay Zepp for processing my manuscripts and articles for my website, the most challenging expenses being my unpredictable dental bills.
   However, since my higher self began to channel these books through my consecrated mind eight months ago, I no longer know what "living within my means" means.
   During these past eight months, my heart's desire has been for my illustrated historical treatise to facilitate a flow of abundance and prosperity into my life as soon as possible, but so far not a single copy has been sold by my distributor-friend Leah of Austin, Texas.
   And I just returned from shopping at the supermarket, where the prices of food (e.g., walnuts) have doubled in recent months.
   My life constitutes an enormous test of faith, and I can only trust spirit to orchestrate!
   With my love and gratitude,
   Arthur

On the morning of 21 August 2007, I made arrangements with lulu.com to have my treatise distributed by Amazon, Barnes & Noble, Borders, and other online booksellers. (Up until this point, I had allowed my friend Leah to distribute my treatise on her website www.fearorlove.com at the special introductory price of $19.95 rather than $24.95 which is the regular price.)

On the afternoon of 21 August 2007, I received the following review from The Mindquest Review, whose editor/publisher Bernie Nelson had recently seen the review of my treatise by James Cox of the Midwest Review and had invited me to submit a copy of my treatise for his consideration.

THE BIBLE'S COVER-STORIES REVEALED
by
Arthur Earl Jones, Ph. D.

Subject: The author presents an amazing dichotomy between those open-minded to truth, and those who suppress truth. He illustrates the suppression of Eighteenth Egyptian Dynasty facts, and how these secrets relate to the Judeo-Christian religion. The purpose is to awaken minds to today's "pivotal point in human history". Subtitle: "The Golden Keys That Unlock History."

Noteworthy: The extraordinary full color photos (8.5 by 11) of ancient figures relevant to the author's new revelations, are worth the price of the book alone. Seven major revelations are back by Biblical history and scientific sources. An example: On the front cover is a full color photo of Queen Tiye, "Mother of Moses and Akhenaten – the founders of monotheistic religion."

Details: Liberty Rising Productions, POB 204264, Austin, TX 78720. 36 pg. 8.5 by 11, $24.95. ISBN: 978-0-9794139-1-9
fearorloveorders@austin.rr.com
www.fearorlove.com

My spontaneous email response to this review by Bernie Nelson, which I managed to transmit on that same day, is as follows:
Dear Bernie Nelson:
    You are clearly the man I have been looking for.
    I have just received your letters dated 13 August 2007 and 16 August 2007, to which I am responding immediately.
    It is so refreshing (as well as encouraging) to finally get an enlightened response from someone who is able to demonstrate that he really understands the meaning and purpose of my illustrated historical treatise, *The Bible's Cover-Stories Revealed*.
    Let me first specify one minor correction in your otherwise superb review: change "back" to "backed".
    Next, let me invite your assistance in creating an effective media kit, which is something I have never done before.
    Finally, I should mention that I am eighty years old and living on my monthly Social Security checks with no financial reserves, which severely limits the extent to which I will be able to avail myself of your services.
    With kind regards and good wishes,
    Sincerely,
    Arthur Earl Jones, Ph. D.

PREVIEWS

The first thing that I did on the morning of 22 August 2007 was to transmit the current message from the Sirian Council of the Galactic Federation channeled by Sheldan Nidle, which predicted radical changes in the very near future, including: 1) removal of the Bush administration; 2) debt forgiveness and prosperity programs, and 3) deflation followed by a new currency system with new credit guidelines and restrictions on banks and corporations. (See Item 30)

The second thing that I did on that morning was to transmit an exuberant exhortation from Ker-On of Venus, a fifth-dimensional emissary of the Galactic Federation channeled by Mike

Quinsey of England, declaring that it was now time for humanity to begin celebrating the victory of the lightworkers over the darkworkers, which prepares the way for planetary ascension. (See Item 31)

And the third thing that I did on 22 August 2007 was to place information regarding my new book on Bowkerlink.com and then to order a barcode.

On 23 August 2007, in an internet article titled: *Hurricane George: How the White House Drowned New Orleans*, investigative journalist Greg Palast broke the shocking news that two years earlier on 29 August 2005, the Bush administration withheld from the Louisiana state police crucial information that the levees had breeched and New Orleans was about to flood as a consequence of Hurricane Katrina.

This constitutes another genocidal crime for which George Bush must be held responsible.

The whistleblower who served as the source for Greg Palast's story is Dr. Ivor van Heerdan, deputy director of the Louisiana State University Hurricane Center, who was the chief technician advising the State of Louisiana on saving lives during Hurricane Katrina.

Between 7:30 and 10:30 on the Thursday evening of 23 August 2007, my higher self channeled through my consecrated mind the first three paragraphs of the Press Release for *Channeling the Apocalypse*.

Between 4:30 and 5:30 on the Friday morning of 24 August 2007, my higher self then channeled through my consecrated mind the last two paragraphs of the Press Release for *Channeling the Apocalypse*.

Let history record that before he died of bladder cancer at age 64 on 24 August 2007, Aaron Russo made enormous contributions to the awakening and enlightenment of humanity by creating the documentary feature film *America: From Freedom to Fascism* and by reporting that Nick Rockefeller had not only revealed the Rockefeller family's agenda for subjugating humanity but had accurately predicted the "war on terror" hoax and the invasion of Iraq and Afghanistan, eleven months before 9/11 occurred.

On 25 August 2007, I woke up with sciatic pain in my right hip, which is something that I have never experienced before, and which gradually subsided.

While surfing the internet, I came across a listing of articles written by Captain Eric H. May during the past two years, zeroed in on his article *Operation Apocalypse: End Timers and End-Game Strategy*, which was published on 31 July 2006 but which I had never read before, received inner guidance to include it in my new book, and then sent him the following feedback by email at nine o'clock that morning.

Captain Eric H. May:

I plan to include your Operation Apocalypse article in my book, *Channeling the Apocalypse*. With my heartfelt gratitude for all of the great work that you have done and will continue to do.

Arthur Earl Jones, Ph. D.

Special Military Correspondent Captain Eric H. May is a former Army military intelligence and public affairs officer, as well as a former NBC editorial writer. His political and military analyses have appeared in The Wall Street Journal, The Houston Chronicle, and Military Intelligence Magazine. Captain May is also the leader of Ghost Troop, a cyber intelligence unit comprised of military, police, and government veterans along with citizen activists. Please see *Operation Apocalypse: End Timers and End-Game Strategy* by Captain Eric H. May in Appendix A.

Later that same morning, I found time to send a follow-up message to Bernie Nelson of the Mindquest Review:
Dear Bernie Nelson:
    During the past several weeks, my attention has been focused and concentrated on the process of writing another book for the specific purpose of confirming and validating the apocalyptic revelations contained in my illustrated historical treatise.
    I have just finished writing a preliminary formulation of the press release for the new book, a copy of which is herewith enclosed...
    As a consequence, I have not yet had an opportunity to read the material that you sent me together with your letter and the review.
    I will communicate further as soon as I have had a chance to consider the various options that you have offered regarding the possibility of working together.
    With kindest regards and good wishes,
    Sincerely,
    Arthur Earl Jones, Ph. D.

On the afternoon of 25 August 2007, while proofreading the manuscript for this book, I received guidance from my higher self to add the following note to page 59 of the verbatim transcript of my telephone session with Archangel Gabriel Benu:
"[Note: With these words, Archangel Gabriel confirmed the genocidal agenda of Maya, the High Priest of Amun, and Paramessu, the recruited assassin, which reversed the course of human history.]"

In the meantime, I received the following email response from Captain May:
"Thanks, Dr. Jones. I'm honored. There is a typo that needs correcting, though. In the article, I mention CNN's Paul Zahn. The correct first name is Paula. Good luck with the book, and please let me know when it comes out. Best regards, CPTMAY."

On the morning of 26 August 2007, I then sent this follow-up message to Captain May:
Thank you, Captain Eric May, for your positive response. I will correct the typo.
    Prepare yourself for a major expansion of consciousness. I am enclosing a preliminary formulation of the press release for my new book *(Channeling the Apocalypse: From the Eighteenth Dynasty to the Current Incarnations)*, which will be self-published in another month or two...

Item 30
Message from the Sirian Council of the Galactic Federation
Channeled by Sheldan Nidle on 21 August 2007

Selamat Jarin! We return, dear Hearts, to discuss much with you! The events swirling around the creation of your new reality continue to move forward. Our Earth allies are busy working out the last legal details concerning the coming resignation of the present US regime. In addition, the dismantling of the Federal Reserve Bank and the introduction of the new global banking system are likewise nearing the final stages. Because of the vital importance of the US Federal Reserve in these matters, a system for changing over from the present financial system to the new one became essential. This new system is to be introduced in three stages: The first is to be part of the debt forgiveness process. Since the core of this debt involves a circuitous and complex procedure ultimately based on the use of US Federal Reserve debentures, it was thought best by all parties to rescind these instruments along with the retirement of the world's debt. The stage is then set for the introduction of the new American Treasury Bank and the new global banking system.

The new banking system comes on line with the formal announcement of a global currency overhaul featuring the reintroduction of hard currency. A great roundup of long-hidden gold reserves, as well as some new gold bullion supplied by the Galactic Federation, makes it possible to take your banking system off the present highly inflated fiat-money footing. Then follows a controlled, massive deflation of prices and other related matters to pre-inflation levels. Once these various price adjustments are completed, a new, more accurate pricing system can replace the old one. These changes will be softened by the delivery of the many prosperity programs. The sharing of these vast sums can permit Earth's many societies to survive this wholesale movement from one monetary order to another. With this done, the final part of step two is to explain how this banking system operates and to announce that it is available to everyone. This global system will highlight the major currencies of Asia, Europe, and the Americas. Naturally, this leads to the reissuing of the world's currencies.

The last of the three steps is to release new, strict guidelines for the use of credit. Because universal abundance is to go hand-in-hand with the setting-up of the new monetary and banking system, it is expected that issuance of credit will be greatly curtailed. This implies that comprehensive measures will be instituted to ensure that this abundance is both maintained and globally sustained. The concept of credit is to revert to its former meaning. The vast expansion of credit, especially in the last half of your twentieth century, is to be prevented from reoccurring by directives formulated by a global committee of old banking hands who intend that the sins of the past not be permitted to contaminate the future. Banks are to be holding houses for wealth and their power limited by strict and detailed regulations. These codes will limit banks to a number of precise services. Money will no longer be an agent separating humanity; indeed, global abundance will be a determining factor in creating the future world of global unity.

The abundance, which has literally taken centuries to amass, is the foundation for what our Earth allies intend to build. Since money, to date, has predominantly been used to acquire and maintain power, the first step of meaningful change is to end the huge monetary disparity that characterizes your societies. Moreover, this leveling of the playing field requires guidelines: It is not simply a matter of distributing vast sums among the poor; in other words, to those who have a very idealistic concept of what is involved in being immensely wealthy. The challenge is to set up a distribution scheme that shifts wealth in a practical manner from its former proprietors to those who are quite innocent of the responsibilities big money confers. To tackle this, a "distribution tree" was set up and the means to maintain the stability of this distribution apparatus put in place. A concomitant is the creation of programs to educate the first recipients of these enormous funds.

This critical process is dependent upon the new transitional governments, which are dedicated to establishing this prosperity-maintaining system. This system is also to be deeply instrumental in ending the roadblocks that were set up to prevent new technologies from coming forth. It will be responsible for encouraging invention in all quarters and supporting an explosion of information in all fields of scientific endeavor. The static condition of your present world is to be morphed into a dynamic environment that quickly makes up for lost time (see previous update). Naturally, this system includes policies tailored to uphold freedom, responsibility, and the individual sovereignty of all. Corporations are to be recast along the lines of "socially responsible partnerships" and the various statute codes that created them, voided. Your present, fractured societies are to be transformed by government edict, personal responsibility, and a new group dynamic into a global community that is motivated to be a hands-on partaker in government and determined to secure the general welfare and the blessings of Liberty for all.

The metamorphosis of your global society is an important aspect of what first contact is all about. Our coming is due in part to your huge innate potential and in part to the decrees of the divine plan. Inside your cellular nuclei is a genetic structure that is mostly lying dormant. Only in the past few decades have these structures begun to be activated--slowly at first, but now at an accelerating pace. These inner changes must now be reflected in your outer global reality, and this is where we come in: Our part in this is to assist our Earth allies in ensuring that these transformations happen according to divine decree. Much is planned and is swiftly nearing the point of manifestation. We are here to tell you that these good deeds are quite close to happening.

First contact is reaching a most exciting point. We mentioned in past messages how diligently our crews are preparing for this blessed event. In fact, the multitudinous hosts of Ascended Masters who are to accompany us have taken up a most sacred series of chants. This outpouring of "intent" signals the proximity of our arrival on your beloved shores. These continuous rituals further heighten our growing excitement over our coming mass reunion with you. The swift approach of these things means that your many body Angels and spiritual guardians are stepping up the pace of your multileveled body changes. The medical teams working on you inform us daily about the escalating demands made on them by Heaven!

Heaven deeply loves you and desires that your present world be transformed by divine action. This spiritual intervention sparked the events about to happen. We monitor all this and use our knowledge to prepare our personnel for what lies ahead. Your role is to allow yourself to undergo an enormous integration of your physical and spiritual bodies. This prepares you for our arrival. We see ourselves as your guides and mentors, and above all, as family. Your changes are likewise transforming your galaxy. We are moving silently, peacefully, and joyfully into a most magnificent aspect of galactic history. Your current history is a microcosm of this, and while not as joyous as ours, is nevertheless a period heralding great change. Above all, this is the glorious moment when you are destined to go from planetary to Galactic Beings.

Today, we discussed the many changes awaiting you. These coming events are precursors to first contact. Rejoice, and know that you are close to the time when truly amazing things are to happen. Be accepting and optimistic during these final waiting moments as you prepare to make your most loving intentions manifest. We now retire. Know in your Heart of Hearts that the perpetual Supply and infinite Abundance of Heaven are indeed Yours! Selamat Majon! Selamat Kasitaram! (Sirian for Rejoice! and Be Blessed in Heavenly Love and Joy!)

Item 31
Message from Ker-On of Venus
Channeled by Mike Quinsy of England on 22 August 2007

You are at a time in this period of awakening, when you should be full of joy and happiness. There is a great Light growing that is lifting up those who seek the truth, as more souls begin to understand their purpose for being here. You are indeed privileged to have been chosen to take part in the end times of this cycle. Many souls are fighting against the old energies that still hold them back, but with the help of others bringing Light to the Earth they are succeeding. Equal opportunity is given to every soul to bring an end to their travels in the lower energies. On one level it only requires the intent to change their path, and that will set a course to fulfilment.

The dark forces are collapsing very rapidly and in spite of the chaos that it is causing, it is creating a shift from what was of the old, to a new enlightened way that will reveal the plan for Man. You are so near to completion of the old cycle, and with it will go the entrenched beliefs that have held you back for eons of time. In the events happening upon Earth see only the opportunity for change, and do not give your energy to those who only see the Apocalypse as the final end to life.

God has not created the misery and despair that exists upon Earth; it has arisen from Man's forgetfulness as to his true being and place in the Cosmos. Dipping deep into the muddied waters of life you have been allowed to experience first hand the depth of negativity, until you have sought the Light of Freedom. You have always known that there was a different way of life, one that would fulfil your dreams of living in absolute peace and harmony. Now the thrust of that belief has become your goal, and you seek the beauty of the Love and Light with its ability to lift you up.

Never before has there been a clearer path defined for your rising up, one that will permanently leave the old behind. What you have invested your life in no longer matters, wealth and fame are but passing stages in your life. Like poverty and loneliness they are simply stops along your path, determined by your need to experience your own creations. There is nothing in your life that has not been brought about by your own actions. Therefore live it out knowing that you are on a path of your own choosing and making. Some will doubt that they could have chosen their present one, but you may be assured that if you could see your greater plan you would fully understand the reasons why.

All life is about experiencing and progressing upwards, and moving back into a higher expression of yourself, seeking the perfection that once was yours. Opening up your heart centre, and allowing the Light to shine out on all around you. Finding your guidance from within and awakening to the subconscious memories of your Higher Self. Come from that place of low estimation of yourself, into one where you acknowledge your divinity. Become that which you are, an expression of your Godself that can be the Light of Freedom and Peace.

There is nothing that you cannot achieve, and even in your wildest dreams you have laid down the possibility of its creation. You are projecting that which you desire, and placing these markers along the path of your life. Now let your imagination know no bounds, as you lift up into realms where your thoughts will bring about instant manifestation. Heed however our advice that you consider what it is you desire, as with your creations also comes responsibility. Pureness and clarity will go hand in hand with your growth into the Light, when you can take your true place in the Universe as fully conscious Cosmic Beings.

As you are now breaking out of the bonds of the lower dimensions, it is difficult for you to comprehend how great is your potential. However, allow for the greatest expression of yourself that you can imagine, and that path will open up for you. Remember that you are a soul given freewill to choose your experiences, and it is your choice as to whether you leave duality. If you wish, you can choose to remain in the lower dimensions for furthering your experiences, until you feel ready to leave them behind.

Many paths are open to you once you ascend, and the end of this cycle is the beginning of a great new adventure that will allow your travels to take you wherever you desire. The end is simply a new beginning, and one that brings you back in touch with all life forms beyond Earth. Life abounds everywhere and no more will you feel isolated and veiled from the truth of your source and Godself. Think expansively and discover your real Self within, and do not be afraid to acknowledge your Godliness. Come out of that shell that has held you back, and allow for a wonderful expansion in your consciousness.

Dear Ones, you do not make the journey to All Knowing alone, and we of the Galactic Federation are just but one group of ascended souls that play a part in your evolution. In service to the higher Forces of Light, when our work is done we shall proceed to another part of the Universe to continue helping others to evolve. Some of you will join us, but many paths are open to you and that choice will be yours.

Meantime we stand fully prepared to move into the next phase of our service to you. We shall be so pleased when the time comes that we can all come together, in the outworking of the final stages leading to Ascension. The changes will be dramatic and take place quickly, and the trauma you have been experiencing will soon be replaced by the descent of peace upon all people. Stress and frustration will soon disappear and a wave of happiness and hope will cover the world.

I am Ker-On a Venusian, and one of many that have been closely associated with the Earth's cleansing and your development. We along with others have contacted Man often to give a guiding hand. Now we will come to assist in your final upliftment, and that gives us great joy. We send as always our loving energies to you all, and offer our hands in friendship and unity in the Oneness of Life.

If you would be so kind as to provide me with a postal address in the meantime, I will be happy to send you a gift copy of my previous publication *(The Bible's Cover-Stories Revealed: The Golden Keys That Unlock History)*.
With heartfelt appreciation,
Sincerely,
Arthur Earl Jones, Ph. D.
PS: Eventually, you will come to understand the relevance of all this.

On the afternoon of 26 August 2007, I transmitted the following message to my list of treasured friends around the world, together with an email link to Greg Palast's current article (Hurricane George: How the White House Drowned New Orleans) which also contained a reference to his recently published book (*Armed Madhouse*).
Dear Friends:
By contrast to what happened in New Orleans two years ago, have you ever seen the film THE TOAST OF NEW ORLEANS (1950) starring Mario Lanza and Kathryn Grayson?
I never get tired of watching their passionate performance of the Love Duet from Madama Butterfly by Giacomo Puccini during the concluding portion of this cinematic masterpiece, which I have seen over a hundred times and which I regard as the supreme example of classical opera at its finest.
I sincerely recommend that you obtain a copy of the DVD version, which became available in July of 2007.
In Love's pure Light,
All-is-one Heartsong.

On 27 August 2007, Alberto Gonzales, the illegitimate Attorney General of the illegitimate Bush Administration of the illegitimate US federal government, announced his resignation, thereby confirming that the New World Order agenda of the Dark Illuminati had entered its terminal phase.

I now invite you to see Appendix C: "Prophetic Message #1 from Kryon", which was channeled by Nancy Tate on 27 August 2007, and which I immediately placed on my website after transmitting it to my list of friends around the world.

I next invite you to see Appendix D: "Prophetic Message #2 from Kryon and Hatonn", which was channeled by Nancy Tate on 29 August 2007, and which I immediately placed on my website after transmitting it to my list of friends around the world.

On the afternoon of 29 August 2007, I made arrangements with lulu.com to have this book distributed by Amazon, Barnes & Noble, Borders, and other online booksellers.

Then, on the evening of 29 August 2007, I sent the following email message to Lyara, whose extraordinary website (www.operationterra.com) I had recently discovered on 12 August 2007.
Dear Sara Lyara Estes:
Greetings in the limitless love of the God I AM that we are, and blessings on

your path.

I have just discovered your extraordinary website this month, and have begun the wondrous process of exploring it.

I immediately wish to humbly acknowledge the profound feeling of gratitude and soul connection that motivates me to contact you.

Please allow me to introduce myself multidimensionally.

My first-dimensional physical body was born shortly before noon on 18 February 1928 in Glendale, California with the given name Arthur Earl Jones.

My third-dimensional mental body received the spiritual name All-is-one Heartsong from the ascended master Saint Germain during the course of a spiritual initiation in 1991.

My sixth-dimensional light body, which functions as my higher self and whose name is Kumara Zora Torith, began to reveal itself in 1988.

My ninth-dimensional aspect, whose name is ZoRaMuEL, began to reveal itself in 1997.

If you would be so kind as to provide me with a postal address, I will be happy to send you a gift copy of the 61-page autobiographical account of my spiritual journey during this lifetime (*Illustration of Spiritual Awakening*) which I wrote in 1998, plus a gift copy of my most recent publication (*The Bible's Cover-Stories Revealed: The Golden Keys That Unlock History*), a 36-page illustrated historical treatise which my higher self channeled through my consecrated mind a few months ago.

In the meantime, I invite you to explore my website at your convenience, beginning with the first two items in each of the four columns.

I am currently in the process of writing a follow-up book *(Channeling the Apocalypse: From the Eighteenth Dynasty to the Current Incarnations)*, the press release for which you will find at the bottom of column 3 on my website.

In Love's pure Light,
Sincerely,
Arthur Earl Jones, Ph. D.
also known as All-is-one Heartsong
(www.planetaryascension.net)

Because Archangel Gabriel had recently informed me that I was about to meet the fourth of four twin-flame soulmates that I was destined to connect with during this lifetime, I wrote the above letter for the specific purpose of determining whether Lyara was the one that Gabriel had been preparing me to meet. Thus, when Lyara responded by first stating that she did not resonate with my website, next asking me to remove her name from my email list, and then wishing me well, I knew immediately that she was not the one.

On the morning of 30 August 2007, I woke up with the following dream: I am visiting a group of people who have survived the American Revolutionary War, and when I reveal myself to them by demonstrating my ability to levitate my body, the people are inspired to improve themselves by expanding their consciousness and developing their abilities.

That evening I made the following entry in my journal: "The energies have become so intensified and the rate of change has become so accelerated that I can hardly keep up with developments at this point."

Then, at three o'clock on the morning of 31 August 2007, my higher self channeled through my consecrated mind the following words, with the clear understanding that they are to precede the words of the press release on the back cover of my new book.

"The negative turning point in human history occurred during the Eighteenth Dynasty of ancient Egypt when the good, the true, and the beautiful were buried. (For further information, see *The Bible's Cover-Stories Revealed: The Golden Keys That Unlock History* by Arthur Earl Jones, Ph. D.)

"The year of 2007 will be remembered as the positive turning point in human history when the good, the true, and the beautiful were resurrected. (For further information, see *Channeling the Apocalypse: From the Eighteenth Dynasty to the Current Incarnations* by Arthur Earl Jones, Ph. D.)"

At precisely 8:46 that morning, I transmitted another update from Germain channeled by my treasured friend Mike Quinsey.

That afternoon, with the help of my friend Zepp Jamieson, I first revised my treatise to meet the requirements of Lulu for online distribution by Amazon, thereby creating the twelfth version of *The Bible's Cover-Stories Revealed*, and then designed the front cover for my book, *Channeling the Apocalypse*.

That evening, I sent forth to my list of over ninety friends around the world a monumental update from the website of Christopher Story (www.globalanalysis.net) to which I appended the following introduction.

> Please give your top-priority attention to this spectacular exposé by Christopher Story of the unprecedented global financial crimes currently being committed by Bush, Cheney and Paulson, involving the theft and misuse of trillions of dollars, for which Ambassador Leo Wanta is the legal trustee.

At two o'clock on the morning of 1 September 2007, my sixth-dimensional higher self blessed my third-dimensional consecrated mind with the following words: "THE HOLY, HOLY, HOLY RECORDING RECORDS."

Around four o'clock that morning, I spent a good hour engaged in meditation and prayer focused on my favorite mantra: "I AM THAT LOVE WHICH IS THE POWER TO TRANSMUTE DISCORD INTO HARMONY."

At seven o'clock that same morning, I woke up with this dream: I am informing a young man that this world is soon going to change and then advising him to follow his heart's desire.

At 10:30 that same morning, while taking my daily walk, the thought suddenly occurred to me that, if the illegitimate Bush regime ordered the US military to attack Iran, it would immediately be rejected by a majority of the American people and could even be rejected by the US military itself.

At nine o'clock that same evening, the thought occurred to me that there are only two scenarios by which the Dark Illuminati could attempt to continue their psychopathic New World Order agenda for deceiving, subjugating, and enslaving humanity: 1) ordering the US military to attack Iran, and 2) simulating a fake invasion of Planet Earth by extraterrestrials using the advanced technology of holographic projections.

At four o'clock on the morning of 2 September 2007, I woke up with this dream: An unusual storm is brewing, which darkens the sky. Security measures are increased, and I am provided with additional financial support, for which I sign, using my initials AEJ.

Then, at 4:30 that same morning, I wrote the following report in my private journal: "Using memory flashbacks to another time in my life 23 years earlier, when attempts were made to control me through substantial gifts to the Spiritual Transformation Center that I established after coauthoring my first book (*Intensive Spiritual Hypnotherapy* by Francuch and Jones) in 1983, and through an invitation from my former Stanford classmate Dr. Frederick Sontag to participate in a large international conference of scholars financed by Reverend Sun Myung Moon of South Korea, which took me to Athens and Jerusalem in 1984, my higher self has today warned me not to accept the dubious offers that I received in the mail from Australia during the past week promising large amounts of money."

At 1:30 that afternoon, I sent the following email message to my growing list of friends around the world:
Dear Friends:
    Here are a few excerpts from an article dated 6 July 1999 on the website of Sara Lyara Estes (www.operationterra.com), which predicts that "less than one-tenth of one percent of humanity", that is, less than one in a thousand human beings on Planet Earth, will graduate from the third dimension to the fourth dimension by means of the planetary ascension process that is destined to take place during the next five years.
    "The Creation is about to be entirely recreated."
    "Each and every Oversoul will be affected in ways that even the Oversouls cannot anticipate."
    "It will be like closing your eyes and then reopening them, only to find that the scene you are looking at has changed drastically."
    "There is no one that is or was in a physical body that can accurately predict what is about to happen or what one will experience after the blink has occurred."
    "There will be many fewer players on the stage when the new drama unfolds."
    "You who are reading this message will be among those who will be there to experience it, but you will be changed from you present form and identity."

"This is the time of the harvest of souls."
In Love's pure Light,
All-is-one Heartsong

Around one o'clock on the morning of 3 September 2007, my consecrated mind received guidance from my higher self to begin the Dedication page with this sentence: ("Life in this polarized world of illusion is essentially a contest between civilized lightworkers, who love the truth, and uncivilized darkworkers, who fear the truth."), and to end the Dedication page with this sentence ("You shall know the truth, and the truth shall make you free." *John* 8:32).

At four o'clock on the same morning, I woke up with the following dream: I am an experienced and capable elder statesman of impeccable integrity responding to an inner calling to step forward at this time of national crisis for the purpose of offering my professional services and leadership skills in undertaking the task of resurrecting and restoring the federal government of the United States of America (which has been hijacked, transmogrified, and desecrated) to its original, authentic, and constitutional position as a beacon of light and the hope of the world, with liberty and justice for all. (Note: It is clear to me that this amazing dream is the work of my higher self and refers to leadership skills that I developed in other lifetimes, such as my lifetime during the latter part of Egypt's Eighteenth Dynasty.)

Here now is the prophetic message which I transmitted to my list of over ninety friends around the world shortly before noon on 3 September 2007, Labor Day.
Beloved Friends:
    My inner guidance tells me that the global contest between civilized lightworkers and uncivilized darkworkers is now on the verge of checkmate, which means that this colossal chess game is about to end in another victory for Love's pure Light.
    My understanding is that there are now only two possible scenarios by means of which the Dark Illuminati could attempt to continue their so-called "New World Order" agenda for deceiving, subjugating, and enslaving humanity, and that both scenarios are destined to fail.
    The first scenario calls for the Bush Administration to order the US military to attack Iran, in which case the American people would immediately repudiate the Bush Administraiton as an agent of the Dark Illuminati.
    And the second scenario calls for the Dark Illuminati to simulate a fake invasion of Planet Earth by extraterrestrials, using an advanced technology of holographic projections, in which case humanity as a whole would quickly see through their fraudulent deception and repudiate the entire New World Order agenda of the Dark Illuminati.
    Do not rule out the possibility that the Dark Illuminati, who constitute the psychopathic core of the global elite, and who are now desperate, could attempt to carry out both scenarios in rapid succession.
    In any case, the American Dream which has gradually turned into an insane Alice-in-Wonderland nightmare, is almost over, and it is now time for all of us to

wake up.
>In Love's pure Light,
>All-is-one Heartsong
>www.planetaryascension.net

Here now is the lighthearted antidote which I used to balance the heaviness of my foregoing message:

Dear Friends:
>I seriously recommend that you get yourself a copy of GROUNDHOG DAY (1993) starring Bill Murray and Andie MacDowell, and that you make a point of reviewing it periodically every time you need a lift.
>
>In this brilliant reincarnation parable devised by Danny Rubin, an obnoxious egotist is required to repeat the same day over and over until he finally learns how to be unselfish and loving.
>
>In my humble opinion, this cinematic masterpiece is unquestionably one of the most important films ever made.
>
>In Love's pure Light,
>All-is-one Heartsong

It only remains to add that, by the end of this Labor Day weekend, I had succeeded in bringing both my private journal and my manuscript for this book up to this pivotal point in time.

At two o'clock on the morning of 4 September 2007, my higher self informed my consecrated mind that it was time to publish a CD recording of The Wake-Up Song, the lyrics and music of which my sixth-dimensional light body had inspired my third-dimensional mental body to compose during the spring of 2003 in response to the horrendous war crimes being committed by the illegitimate Bush Regime in the name of the American people.

Just one hour later, at three o'clock on the morning of 4 September 2007, my higher self inspired my consecrated mind with the idea of forming a creative team by selecting a manager with legal expertise to negotiate a contingency percentage with a promoter such as Bernie Nelson, the ultimate purpose being to joyfully facilitate the awakening of humanity at this pivotal point in human history. (See Appendix E)

NEFERTITI

At three o'clock on the morning of 5 September 2007, my higher self then surprised me by giving my consecrated mind specific instructions to insert in my book at this point another excerpt from my eighteenth session with Archangel Gabriel Benu on 5 June 2007 for the specific purpose of demonstrating the capacity of higher consciousness to solve any mystery by using absolute knowing to reveal the truth.

Allisone: I'm going to start by asking a couple of questions about two movies. In the film *The Immortal Beloved*, the theory is advanced that Beethoven's beloved was the woman who married his brother when she failed to receive Beethoven's love letter and mistakenly thought that he had rejected her, the further implication being that Beethoven's nephew Karl was actually his own son by this woman. Is this true?

Gabriel: Yes, it is.

Allisone: Did the higher self of the author Bernard Rose reveal this to him? Do you have any idea how he got that insight?

Gabriel: Let me look. I am looking at that, but I am also looking at him having access to letters.

Allisone: I see. I'm sure he did a lot of research.

Gabriel: Yes.

Allisone: And he may have just jumped to a logical conclusion.

Gabriel: He knew.

Allisone: Uh-huh.

Gabriel: He did some research, and then he said to himself, "You know, I just feel this. I know this."

Allisone: Good for him. So it was an inner knowing.

Gabriel: Yes.

Allisone: Not just a guessing.

Gabriel: Right.

Allisone: Yes, that's what I sensed. Okay. In the film *Amadeus*, the theory is advanced that Mozart was the target of covert malicious actions by another composer by the name of Salieri, who simultaneously admired, envied, and hated Mozart.

Gabriel: That is correct.

Allisone: Did Salieri contribute to Mozart's death?

Gabriel: Yes, he did.

Allisone: I'll be even more specific and ask: Did Salieri poison Mozart?

Gabriel:	Yes, he did.
Allisone:	Really!
Gabriel:	Yes.
Allisone:	He arranged for Mozart to be poisoned.
Gabriel:	He arranged for him to be poisoned.
Allisone:	That would explain why Mozart died at such an early age.
Gabriel:	Right.
Allisone:	Okay. Well, that poison question leads me into some questions regarding my treatise, which has just been published, as you know.
Gabriel:	Right.
Allisone:	What is the undetectable poison that Paramessu used to assassinate Akhenaten and his family?
Gabriel:	This is one that actually cannot be reproduced in this time-space, but it is a combination of many different oils together.
Allisone:	Okay.
Gabriel:	It was not ingested. It was rubbed on the skin.
Allisone:	Really?
Gabriel:	Yeah.
Allisone:	That's an interesting detail. Not ingested, but rubbed on the skin.
Gabriel:	Not ingested, but rubbed on the skin.
Allisone:	That would make it much easier to accomplish.
Gabriel:	Not only that, but what I would say is that, when something like this occurs, it does not show up in the embalming process that they do.
Allisone:	Yeah, I understand. You emphasized that it was undetectable.

Gabriel: Right.

Allisone: Well, I very much appreciate this, and I think I'll go on to the next question.

Gabriel: Alright.

Allisone: How did Paramessu manage to administer the undetectable poison in the case of Akhenaten?

Gabriel: It would be what looks like a handshake. No, not a handshake. Let me see. It has to do with the hands. It is . . . Ah! The individual had a headache.

Allisone: Uh-huh.

Gabriel: And so this one said: "Let me massage your temples." And it went right to the brain.

[Note: Paramessu disguised himself as an expert massage therapist and, after applying the lethal massage oil, he carefully washed his hands in a neutralizing solvent.]

Allisone: And the implication would be that Akhenaten, at that point, trusted Paramessu, who was a military officer, ...

Gabriel: Exactly.

Allisone: ...and didn't realize, had no idea, what was about to happen.

Gabriel: Right.

Allisone: Although he may have sensed that his life was in danger, because Queen Nefertiti and Queen Tiye had already been assassinated.

Gabriel: Right. He knew it was in danger, but he didn't think it was from him.

Allisone: Yeah. Okay. Was a similar method used previously with Queen Nefertiti and Queen Tiye?

Gabriel: Yes.

Allisone: Some kind of a massage.

Gabriel: A massage. But Queen Nefertiti had a feeling . . .

Allisone: Uh-huh.

Gabriel:	. . . and went immediately and bathed her head and her body.
Allisone:	Uh-huh.
Gabriel:	And so it was not what put her under.
Allisone:	Oh, really!
Gabriel:	No.
Allisone:	Queen Nefertiti was not poisoned?
Gabriel:	She was, but it did not kill her.
Allisone:	It did kill Queen Tiye?
Gabriel:	Yes, it did.
Allisone:	So how was Queen Nefertiti killed, then?
Gabriel:	In two different ways. She actually left the body.
Allisone:	Uh-huh.
Gabriel:	And left the body in a state of looking like she had been poisoned to death.
Allisone:	Uh.-huh.
Gabriel:	She actually moved from that area.
Allisone:	She moved from what area?
Gabriel:	From Egypt. Actually from that dimension.
Allisone:	Uh.
Gabriel:	Her body remained there.
Allisone:	I see.
Gabriel:	She transcended the body.
Allisone:	Really! How interesting!

Gabriel: Yeah.

Allisone: So she witnessed the death of Queen Tiye . . .

Gabriel: Right.

Allisone: . . . by poison.

Gabriel: Right.

Allisone: And an attempt was made by Paramessu to poison Nefertiti.

Gabriel: Correct.

Allisone: But it didn't work, and she chose to leave her body.

Gabriel: She chose to leave the body.

Allisone: And then the face of her mummy was later damaged.

Gabriel: Correct.

Allisone: So she wasn't . . . she wasn't struck a blow at that time.

Gabriel: No.

Allisone: The damage to her mummy occurred afterward.

Gabriel: Right.

Allisone: Okay. Thank you. That's helpful.

Gabriel: Because this one was so frustrated that he did not take her life.

Allisone: Um.

Gabriel: The one that poisoned her or attempted to.

Allisone: Paramessu was so frustrated . . .

Gabriel: . . . so frustrated because of what she did. She was standing in front of him. She literally dropped the body like you would drop a rag.

Allisone: Wow!

Gabriel: And he saw her leave.

Allisone: How interesting!

Gabriel: Yeah.

Allisone: Okay. Let's see.

Gabriel: You would not read that in history books.

Allisone: Of course not. [laughs] That certainly implies that Nefertiti was very highly evolved.

Gabriel: Yes, she was.

Allisone: Okay. Next question. Let's see. . .

Gabriel: By the way, it did create almost a feeling of madness in this man. When he saw this, he didn't know what to believe.

Allisone: In other words, Paramessu was really shaken by what Nefertiti did.

Gabriel: Completely!

Allisone: Huh! Interesting.

Gabriel: Because she told him that she would haunt him 'till the end of all days'.

Allisone: Uh-huh! I see. She was actually able to speak to him before she left her body.

Gabriel: Yes, she did.

Allisone: Okay. This is a very interesting detail that you are sharing with me.

Gabriel: And she left . . . it looked like almost a . . . She kept the physical looking like the essence of leaving. So it looked like she had just disrobed.

Allisone: I see.

Gabriel: Which terrified him!

Allisone: Huh! He was frustrated and terrified!

Gabriel: Yes! Because what she told him is that she would haunt him 'till the end of all days', not just his days, but all days.

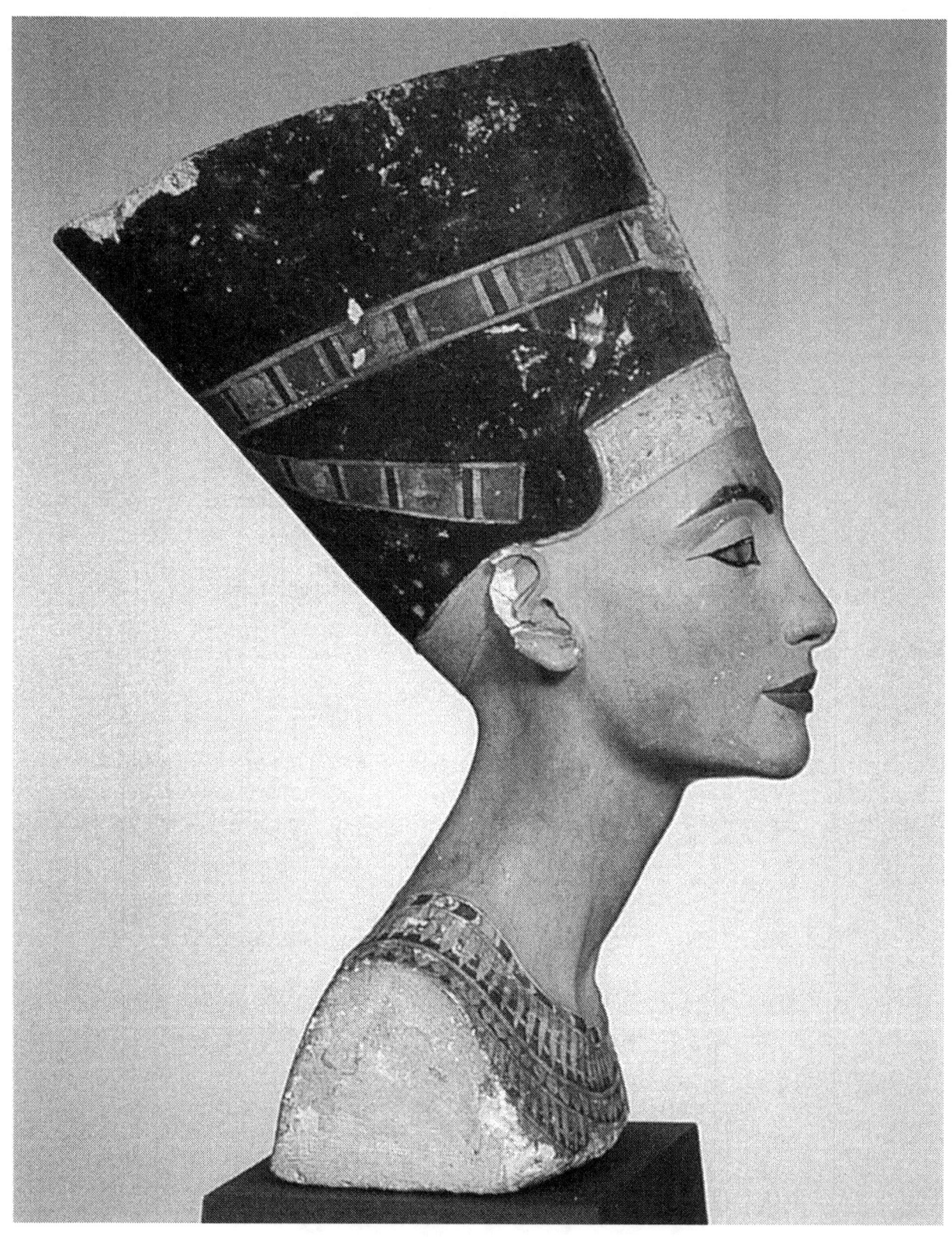

Item 32: Queen Nefertiti

Allisone:	All days.
Gabriel:	That what he had done was . . . He thought he had killed the best that Egypt had to offer.
Allisone:	Sure.
Gabriel:	And she let him know that they were going on.
Allisone:	Yeah. In other words, there were going to be consequences that she would see to.
Gabriel:	Right.
Allisone:	And I gather that she fulfilled her promise.
Gabriel:	Oh, yes! She did!

[The clear implication is: 1) that Nefertiti was poisoned by Paramessu, but was able to dilute the poison by immediately washing herself; 2) that she responded by first promising to haunt him till the end of all days and by then suddenly departing her body voluntarily, which had the desired effect of terrifying him; but 3) that Paramessu then acted out his frustration and anger by delivering the postmortem wound to her face, which made it impossible for Nefertiti to revive and reinhabit her body.]

On the evening of 5 September 2007, I enjoyed Shirley MacLaine's New Age masterpiece, *Out On A Limb* for what must have been about the twelfth time in ten years, using my recently-acquired full version for the third time.

OSAMA

Then, early in the morning of 6 September 2007, my higher self again surprised me by asking my consecrated mind to insert in my book at this point several excerpts from my eighth session with Archangel Gabriel Benu, which had taken place five years earlier on 12 August 2002.

Karen Cook:	Hello
Allisone:	Hi, Karen. This is All-is-one Heartsong in Mount Shasta.
Karen Cook:	Hi there.
Allisone:	This will be my eighth telephone session over the past six years, and I want to express once again my heartfelt gratitude for your dedicated service to the enlightenment of humanity, which makes it possible for me to communicate with Archangel Gabriel Benu in this way.

Karen Cook: Okay, wait just a moment while I get him for you.

Allisone: I love you.

Gabriel: Greetings!

Allisone: Greetings, Archangel Gabriel Benu.

Gabriel: How be you?

Allisone: I be in joy.

Gabriel: That's good! It is always good to be in joy.

Allisone: I would like to begin this session by reaffirming my choice to be in consecrated service to God and to humanity so that we can continue working together for the benefit of all.

Gabriel: So be it. I will relay the message.

Allisone: I am acutely aware of the fact that my consciousness is gradually expanding from my former identity as Dr. Arthur Earl Jones through my present identity as All-is-one Heartsong to my future identity, which I think of in terms of my soul name ZoRaMuEL.

Gabriel: Yes.

Allisone: And I welcome your assistance in accelerating the process of expanding my consciousness.

Gabriel: Not difficult. I will endeavor to be with you along your divine pathway.

Allisone: I know that you are always with me.

Gabriel: Yes, I am.

Allisone: Let's begin this way. Is our universe currently in the process of merging with a parallel universe as predicted by Saint Germain in 1987?

Gabriel: Yes.

Allisone: Is this what is causing the halo of gamma-ray energy which now surrounds our Milky Way Galaxy?

Gabriel:	It is partly that, but is also the fact that you are now right smack in the middle of the Photon Belt.
Allisone:	Are we talking about the field of photon energy within our galaxy or surrounding our galaxy?
Gabriel:	Surrounding your galaxy. It has been building as the years have gone by, and now it is at the zenith of it.
Allisone:	And this is what facilitates our planetary ascension process?
Gabriel:	Yes, it does.
Allisone:	Yeah. Okay. Next question. How much longer will the global elite be able to exercise control over humanity?
Gabriel:	Less than six years.
Allisone:	In our previous session, you indicated they could begin to lose control as soon as 2004.
Gabriel:	That is correct.
Allisone:	But they'll be around until at least 2006.
Gabriel:	Correct.
Allisone:	Which faction of the Dark Illuminati are in control of the global elite: 1) the Jesuit Order, 2) the Rothschild family, 3) the Hanover-Windsor family, or 4) the Reptilian extraterrestrials?
Gabriel:	Rothschild.
Allisone:	Aren't the Reptilians in control of the Jesuits and the Rothschilds and the Hanover-Windsors?
Gabriel:	No, the Rothschilds are the ones who are in control, and the Reptilians answer to the Rothschilds because they are the one that gave them permission to come onto this planet.
Allisone:	Really?
Gabriel:	Yes, but I will tell you that the other two factions are very, very strong, except for the fact that, like all elite-status individuals, they begin to rot from the inside.

Item 33: Jeroboam Rothschild (alias Georges Mandel) at the age of 54 with Paul Reynaud (the newly-elected Premier of France, who was officially his boss but actually his servant) as pictured in the 27 May 1940 issue of Time Magazine shortly before France surrendered to Germany on 22 June 1940.

Allisone: Yes, I understand. So, if I heard you correctly, it's the Rothschild family that invited the Reptilian extraterrestrials to participate in humanity.

Gabriel: That is correct.

Allisone: So the Rothschilds are really at the heart of the whole darkworkers' conspiracy.

Gabriel: The Illuminati.

Allisone: And they operate in part through the Jesuit Order.

Gabriel: Right.

Allisone: Okay, I've got the picture. In our previous two sessions, you indicated that ruling members of the global elite such as Queen Elizabeth, the Rothschilds, the Rockefellers, Henry Kissinger, and George Bush the First are actually shapeshifting reptilian space beings disguised as human beings. Can you confirm that?

Gabriel: I would say that they are able to shapeshift with no problem whatsoever.

[Note: By answering in this way, Gabriel indicated that they are reptilian human beings, not reptilian space beings.]

Allisone: But are they basically reptilians?

Gabriel: They are basically reptilians of a reptilian ancestry that are living on Earth.

Allisone: I see. So they are different from ordinary human beings.

Gabriel: Yes.

Allisone: Approximately how many reptilian human beings are there on Planet Earth at present? Just a rough estimate.

Gabriel: A rough estimate. Seventy-five million.

Allisone: Seventy-five million!

Gabriel: Yeah. They have been here a long time. But one thing to take into consideration, and that is that not all reptilians are negative.

Allisone: Yeah, of course.

Gabriel: There are many who are very fine doctors, very fine healers.

Allisone: So there are seventy-five million reptilian human beings.

Gabriel: Worldwide, not just here in America.

Allisone: I understand. Okay. What is the general intention of the reptilians toward humanity?

Gabriel: The intention of the first group, the warriors, was takeover, because their planet is having some difficulties.

Allisone: Uh-huh.

Gabriel: But the second group, the healers, are here to assist humanity.

Allisone: Let me ask this question, then. How many warrior reptilians are there on Planet Earth at present?

Gabriel: Less than seven thousand.

Allisone: I see! Oh, that is a big revelation!

Gabriel: Very big.

Allisone: That really helps me to understand the situation.

Gabriel: Good.

[Note: To avoid confusion, a clear distinction needs to be made between reptilian extraterrestrials (such as the visiting Greys from Zeta Reticuli) and reptilian human beings (of which there are about seventy-five million positive healers and only about seven thousand negative warriors such as the Rothschilds, the Hanover-Windsors, the Rockefellers, and the Bushs).]

Allisone: Next question. According to Arizona Wilder, whose real name is Jennifer Green, these reptilian shapeshifters need to drink the human blood of blond, blue-eyed Aryan stock in order to maintain their disguise as human beings. Is this true?

Gabriel: No.

Allisone: Not true. So they don't engage in human sacrifice.

Gabriel: They have.

Allisone: Mhmm.

Gabriel: But it hasn't benefited them, so they have decided on new rituals that they go

	through.
Allisone:	I see. So the answer is yes but no.
Gabriel:	Right. What she has done is to give information that is very old.
Allisone:	That's what I want to get into with this question. Is it true that Jennifer Green, alias Arizona Wilder, was programmed as a trauma-based mind-controlled slave by Josef Mengele, the Nazi commandant of the Auschwitz death camp, after he was secretly brought to the United States after the Second World War?
Gabriel:	That is correct.
Allisone:	And was Josef Mengele a reptilian?
Gabriel:	Yes.
Allisone:	And is Jennifer Green a reptilian?
Gabriel:	Yes.
Allisone:	Yes. You're sure about that?
Gabriel:	I am positive.
Allisone:	Okay, that explains the whole situation. I'm glad that I was able to come up with the right questions. Thank you much.
Gabriel:	But I will tell you that she is not aware of it totally.
Allisone:	I see. I understand. That figures. Of course. Okay. Now, during our previous session, you specified that the assassination of President Kennedy in 1963 was ordered by a member of the Rothschild family rather than by a member of the royal Hanover-Windsor family of England.
Gabriel:	Correct.
Allisone:	My question is this. Was Kennedy's assassination then arranged by the British Intelligence Chief William Stephenson or by Aristotle Onassis or both.
Gabriel:	Both.
Allisone:	Both. That's all I need to know. Thank you much.

Item 34: Osama bin Laden

[Note: Many years earlier, during a private session with the ascended master Saint Germain, speaking through his dedicated full-body channel Azena, I had already learned in 1987 that one of the key assassins of President John F. Kennedy in 1963 was the notorious CIA agent Howard Hunt. Let history record that it was the assassination of President Kennedy on 22 November 1963, followed by the Vietnam War and the proliferation of drugs and pornography, which clearly signaled the intention of the Dark Illuminati, operating through the Tavistock Institute and subsidiary think tanks, to drive humanity crazy by transforming our world into an insane Alice-in-Wonderland nightmare from which we have been trying to wake up ever since.]

Allisone: Next question. Did Osama bin Laden and the CIA work together in planning the terrorist attack on the World Trade Center and the Pentagon?

Gabriel: No.

Allisone: They didn't?

Gabriel: No. The CIA and the FBI were advised that this was going to occur, but they had been advised of this for over twenty years.

Allisone: Yes.

Gabriel: The man is a sociopath, and it was basically in retaliation. He helped the CIA many many times in fighting the Russians.

Allisone: Yes, I understand.

Gabriel: But what happened was that he told them in one specific meeting to never ever bring military arms into Saudi Arabia.

Allisone: I understand.

Gabriel: And they did!

Allisone: Uh-huh.

Gabriel: And so he took it as a betrayal.

Allisone: So he wasn't operating as a CIA asset or agent when he planned the terrorist attack?

Gabriel: Not at all. That was enough to tip his mental stability.

Allisone: I see.

Gabriel: And what he wanted to do was to make a statement to make the towers stand as an emblem for terrorism.

Allisone: I understand.

Gabriel: But no, they knew about it!

[Note: During a subsequent session, Archangel Gabriel Benu explained further that the Dark Illuminati intentionally provoked Osama bin Laden to carry out his insane desire for revenge by attacking the World Trade Center and the Pentagon, which he regarded as symbols of the Great Satan, while covertly helping him to organize the original al Qaida, which was composed of American demolition experts in the United States.]

Allisone: I think that answers the question. And we are now in the last few seconds of the last minute of my session. [laughs]

Gabriel: Good.

Allisone: Good timing. I'm so grateful for your assistance.

Gabriel: Well, I am pleased to assist you, my friend.

Allisone: My love for you and my gratitude are beyond all words. And I look forward to further sharing in the days to come.

Gabriel: Yes, and we will, my friend.

Allisone: Thank you so much.

Gabriel: Blessings.

Allisone: Blessings.

Having completed this illuminating digression to an earlier session with Gabriel in August of 2002, less than a year after the apocalyptic terrorist attack on 11 September 2001, let us now return to the ongoing record in my private journal for September of 2007.

At seven o'clock on the morning of 7 September 2007, with tears of love and gratitude in my eyes, I read the worldwide internet tributes to the great Italian tenor Luciano Pavarotti, who had died of pancreatic cancer on the previous day at the age of 71, and whose departure served as a magnificent example of those lightworkers who, having completed their mission, were now taking their leave.

Then, around noon on 7 September 2007, I received the following email message from my treasured friend Rebekah, who lives in Washington, D.C.

Dear Allisone:

Here are several questions regarding your marvelous treatise, which I loved reading.

1) How did the ascended master Thoth make arrangements for Abram (Abraham) and Sarai (Sarah) to join their Hebrew lineage with the Egyptian lineage?

2) You state that Sarai used the name Isis when serving as the Pharaoh's concubine. Is this the same Isis of "Isis and Osiris" fame, or was she named after the legendary Isis? (You can see I don't know my history.)

3) Were you Ay?

4a) Was Horemheb's desecration of Ay's tomb and annihilation of Akhenaten's reign because of polytheism versus monotheism?

4b) Did Pharaoh Thutmose III demolish evidence of Hatshepsut because she was racist and sought to marginalize him and his lineage because of her bigotry?

5) What do you think the ramifications will be of A) the revelation of cover stories in the Bible and B) the fact of an ancient Jewish-Arab lineage?

Love, Rebekah

On the evening of 8 September, I responded to Rebekah's questions by sending her the following email message:

Beloved Rebekah:

Here are my answers to your excellent questions, which demonstrate that you have read and understood my treatise without any previous knowledge of Egypt's Eighteenth Dynasty.

1) According to Archangel Gabriel Benu, my soul was one of 17 souls who participated in the soul group that incarnated as Abram, who eventually became known as Abraham. My understanding is that the ascended master Thoth communicated telepathically with Abram in the same way that he later communicated telepathically with Joseph the Israelite.

2) Sarai was not Isis, the ascended master of ancient Atlantis, but chose that alias from Egyptian mythology as a means of making herself more acceptable to the Egyptian priesthood.

3) According to Archangel Gabriel Benu, my soul was one of 27 souls who participated in the soul group that incarnated as Ephraim, the younger son of Joseph the Israelite who eventually became known as Pharaoh Ay.

4A) First, because the very idea of a Hebrew-Egyptian hybrid becoming an Egyptian pharaoh was anathema to the Amun priesthood of Egypt. Second, because the very idea of replacing Egyptian polytheism with Hebrew monotheism was also anathema to the Amun priesthood of Egypt. And third, because Horemheb was a very ambitious and ruthless man.

4B) Having failed to provide Pharaoh Thutmose II with a male heir, Queen Hatshepsut's attempt to marginalize Pharaoh Thutmose III was rooted in her deep-seated feeling of inadequacy, which manifested as racial prejudice and bigotry that were encouraged and exacerbated by the High Priest of Amun.

5A) The apocalyptic revelation of akashic truths through the process of uncovering these cover stories in the Bible will initially threaten and eventually transmute the false belief systems of Egyptian fundamentalists, Jewish fundamentalists. and Christian fundamentalists alike.

5B) The Ishmaelite lineage of the Arabic people, the progenitors of which were the Hebrew Abram and the Egyptian Hagar, is not controversial, but the other Hebrew-Egyptian lineage, which began with the Hebrew Sarai and the Egyptian Pharaoh Thutmose II, and which was then compounded by Joseph the Israelite and his Egyptian wife Asenath, always was and still is extremely controversial.

In Love's pure Light,
All-is-one

At 12:24 on 9 September 2007, I transmitted to my list of over ninety friends around the world the current update (dated 8 September 2007) by Christopher Story, prefaced by the following introduction.

Dear Friends:

This current update by Christopher Story contains incontrovertible confirmation that the global contest between civilized lightworkers and uncivilized darkworkers is now at the point of checkmate.

Prepare yourselves for momentous transformative events during the next ten days.

In Love's pure Light,
All-is-one Heartsong
www.planetaryascension.net

Here now is another example of the way that I periodically encouraged my friends to lighten up and open their hearts as we approached the end of our insane Alice-in-Wonderland nightmare:

Dear Friends:

I also recommend that you get yourself a copy of SLEEPLESS IN SEATTLE (1993) starring Tom Hanks and Meg Ryan, and that you make a point of reviewing it periodically.

Working through the inspired efforts of an eight-year-old boy who is attempting to find a new wife for his widowered father, spirit orchestrates the ultimate romantic rendezvous at the top of the Empire State Building on Valentine's Day, which brings together a man and a woman who are made for each other.

It is worth noting further, that Nora Ephron succeeded in following this masterpiece of romantic comedy with an ingenious rematch titled, YOU'VE GOT MAIL (1998).

In Love's pure Light,
All-is-one Heartsong.

COMPLETION

On the evening of 9 September 2007, I composed the table of contents and the list of illustrations for this book, and was amazed by how easily everything fell into place.

At eight o'clock on the morning of 10 September 2007, I transmitted to my list of friends around the world this introduction to the current channeling by Mike Quinsey.

Dear Friends:

Ker-On of Venus, a fifth-dimensional emissary of the Galactic Federation channeled by Mike Quinsey of England, has today blessed us with a momentous message that includes the following key passages.

"This month is full of promise and the potential to take a decisive step forward."

"It is going to result in revelations that will end the attempts of the dark to extend their world power."

"Great Light is descending upon Earth, and no power will stop it from manifesting the changes for good and the ultimate success of the Creator's plan for Man."

"Soon the pathway to Ascension will become clear."

In Love's pure Light,

All-is-one Heartsong

At ten o'clock that same morning, I took thirty more pages of handwritten notes to my friend Zepp Jamieson, who is a computer wizard when it comes to word processing and graphic design, one beautiful example of which is the watermark design on the dedication page of this book.

After lunch that afternoon, at the request of my landlady Priscilla Dawson, I spent a couple of hours clearing the dead leaves in my back yard, which caused me to become acutely aware of the fact that my physical body was now almost eighty years old.

At three-thirty, I walked over to the weekly Farmer's Market to buy some fresh carrots, cucumbers, and heirloom tomatoes from my friend Sarah Post, who brings her prime produce from Mountain Home Farm to Mount Shasta every Monday afternoon during August and September.

I was then guided by my higher self to spend the rest of that day in peaceful meditation and prayer.

I went to sleep a few minutes before nine o'clock and woke up a few minutes before midnight, wondering how I was going to compose an appropriate epilogue for this book, which was rapidly approaching completion. At exactly 12:03 a.m., I made the empowering choice to surrender my mind to the Holy Spirit, and my higher self immediately began to transmit to my conscious mind the first words of the Epilogue, the last words of which were transmitted around 12:50 a.m.

At six o'clock on the morning of 11 September 2007, I woke up with the following dream: My wife and I are spending an afternoon visiting a family of several adults in their apartment, where the loving feelings are so nourishing and the harmonious energies are so attractive that we find it extremely difficult to leave. (Note: My interpretation of this dream is that it represents my soul family on higher dimensions of consciousness, whose harmonious frequencies I found difficult to leave when I volunteered to undertake the task of incarnating into the discordant third dimension of separation consciousness on Planet Earth to help facilitate the awakening, enlightenment, and ascension of humanity.)

After my usual breakfast (which consisted of a glass of fresh orange juice, a cup of Yerba Matte tea, one slice of toasted multiseed bread with almond butter, cayenne pepper, cinnamon, and honey plus about thirteen vitamin and mineral supplements), I set forth on my usual two-and-one-half-mile walk.

After pausing to feast on the abundance of blackberries near the KOA campground, I next celebrated this beautiful day with the following words: "Hello, beautiful Shasta Mountain. I am grateful for your presence in my life. Greetings to you, Mother Earth. I love you, and I choose to be one with you as we ride this wave of planetary ascension. God I AM, incarnate on Planet Earth, with every cell of my body temple vibrating in harmony, and limitless love flowing through my heart to all of humanity."

I then walked up Butte Avenue to Everitt Memorial Highway and began to return to my apartment on Orem Street, pausing for a moment near the fire hydrant at the corner of Rockfellow Avenue to transmit healing energies of love to a special friend in the form of a young tree that was recuperating from the ordeal of twice being poisoned with weed-killing chemicals by the unenlightened landscape gardeners at the Sisson Middle School.

Thus, it was about noon by the time I reached Zepp's office with my handwritten version of the Epilogue, which he would soon incorporate into the manuscript for this book.

After a delicious lunch composed of Sara Post's heirloom tomatoes, cucumbers, and some mixed greens, together with the Daily Advantage combination of vitamins and minerals concocted by Dr. David Williams, I prepared to fast as usual for the rest of the day by drinking a glass of lime-and-lemonade sweetened with orange blossom honey and then lying down for a brief rest before working on my manuscript.

Around six o'clock on the evening of 11 September 2007, I transmitted to my list of lightworking friends around the world Sheldan Nidle's current update, prefaced by the following introduction:
Beloved Friends:
    This momentous message from the Sirian Council of the Galactic Federation, channeled by Sheldan Nidle on 11 September 2007, confirms that the global contest between lightworkers and darkworkers has now reached the pivotal point of checkmate and that the global political, economic, and social system of Planet Earth is now on the verge of undergoing a profound and radical positive transformation.
    Stay centered and alert, and be prepared for profound and radical positive changes in the immediate future.
    In Love's pure Light,
    All-is-one Heartsong.

Around 9:30 on the morning of 12 September 2007, I transmitted to my friends around the world an update by Ag-agria of Sirius, channeled by Mike Quinsey of England, which contained the following key passages:

"These are rapidly moving times, and events are beginning to come into being that will test your calmness."

"Indeed, when the dark are deliberately creating chaos, it is most important that you are peaceful and stand fast to deflect that energy."

"The scales of Light and Dark energies are finally balanced, and it determines the level of mass consciousness. However, the dark will not be allowed to overcome the Light no matter what attempts they make to unsettle you. It is in fact a minority that hold the Light and continue to attract it to Earth, and many of you came into this lifetime specifically to carry out such a task. Even more are awakening to such responsibilities, and the Light will now remain in a leading position continuing to grow at an increased rate."

"The forces for change increase almost daily, and the energies cannot be held back much longer. Once the breakthrough occurs, you will see all of our plans for you come to fruition very quickly. There is an optimum time when we shall be allowed to intervene, but that is unnecessary at present."

"You are sovereign beings and you are beginning to take back your freedom, and that is breaking the hold of the dark upon you . . . we see your energies for peace becoming a formidable force for change. It will eventually come to the whole world, but first those who have abused their authority and led you towards oblivion must be removed."

"Waiting in the wings are the most wonderful Beings that comprise the Galactic Federation . . . We are at a vantage point where we can monitor all events upon Earth, and also gauge the level of consciousness you have reached."

"Very soon, those who have misled you will have been removed, and then you will see a magical change in people's attitudes."

"A natural love and respect for each other will allow a great coming together, and we will also join you in that energy. We Are All One, and that is the most important message of this time."

I next read an article by Gareth Porter, which had just been emailed to me by my friend Zepp, revealing the extraordinary conflict that had developed over the previous six months between General David Petraeus, who serves as the military front man for George W. Bush, and Admiral William Fallon, chief of the Central Command (CENTCOM), who had openly defied the Bush Administration by publicly declaring that an attack on Iran by the US military would not occur during his watch. (See Appendix F)

After meeting with Zepp that afternoon for the purpose of attempting to resolve a technical problem which had arisen regarding the distribution of my treatise by Lulu, I then spent that evening composing a request for assistance, which I sent to Lulu's CEO Bob Young by email on the following morning. (See Appendix H)

Item 35: Admiral William Fallon

At three o'clock on the morning of 13 September 2007, I woke up with the following dream: I am a monk in a monastery who is learning how to quiet his mind by turning inward for silent meditation. (Note: This dream appears to be a remembrance of my previous lifetimes in Tibet.)

After sending my email message to Lulu's CEO around eight o'clock that morning, I ate my usual breakfast, which I then supplemented by again feasting on the abundance of blackberries near the KOA campground during my usual morning walk.

That afternoon, after treating myself to a delicious lunch at Lily's Restaurant (chicken pesto linguini, specially prepared by my friend Ron, who owns the restaurant), I worked with Zepp on the manuscript for my book and then relaxed in the evening by watching *Heaven Can Wait* for the umpteenth time.

At 3:40 on the morning of 14 September 2007, my higher self advised my conscious mind to make a clear distinction between two different aspects of the Divine Plan for the end of this current cycle on Planet Earth: 1) Divine Exposure, as exemplified by Archangel Gabriel Benu's confirmation of my treatise and the additional revelations contained in this book; and 2) Divine Intervention, as exemplified by the momentous message from the ascended master Adama of Inner Earth, channeled by Nancy Tate on 13 September 2007. (See Appendix G)

When I got up to fix my breakfast at six o'clock that morning, the weather had turned so cold that I decided to turn on my radiant heaters for the first time in about six months.

After breakfast, I sat down at my computer and went directly to Truthout, where the desperate expression on the face of a traumatized young Sunni girl whose family had just been forced to flee from the current violence and chaos in Baghdad brought tears of compassion to my eyes, followed by these spontaneous words through my mouth: "Germain, it's time for us to end this nightmare!"

I then read the thoughtful article titled "'The Eleventh Hour' and Generation Z" by Truthout's environmental editor Kelpie Wilson, which, in addition to reviewing Leonardo DiCaprio's recent documentary about the ominous ecological crisis currently confronting us on Planet Earth, also reviewed a similar documentary just released by Tim Bennett, titled "What a Way to Go: Life at the End of Empire."

After working with Zepp on the Appendices for my book, I fixed myself another tomato and cucumber salad for lunch, and then spent the whole afternoon organizing the illustrative items for the first forty pages of this book. In the evening, I relaxed, meditated, and listened, first to Prokofiev's First Violin Concerto performed by David Oistrakh, and then to Cosmic Messenger by Jean-Luc Ponty, in whose work musical expression may be said to have reached its ultimate conclusion.

At four o'clock on the morning of 15 September 2007, I received guidance from my higher self to include a portrait of my beloved friend Grace, together with one of her poems. And so I drove up to Morningstar later that morning to inform Grace of this development and to obtain her permission. Imagine my delight when Grace not only gave me permission to include her poem, "Resurrection", together with her portrait, but also shared with me several poetic masterpieces to which she had just given birth during the past few days.

After participating in the local Peace Gathering of lightworkers at the Mount Shasta City Hall, which was an integral part of the nationwide movement to protest the US attack against Iraq and Afghanistan plus the threat of a US attack against Iran, I fixed myself a simple lunch, consisting of an apple and a banana, together with some cashews and pistachios, and then spent the afternoon proofreading the most recently processed portion of my manuscript.

While surfing the Internet for news that evening, I noted that the US dollar was continuing to depreciate and the price of gold was rising about $700 per ounce, as a consequence of which the US Mint had just suspended the sale of its gold coins.

I then devoted the rest of the evening to watching my DVD of the film *Pretty Woman* for what must have been about the fifth time.

At six o'clock on the morning of 16 September 2007, I woke up with the following dream: I am observing three men who are obsessed with the idea of establishing a gold mine, which I regard as an unrealistic fantasy.

After my usual breakfast, I continued the process of proofreading the most recent pages of my manuscript. And, once again, I felt motivated by the realization that, by sharing my personal experiences through the publication of this book, I will be fulfilling the purpose for which I volunteered to undertake this incarnation on Planet Earth.

Shortly before noon, I set forth on my daily walk with the intention of feasting yet again on the blackberries at the KOA campground. But my walk soon turned out to be another instance of "life is what's happening while you're busy making other plans" when a lightworker who introduced himself as David Casebeer proceeded to engage me in a conversation that ranged from the pioneering breakthroughs of Dr. Leonard Horowitz to the imminent termination of the Dark Illuminati.

And so, instead of feasting on blackberries, I decided to treat myself to a three-cheese omelet at Lily's Restaurant, after which I transmitted the following invitation to my list of friends around the world.
Beloved Friends:
    For a classic, deeply moving, and absolutely unforgettable example of soul recognition, I invite you to see the ending of the cinematic masterpiece HEAVEN CAN WAIT (1978), starring Warren Beatty and Julie Christie. In my humble opinion, it is that final scene, together with its musical theme, which elevates this entertaining movie into one of the great films of all time.
    In Love's pure Light,
    Allisone Heartsong

I spent the remainder of that afternoon organizing the illustrations for this book and then reading the manuscript for a booklet titled *Unzipping Reality* which my friend Leah La Chapelle had just sent to me for my editorial advice.

That evening, I was guided by my higher self to watch my video copy of *Whale Rider* for what must have been about the seventh time since it was released in 2003, and was amazed to find myself being repeatedly moved to tears throughout the film as the realization gradually dawned on me that this cinematic masterpiece about whale consciousness constitutes an enlightened vision of humanity's future that will provide a fitting conclusion for this book.

From two to three o'clock on the morning of 17 September 2007, my higher self then proceeded to transmit through my consecrated mind something titled "Twelve Steps to God-Realization", which was clearly in response to my experience of reading the manuscript for Leah's booklet, and which is nothing less than a concise summary of all the wisdom I have gained during this lifetime. (See Item 36)

At seven o'clock on the morning of 17 September 2007, I woke up with the following dream: I am an experienced psychotherapist who is inviting one of my emotionally disturbed patients to increase the frequency of therapy sessions from three times a week to five times a week. (Note: I spent 26 years in full-time private practice as a professional psychotherapist in New York City from 1952 to 1978 before moving back to California with my wife and children, where I spent several more years as a professional deep-trance facilitator for the purpose of providing my clients with conscious access to their higher selves.)

After breakfast, I spent over an hour at Zepp's office making a number of corrections on the manuscript, drove to the supermarket to buy some food supplies, fixed myself a lunch composed of an apple, a banana, and some cashew and pistachio nuts, and then devoted the whole afternoon to the task of organizing the illustrations and integrating them with the text of the book.

Without knowing anything about the film except that it featured Jodie Foster, whom I had come to regard as one of my favorite actresses, I decided to spend the evening at the local theater watching something mislabeled *The Brave One*. When it turned out to be about a series of murders by a vigilante seeking revenge for the brutal murder of her fiancé in New York City's Central Park, I immediately chose to reduce the emotional impact by repeatedly reminding myself that this was an illusion within an illusion based on sophisticated cinematic deception, which happens to be the ultimate truth underlying all of the films that I have referred to in this book.

I spent the late morning of 18 September 2007 working with Zepp to integrate the initial pages of the text with the various other items that make up the first fifteen pages of this book.

In view of the fact that I wanted to include a few revealing quotations and several explanatory articles as well as photographs, we decided to simply call these things a list of items rather than a list of illustrations.

Item 36

Twelve Steps to God-Realization

1) Choose to use your free will to make empowering choices rather than disempowering choices.

2) Choose to learn, grow, evolve, and expand your consciousness rather than to maintain the status quo.

3) Choose to be a civilized lightworker who loves the truth rather than an uncivilized darkworker who fears the truth.

4) Choose to place your third-dimensional mind in the service of your fourth-dimensional heart, so as to become an enlightened human being with an open heart rather than an unenlightened human being with a closed heart.

5) Choose to live from the inside out rather than from the outside in, so as to never give your power away to anyone or anything perceived to be outside of yourself.

6) Choose to heal the illusion of separation by redefining polar opposites as polar complements, so as to shift out of separation consciousness into unity consciousness.

7) Choose to release all judgmental emotions by practicing unconditional forgiving love in every situation.

8) Choose to be that love which is the power to transmute discord into harmony.

9) Choose to make positive use of the universal law of attraction by keeping your attention focused on what you do want rather than on what you don't want.

10) Choose to live in alignment with the universal law of allowance by honoring the right of others to exercise their free will for the purpose of gathering wisdom from experiencing the consequences of their choices.

11) Choose to fly into the sun as an enlightened and empowered sunbeam so as to become one with our Creator Source.

12) Choose to be a God-Realized lover of all that is.

That afternoon, I also made a decision not to transmit the current update from Christopher Story to my list of friends around the world so as not to unnecessarily complicate their lives with nonessential distractions.

However, I did transmit the current update from the Sirian Council of the Galactic Federation channeled by Sheldan Nidle, which included the following momentous passage: "You are very close to some major announcements as well as to the disbursement of your much-promised prosperity. In effect, this reality, long run by the dark and its greedy and callous minions, is about to be amazingly transformed. All that we have been telling you about is now close to fruition, starting, of course, with the abundance deliveries. It is the successful completion of the deliveries that starts the cascade of dominoes that brings down the present US administration. Over the past few years, this group of shrewd and self-serving malefactors has led your world down a precarious path of mischief and mayhem, designed to benefit only their friends, family, and corporate associates. Now, the time finally comes to jettison these defiant ones and move your world to a better place. It is this desire that has driven both our Earth allies and us, and we are pleased to state that the planetary gear-change we all want is almost upon us at last. Those who are preparing to make the series of announcements, as well as those scheduled to form the new transitional governments, are very diligently setting into motion the final maneuvers that are to swiftly transform your current bleak reality."

On 19 September 2007, I spent the whole morning working with Zepp on the task of finalizing the first twenty-one pages of this book, including a decision to include Item 5: Dimensions of Consciousness on page 8. Needless to say, finalization of the Table of Contents on page 3 and the List of Items on page 12 had to be postponed until later.

Upon leaving Zepp's office shortly after noon, I could feel that my higher self was so pleased with what I had accomplished that I decided to celebrate by treating myself to a delicious lunch at Lily's Restaurant, even though my mind was of the opinion that I could not afford the twenty dollars that it cost.

Upon returning home after lunch, I turned on my computer to check for email messages and found the following treasure waiting for me: "Hi Dad, I haven't heard from you in a while and just wanted to check that you are doing okay. Love, Cinnamon."

Because many weeks had passed since I last heard from my younger daughter, I responded immediately with the following reply:
Beloved Cinnamon:
    I'm very happy to hear from you, and hope that you are well.
    I am healthy, happy, and very focused on completing my new book (Channeling the Apocalypse), which I hope to self-publish in October.
    Do not hesitate to call me any time at your convenience, because sharing thoughts and feelings with you continues to be my top priority.
    Your father who loves you.

After briefly checking the world news, I then took a nap from three to five o'clock and next decided to take a short jaunt around the block by walking up Lake Street and jogging down Orem Street, even though the weather had turned cold and raindrops were beginning to fall.

When I then checked my computer for emails at six o'clock, I discovered the following message from my younger daughter:

Hi, Dad,

  Thanks for letting me know you are doing well. I am glad you are happily focused on your new book.

  I am still experiencing poor health with new neuromuscular symptoms–muscle pain, twitching, and occasional tremors. Unfortunately, my health insurance got changed out from under me, so I lost the only M.D. I had that I really respected.

  The cats are also having their health issues, so I went to see Dr. Hoskins, my old boss [at the local clinic for veterinary medicine] for whom I have tremendous respect. He seems somewhat interested in helping me figure out what is making me sick. His first thought was chronic Lyme's disease. So we discussed the experience of one of the vets there who was sick with Lyme's for several years.

  Anyway, the green drinks still seem to help. Scott [her husband], Ella, Cappy and Scout [her dogs] are all doing well.

  Love, Cinnamon.

PS: I have started taking shepherding lessons from Bill, a wonderfully patient and insightful man from Montana, and thought you might enjoy a few pictures. 1) Cappy holding sheep. 2) Cappy waiting for a command. 3) Bill explaining some aspect of shepherding to me with infinite patience. 4) Cappy taking direction to circle sheep as opposed to scattering them. I omitted the picture of him creating pure mayhem.

Instead of watching a lighthearted video for the purpose of relaxing, I immediately decided to change my plan for that evening by composing the following message, which I sent to my younger daughter at 8:01 p.m. on 19 September 2007.

Beloved Cinnamon:

  Thank you for your follow-up message, informing me about your current neuromuscular symptoms and entertaining me with your shepherding pictures.

  I want you to know that I am choosing to be right with you, as always, as you go through whatever trials and tribulations come your way.

  It is clear to me that, in undertaking shepherding lessons with Bill, you are making an empowering choice to follow your heart's desire, which means that you are actively following the path that leads to wisdom and mastery.

  In order for me to understand more fully where you are currently at on that path, I would like to invite you to answer this key question: If we make a clear distinction between the scientific orientation exemplified by your mother, and the spiritual orientation exemplified by your father, what mental map of reality are you currently choosing to use for the purpose of finding your way through this wondrous world of third-dimensional consciousness on Planet Earth?

  I encourage you to take your time in formulating your current answer to this

key question, which may prove to be extremely helpful as we work together for the purpose of solving the challenging problem with which you are presently confronted.
Your father who loves you.

I woke up at six o'clock on the morning of 20 September 2007 feeling like an Olympic athlete preparing for a major event, which was my typical orientation that I had consciously cultivated since the year 2000, the major event being nothing less than planetary ascension. However, it was not until the beginning of my 80th year on 18 February 2007 that I expanded this orientation to include doing ten sit-ups and fifty bicycle kicks before getting out of bed each morning.

After a quick breakfast and a short walk, I continued to work with Zepp on the task of finalizing the first part of my manuscript, and we then placed "Twelve Steps to God-Realization" on my website.

That afternoon, one of my many friends brought to my attention an extraordinary article by Judith Moriarty on how to destroy a nation. (See Appendix I)

At six o'clock on the morning of 21 September 2007, I woke up with the following dream: I am a teacher at a school for masters which involves a series of initiations. Students are first assigned to the garbage detail and are then assigned to clean the latrines, the essential purpose of these assignments being to first arouse and then overcome ego resistance so as to cultivate an enlightened orientation of humble service. When two students are next assigned to work in the library, one makes the unenlightened choice to just take it easy, whereas the other makes the enlightened choice to go all out for the purpose of rendering humble service and is immediately rewarded by being assigned to assist the Dean of Students, a wise woman who will serve as his mentor.

At 8:49 that morning, I transmitted the current update from Germain with this introduction:
Dear Friends:
Channeled by Mike Quinsey in England, the ascended master Saint Germain, who is overseeing humanity's planetary ascension process, has today blessed us with a major message that includes the following key passages:
"Now you stand on the verge of victory."
"Together we are an invincible force that is poised to bring about the fall of the dark."
"This cycle was always destined to provide the stepping-stone to the higher dimensions of Light."
"There is an understanding that the present regime must give way to the power of Love and Light."
"The corruption and deceit that has been commonplace amongst your leadership will cease when they are removed."
"Know that you are about to permanently lift up out of the dark energies, and they shall be cleansed from the Earth for all time."

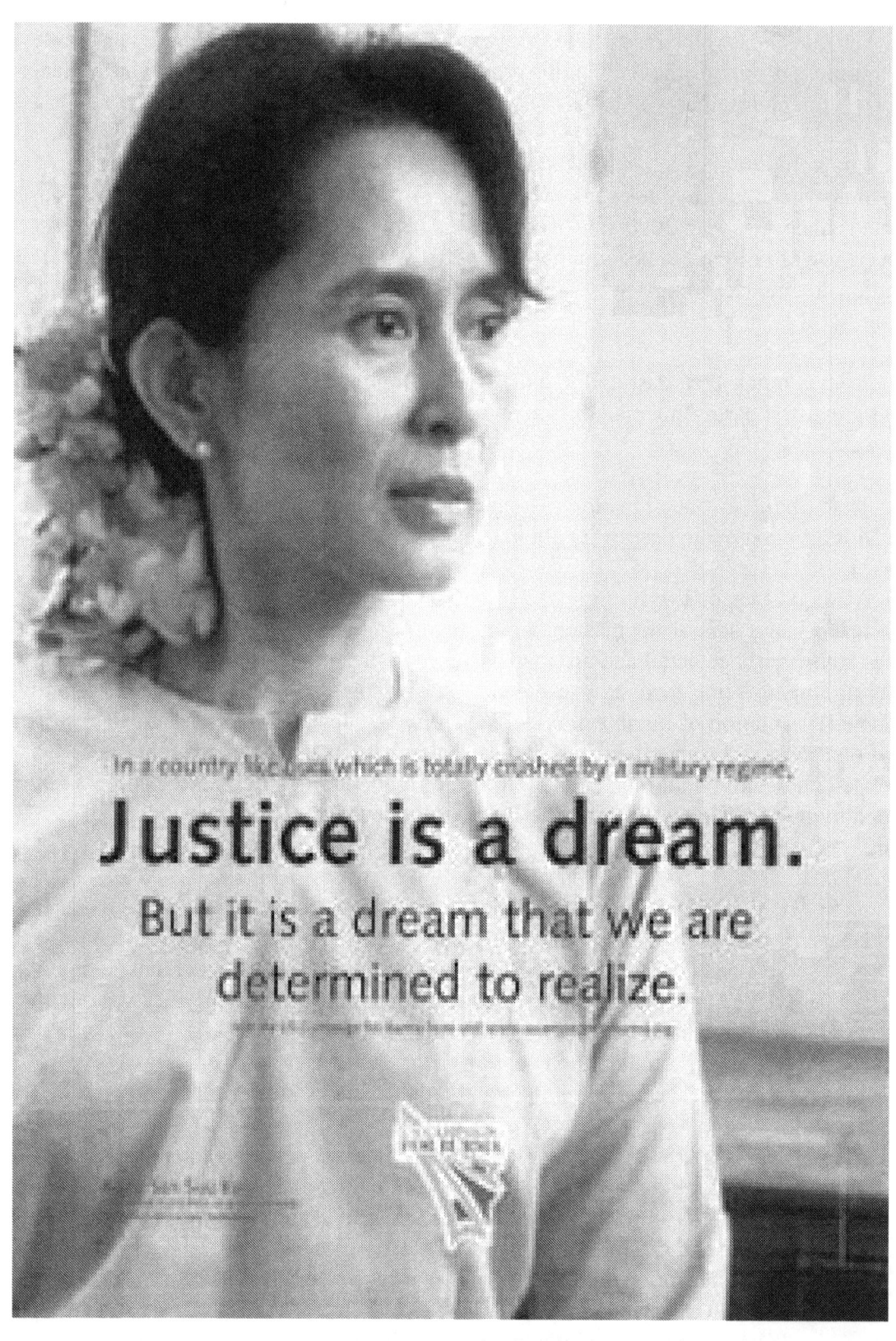

Item 37: Aung San Suu Kyi

"You are at the door of the new dimension that is descending upon Earth, one that will bring release from the cycle of duality."
In Love's pure Light,
All-is-one Heartsong

I then met with Zepp from one to three o'clock for the purpose of ironing out the minor problems that I had discovered on the previous afternoon, after which Zepp shared with me a video news clip of Olbermann's devastating commentary on the way that George Bush is currently using General Petraeus as his front man to perpetuate the disastrous US occupation of Iraq.

Upon waking up from an afternoon nap around five o'clock, I received inner guidance from my higher self to place an order with Amazon for two books by Dr. Joann Fletcher (*The Search for Nefertiti* and *Chronicles of a Pharaoh: The Intimate Life of Amenhotep III*.)

I was then inspired to listen again to my CD of Cosmic Messenger by Jean-Luc Ponty before concluding the day with yet another viewing of *The Big Blue*, which I use to align with dolphin consciousness.

At seven o'clock on the morning of 22 September 2007, I woke up from a dream that was too elusive to record and, after enjoying my usual breakfast, turned on my computer to read, with tears in my eyes, that Aung San Suu Kyi (whom most people, including myself, have regarded as the rightful leader of the Burmese people ever since her election in 1990 was blocked by a military coup d'etat) had just wept as she walked out of her house in Rangoon (where she has been under house arrest for most of her life since that time) to meet in silent prayer with a contingent of the more than ten thousand Buddhist monks who, for the past six days, have been marching in protest against the repressive military junta (five thousand in Rangoon, and five thousand in Mandalay).

At 9:39 that morning, I then sent forth the following email message to my list of friends around the world:
Dear Friends:
As you may know, we are now at pivotal point, where major transformative events are taking place behind the scenes prior to public announcement during the immediate future.
As you may also know, unconfirmed rumors are flying on the internet in the absence of confirmed facts.
And here is a summary of the current unconfirmed rumors:
"Rumors persist regarding the imminent departure of Bush, the pending arrest of Paulson and Cheney, and Paulson's closed door meeting with Congress on the afternoon of September 19, advising that we have now joined the new Global Banking System."
I recommend that we regard these unconfirmed rumors as working hypotheses which remain to be confirmed.
In Love's pure Light,
All-is-one Heartsong

Later that morning, I received an email message from my friend, Donald Nobach (who has led the peace gatherings and anti-war protest marches in Mount Shasta for the past several years), reporting that Homeland Security Director Michael Chertoff has just announced that, beginning in 2008, American citizens will not be allowed to travel by air unless they have clearance from the Department of Homeland Security. (Needless to say, I interpreted this announcement by Chertoff as the last dying gasp of the Dark Illuminati, who simply cannot accept the fact that they have lost and that the chess game is over.)

After taking my morning walk to the KOA campground so that I could again feast on the abundance of blackberries, I decided to have lunch at Lily's Restaurant so that I could again enjoy their three-cheese omelet.

I then spent the afternoon catching up on my journal entries regarding recent developments, and finally got around to transmitting "Twelve Steps to God-Realization" to my list of friends around the world before the end of that day.

That night, around two o'clock, I had the following dream, which I quickly recorded before going back to sleep: When the heart chakra opens, the enlightened human being is motivated to create circles of twelve which are then connected together to form a network of lightworkers that gradually transform the whole of humanity on Planet Earth.

On the morning of 23 September 2007 (Autumn Equinox), I woke up a few minutes before six o'clock, had a quick breakfast, and turned on my computer a few minutes before seven o'clock to read the following news report: "About 5,000 Burmese monks have been joined by nuns for the first time on the seventh day of protests calling for an end to the military government. Cheered on by 10,000 onlookers, up to 150 nuns joined the march through the heart of Rangoon. But unlike a day earlier, police barred a group of monks from entering the road that leads to the home of detained opposition leader Aung San Suu Kyi. The protest is the biggest public show of opposition since the 1988 uprising."

At 8:55 that morning, I then transmitted to my list of friends around the world the following email message:
Beloved Friends:
    In celebration of this Autumn Equinox, I would like to share with you a dream which I had on 6 January 2007, which is now over eight months ago.
    Here is the verbatim transcription of how I recorded that dream and my interpretation of that dream in my personal journal.
    "Dream: Align to change from Autumn Equinox to Winter Solstice.
    "Interpretation: This remarkable dream seems to be a message from my higher self predicting radical change from September 23 to December 22 during the latter part of 2007."
    In Love's pure Light,
    All-is-one Heartsong

After working on my manuscript for a couple of hours, I next went for a walk in the sunshine, and then fixed myself another tomato and cucumber salad.

An unusual sequence of events then proceeded to unfold, which I shall now describe very carefully.

After taking my laundry to the laundromat sooner than usual, I next lay down on my bed to meditate for a few minutes, and was then guided by my higher self to review the record in my personal journal regarding what I had experienced one year earlier around the end of September and the beginning of October in 2006.

In the process of reviewing that material, I discovered an extremely significant detail which I had overlooked while writing the Prelude section of my manuscript during the fourth week in June of 2007.

This extremely significant detail consisted in the following extraordinary sentence which my higher self had channeled through my consecrated mind at three o'clock on the morning of 12 October 2006.

"If the secret agenda of George W. Bush has been to transform the United States of America from humanity's beloved exemplar of liberty and justice for all to the most hated nation in the world, then the simple truth of the matter is that he has succeeded brilliantly in achieving his goal."

According to the entry which I wrote in my journal later that day, I immediately submitted this remarkable statement to www.truthout.org in care of the Executive Director Marc Ash and the Managing Editor Scott Galindez, inviting them to use it as a one-sentence Op-Editorial bearing the title "Epitaph for Uncle Sam."

What makes this remarkable statement so extremely significant is the fact that, just one year later, I would now label it "Epitaph for George Bush."

It is this simple fact which provides us with a precise measurement of the radical transformative change that we have lived through during the pivotal year from October of 2006 to October of 2007.

It only remains to add that I celebrated the occasion by listening to Beethoven's Ninth Symphony that evening before going to bed.

At five o'clock on the morning of 24 September 2007, I woke up with a most unusual dream, which I recorded as follows: After separating my limited self from my unlimited self for the purpose of gathering wisdom, I am now merging my limited self with my unlimited self to become fully empowered.

This dream was accompanied by extremely elusive imagery that included an image of me scribbling words on paper which were completely illegible.

After getting out of bed to scribble down on paper the words recorded above, I turned on the stove in my kitchen and the radiator in my living room before closing the window and getting back into bed.

I then spent the next forty-five minutes doing deep-breathing exercises and contemplating my dream while waiting for the apartment to warm up.

Around 5:45, I did my fifty bicycle kicks, and at six o'clock I did my ten sit-ups with the determined attitude of an Olympic athlete preparing for a major event.

I then got up, turned on the lights, and proceeded to fix my usual breakfast with two pieces of rye crispbread instead of one slice of toasted multiseed bread.

Around seven o'clock, I turned on my Dell computer and read the loving tributes to the incomparable mime artist Marcel Marceau, who "had a rare gift–that of communicating with each and every one of us, beyond the barrier of language."

I next read the news report that one hundred thousand people had just marched peacefully through the city of Rangoon with the Buddhist monks, who were now calling for the entire country to join with them in their campaign to overthrow the intolerably repressive military government.

Shortly after eight o'clock, I then transmitted a key message from Ag-agria of Sirius, prefaced by the following introduction:

Beloved Friends:

Ag-agria of Sirius, a fifth-dimensional emissary of the Galactic Federation channeled by Mike Quinsey in England, has today blessed us with a key message that includes the following passages.

"So much is happening right now, and it is coming together to create the perfect circumstances that will bring a quantum leap forward."

"What is taking place is a world event, and our help and influence has been just as evident in other countries outside of the West."

"Look for example at the non-violent uprising by the monks in Burma, and how it has taken on a demonstration for peace."

"Your mass consciousness is growing to a massive size, and its energy is serving to awaken people to their own power."

"It is an unstoppable force of Light."

"Matters are reaching a point where the dark are creating their own demise."

"We now await their final attempt to avoid events that shall spell the end of them."

"You can therefore stand aside and watch their last acts of defiance."

In Love's pure Light,

All-is-one Heartsong

After my morning walk, I took the next batch of handwritten pages to Zepp, asked him to place the message from Ag-agria on my website, and then guided him through a complex series of corrections on the manuscript.

I next prepared a delicious lunch, consisting of an avocado with salsa plus some fresh carrot juice, and then spent the rest of the afternoon organizing the first forty pages of my manuscript.

I went to bed early that night, asking my higher self to help me refine Item 6: The Dividing of the Ways, and to my amazement my higher self responded by waking me up between ten and eleven o'clock that very evening to provide my consecrated mind with a refinement which transformed my article into a profoundly heartfelt acknowledgment of Archangel Gabriel and the ascended master Saint Germain as my beloved mentors.

I woke up on the morning of 25 September 2007 feeling exceptionally energized, and after my usual exercises, my usual breakfast, and my usual walk, I spent two full hours working with Zepp to finalize the first thirty-three pages of my manuscript.

I then celebrated this accomplishment by going to Lily's Restaurant for a light lunch that consisted of orange-beet soup, a mixed green salad with avocado dressing, and a slice of key lime pie, most of which I took home with me in a box because it was more than I could eat.

As I was leaving the restaurant, which has become for me almost like a home-away-from-home, my higher self specified that my favorite waitress, whom I know only as Kim, should be included in this book because she loves people as much as I do and fills that restaurant with Love's pure Light whenever she is present.

After sleeping soundly for three hours, I woke up from my afternoon nap at 4:30 and immediately began to organize pages 34 to 45.

For some reason, Zepp had left blank a space large enough for a six-line paragraph at the bottom of page 31, so I asked my higher self for guidance as to how I might fill that empty space and immediately received guidance to compose a six-line paragraph which summarized several email messages about Calleman's interpretation of the Mayan's calendar that I had previously regarded as being too complex and lengthy to include, which I inserted on page 29.

I was then inspired to complete the day by watching my recently acquired videotape of *Resurrection* for the second time, having previously seen a rented version only twice before.

After sleeping more restlessly than usual, I woke up at 7:30 on the morning of 26 September 2007 feeling more determined than ever, and decided to vary my routine by substituting one of Katie Anna's leftover organic rice cakes for my usual rye crispbread. (Please understand that my higher self has specifically asked my consecrated mind to record even the most trivial details of my personal experience at this pivotal point in human history.)

I then opened my computer and immediately began to transmit a message from SaLuSa of Sirius, prefaced by the following introduction:

Dear Friends:

SaLuSa of Sirius, a fifth-dimensional emissary of the Galactic Federation channeled by Mike Quinsey of England, has today blessed us with a clear explanation of the dividing of the ways which we are currently passing through.

"The movement of energies is gathering pace, and you are forming a massive grid of Light that is spreading all over."

"Even those who are under the spell of the dark and obey their orders are beginning to take a wider view of their responsibilities to their fellow man."

"There is no oath to your administration or country that takes precedence over your allegiance to God."

"Inwardly all know when they are being called upon to serve another Master, and it is their choice entirely."

"Having exercised your freewill as to whom you serve, it is your responsibility for any actions you take."

"It is therefore beholden unto you to establish where your loyalty lies, and act accordingly."

"What we have referred to as the parting of the ways comes about through your choice."

"You have divided into two camps, and those who have no desire to leave the old behind will remain in the lower vibrations."

"You may wonder why you have accepted the opportunity to experience life in the lower realms, and you did so because you could see how it would benefit you."

"Duality has provided the challenge that has speeded up your evolution, without which your growth would have been considerably slower."

In Love's pure Light,
All-is-one Heartsong

While surfing the Internet, I next decided to counteract the disinformation campaign which the Bush regime was waging against Iran in general and the President of Iran in particular by sending the following email message to my list of friends around the world.

Dear Friends:

I invite you to read and contemplate these excerpts from the concluding portion of the speech by Iranian President Ahmadinejad to the United Nations General Assembly on 25 September 2007.

"Humanity has passed a perilous precipice, and the age of monotheism, purity, affinity, respecting others, justice, and true peace-loving has commenced."

"It is a divine promise that truth will be victorious and the Earth will be inherited by the righteous."

"The era of darkness will end."

"The tender-hearted and humanity-loving governments will replace the aggressive and domineering ones."

"Human dignity will be regained."

"The pleasing aroma of justice will permeate the world, and people will live together in a brotherly and affectionate manner."

"I wish for a bright future for all human beings and the dawn of the liberation of and freedom for all humans, and the rule of love and affection all around the world, as well as the elimination of oppression, hatred, and violence, a wish which I expect will be realized in the near future."

In Love's pure Light,
All-is-one Heartsong

After lunch, I turned on my computer, reviewed the news (which included a report that the military government in Burma had begun to resort to violence), transmitted an email message regarding the current rumors (which included a report that arrest warrants had been issued for Bush I, Bush II, Cheney and Paulson), and then sent forth the following recommendation:

Dear Friends:

Have you seen the film RESURRECTION (1980) starring Ellen Burstyn and Sam Shepard?

This cinematic masterpiece tells the unforgettable story of an ordinary woman who experiences clinical death as the result of a car accident and then returns to life with the extraordinary ability to heal other people by means of her unconditional love, which allows her to become one with them empathically.

Although it has now become rare and hard to find, copies of this VHS videotape may still be obtained through Amazon.

After spending the rest of the afternoon organizing the next several pages of my manuscript, I was then guided to watch the film *Joshua* for the umpteenth time.

At 5:30 on the morning of 27 September 2007, my higher self surprised my consecrated mind with the following highly unorthodox definition of religion: "Religion can best be defined as the conceptualization, distortion, and perversion of spiritual truth by the human mind in third-dimensional separation consciousness."

After breakfast, I informed my list of friends regarding the current rumors on the internet, drove up to Morningstar to obtain Grace's approval for the formatting of her poem in my manuscript, and then spent two hours with Zepp finalizing the sequence of pages up to CONTROVERSIES on page 46.

After lunch, I devoted the entire afternoon to the task of organizing the next one hundred pages and then took a short walk before watching my video copy of *You've Got Mail* for what must have also been the umpteenth time.

At three o'clock on the morning of 28 September 2007, my higher self gave me a whole list of questions to ask my beloved friend Rebekah for the purpose of determining whether she was the appropriate singer to record my Wake-Up Song, which my higher self had inspired my conscious mind to compose in the spring of 2003.

One hour later, at four o'clock that morning, I received specific instructions from my higher self to contact the young London-based Burmese blogger Ko Htike, who has been attempting to keep information from Burma flowing on the Internet despite massive governmental censorship.

Let history record it was on the morning of 28 September 2007 that George W. Bush made a desperate attempt to salvage his reputation as a ruthless war criminal by condemning the murderous suppression of the Burmese people in the vain hope that he could thereby persuade the world to regard the Burmese regime as the "bad guys" and the Bush regime as the "good guys."

Sleeping later than usual that morning, I finally woke up at eight o'clock with a clear recollection of the following dream: I am with Captain Eric May, whose parents have called forth maximal protection for their beloved son.

After breakfast, I met with Zepp from ten to twelve o'clock for the purpose of finalizing pages 47 to 140 of my manuscript.

I then celebrated this accomplishment by going to Lily's Restaurant for lunch, which consisted of a mixed green salad and my favorite chicken pesto linguini prepared by my friend Ron.

Immediately after lunch, I transmitted the following email message to Ko Htiki, the young London-based Burmese blogger to whom my higher self had asked me to send a specific recommendation.

Dear Ko Htiki:

Please allow me to introduce myself. My professional name is Arthur Earl Jones, Ph. D. I am a psychologist and psychotherapist by profession, am now eighty years old, and have been a devoted admirer of Aung San Suu Kyi for many years.

My spiritual name, which I received from the ascended master Saint Germain in 1991, is All-is-one Heartsong.

The ascended master Saint Germain and the archangel Gabriel have been my spiritual guides and mentors since 1982, and I have served as a humble channel for spirit since that time.

Confirmation of these facts may be found on my website (www.planetaryascension.net) which I established on 17 May 2002 using my spiritual name All-is-one Heartsong.

If you would like to receive further proof and would be so kind as to send me your postal address, I will be happy to send you a 61-page autobiographical account of my spiritual journey during this lifetime (*Illustration of Spiritual Awakening*).

Last night, at four o'clock in the morning of 28 September 2007, I received guidance from my higher self (a sixth-dimensional light body whose name is Kumara Zora Torith) to contact you for the specific purpose of giving you this message to transmit to the Buddhist leadership of the current protest movement in Burma.

Spirit recommends changing tactics from public marches to a series of three-day general strikes, which could begin as soon as October 1 to 3.

Sincerely,
Dr. Arthur Earl Jones
also known as
All-is-one Heartsong

Later that afternoon, I transmitted the following email message to my younger daughter Karen Cinnamon, who had just sent me a detailed account of her medical symptoms and their possible causes:

Beloved Cinnamon:

I welcome your communication and will respond in several steps because I am now in the final stage of completing my new book.

I have read the article by Marjorie Tietzen and am in general agreement with it as far as it goes, my only reservation being that she doesn't understand what I call the Big Picture (reality as viewed from the perspective of the sixth-dimensional higher self) and therefore gives a fear-based presentation of what I call the Little Picture (illusion as viewed from the perspective of the third-dimensional human mind).

Before we get into the specific details, I recommend that we start with the general fundamentals and begin by clarifying the relation between the spiritual orientation exemplified by your father and the scientific orientation exemplified by your mother.

Instead of regarding these two different orientations as polar opposites, I propose that we regard them, not merely as polar complements, but rather as a special theory that is contained within a general theory, where the scientific orientation of our third-dimensional human mind is simply a special case within the spiritual orientation of our sixth-dimensional higher self.

Thus, whereas our higher self sees and understands the Big Picture, our limited human mind is only able to perceive and interpret or misinterpret the Little Picture, which is a tiny fraction of the Big Picture.

Please give me your feedback at your convenience, and we will then be in a position to take the next step.

Your father who loves you.

That evening, I relaxed and refreshed my mind by watching *Sleepless in Seattle* for what must have also been the umpteenth time.

After breakfast on the Saturday morning of 29 September 2007, I finally got around to transmitting a magnificent message from Ker-On of Venus, a fifth-dimensional emissary of the Galactic Federation channeled by Mike Quinsey of England on the previous day, and I then spent the rest of the morning checking the news and recording my recent experiences.

Following an avocado and salsa lunch, I devoted myself to the task of organizing the next pages of my manuscript including Items 30 and 31, and it was not until five o'clock in the evening that I finally got around to taking a short walk in the sunshine.

I then decided to entertain myself by watching a mediocre fantasy-film of Tom Hanks and Meg Ryan called *Joe and the Volcano* for what was probably the third and last time.

At seven o'clock on the morning of 30 September 2007, I woke up with guidance from my higher self about how to formulate my next email message to my younger daughter Karen Cinnamon. Hence, immediately after breakfast, I transmitted the following formulation.

Beloved Cinnamon:

Our first step is to make a clear distinction between what I call the Little Picture (of the physical universe and the laws of physics and quantum mechanics), which is a product of the scientific thinking of the human mind in the third dimension of consciousness, and what I call the Big Picture (of the twelve dimensions of consciousness and the metaphysical laws of attraction, karma, and reincarnation), which is a product of the spiritual knowing of the higher self on the sixth dimension of consciousness.

Our second step is to make a clear distinction between the unenlightened scientific orientation which misconceives consciousness as an epiphenomenon of physiological processes, and the enlightened scientific orientation, which recognizes that physical and physiological processes are decisively influenced by the conscious intention of the observer.

Our third step is to make a clear distinction between the benevolent use of science by lightworkers for the purpose of benefiting humanity, and the malevolent misuse of science by darkworkers for the purpose of subjugating humanity (which is what the article by Marjorie Tietzen on the intentional invention of incapacitating illnesses is all about).

Please give me your feedback regarding these three preliminary steps, and we will then be in a position to proceed with our exploration of your current situation.

Your father who loves you.

I then spent the rest of the morning organizing the next thirty-five pages of my manuscript before going to Lily's for a three-cheese omelet brunch.

The remainder of that day was devoted to proofreading the most recent pages of my manuscript.

At five o'clock on the morning of 1 October 2007, I woke up with the following dream: I realize that I have succeeded in collecting a complete set of recordings in the form of twenty-four videotapes of twenty-four different speakers at a conference, of which I am one of the presenters.

I interpreted this dream to be the signal from my higher self which I had been asking for, indicating that Volume One of my book *Channeling the Apocalypse* was now complete and that Volume Two could begin in October of 2007.

After breakfast, I turned on my computer and went directly to Tree of the Golden Light, where I selected ET Contact and zeroed in on Mike Quinsey's channeling of a message from Diane of Sirius, which contained nothing new except for this important prediction on the very first line: "Many events are coming to a head, and soon one will explode on the scene, and you will realize that you have witnessed the first important change."

I transmitted Diane's message to my email list of over ninety friends around the world and recorded my experiences while contemplating the fact that I now had a clear signal from my higher self indicating that I could proceed immediately with the task of publishing Volume One of *Channeling the Apocalypse*.

I then proceeded to check the world news, which began with the fact that the military government in Burma had shut down the Internet access to the entire country on 28 September 2007.

Some three thousand Buddhist monks were then taken from their monasteries and placed in make-shift prisons on the outskirts of Rangoon, where they were currently refusing to take food from their jailers.

The Japanese Deputy Foreign Minister Mitoji Yabunaka had just arrived in Burma to ensure a full investigation into the death of Japanese video journalist Kenji Nagai, who had been shot at close range by a Burmese soldier on September 25, when many people were killed by the ruthless military junta at the height of their violent suppression of the massive non-violent protest marches.

And UN special envoy Ibrahim Gambari had already met with opposition leader Aung San Suu Kyi on September 30 prior to meeting with Burma's military leader General Than Shwe on October 2.

After taking a short walk, I worked with Zepp for the rest of the morning to organize the manuscript up to the portrait of Osama bin Laden.

I then had an apple, banana, and nut lunch and devoted the entire afternoon to the process of preparing the next portion of my manuscript for finalization.

At 5:30 that evening, I turned on my computer and went directly to the website of Ko Htike, the young London-based Burmese blogger, who had just learned that a group of nearly 200 monks were ruthlessly bludgeoned to death at their monastery near the Ngwe Kyar Yan neighborhood on Wei-za-yan-tar Road in Rangoon (Yangon) on Sunday, 30 September 2007.

Here is the verbatim record of the report by Ko Htike which was dated 30 September 2007, and posted on 1 October 2007.

"We just got phone call with our sister living in Yangon (Rangoon) about a few hours ago.

"We saw on BBC world, saying that 200 monks were arrested. The true picture is far worse!!!!!!!!

"For one instance, the monastery at an obscure neighborhood of Yangon (Rangoon) called Ngwe Kyar Yan on Wei-za-yan-tar Road had been raided early this morning.

"A troop of lone-tein (riot police comprised of paid thugs) protected by the military trucks, raided the monastery with 200 studying monks. They systematically ordered all the monks to line up and banged and crushed each one's head against the brick wall of the monastery. One by one, the peaceful, non-resisting monks fell to the ground, screaming in pain. Then, they tore off the red robes and threw them all in the military trucks (like rice bags) and took the bodies away.

"The head monk of the monastery was tied up in the middle of the monastery, tortured, bludgeoned, and later died the same day, today. Tens of thousands of people gathered outside the monastery, warded off by troops with bayoneted rifles, unable to help their helpless monks being slaughtered inside the monastery. Their every try to forge ahead was met with the bayonets.

"When all is done, only 10 out of 200 remained alive, hiding in the monastery. Blood stained everywhere on the walls and floors of the monastery.

"Please tell your audience of the full extent of the fate of the monks, please please!!!!!!!!!

"'Arrested' is not enough expression. They have been bludgeoned to death."

In response to the shocking news of this outrageous atrocity, I immediately stopped working on my manuscript and decided to spend the remainder of the evening in silent prayer and meditation.

I then spent that entire night loving myself free of the acute emotional pain which I experienced as I empathized with the plight of the Burmese people, whose tragic situation epitomized the insane Alice-in-Wonderland nightmare from which humanity was desperately trying to wake up.

Item 38: October 2007 meeting of Aung San Suu Kyi with UN envoy Ibrahim Gambari

Item 39: General Than Shwe, Burmese tyrant

Item 40
Thousands of protesters executed in Burma

Thousands of protesters, including monks, have been executed and their bodies dumped in Burma's jungle, a British newspaper reports.

Citing a former intelligence officer for the country's ruling junta, the Daily Mail reported late Monday that security forces were ordered to take part in a massacre of the revered monks.

"Many more people have been killed in recent days than you've heard about. The bodies can be counted in several thousand," Hla Win, a senior official who defected, told the newspaper from his border hideout as he fled to Thailand.

The junta, however, has confirmed only 10 deaths so far.

Win told the newspaper he fled with his son after he heard of the executions.

"They were to be killed and their bodies dumped deep inside the jungle. I refused to participate in this," he told the Daily Mail.

A picture accompanying the article shows a saffron robed body lying face down in a river, with the caption identifying it as an executed Buddhist monk.

Human rights groups are still trying to learn more about the severity of last week's crackdown. Some groups estimate as many as 1,500 people have also been jailed, including up to 1,000 monks.

Crackdown's severity unknown

According to one Asian diplomat, monks are paying a heavy price for their leadership in the protests.

All the arrested monks have been defrocked — stripped of their highly revered status and made to wear civilian clothes, he said. Some of them are likely to face long jail terms, the diplomat said on condition of anonymity.

It has been difficult to get accurate information out of the country. Military rulers have restricted internet access and mobile phone service.

Soldiers have gone to hotels in search of foreign journalists operating without permission.

At least four local journalists have been arrested and others have been detained or harassed, Reporters Without Borders and the Burma Media Association said in a statement.

Security forces used 'utmost restraint'

In a speech to the United Nations General Assembly on Monday, Burma's foreign minister defended the junta's actions, saying security forces exercised the "utmost restraint" and only took action against protesters when the "mob became unruly and provocative."

"Normalcy has now returned in Myanmar," said U Nyan Win.

The minister accused "political opportunists" of fuelling protests to create a showdown in the country that they could benefit from.

"The situation would not have deteriorated, had the initial protest of a small group of activists against the rise in fuel prices not been exploited by political opportunists," Nyan Win said.

"They sought to turn the situation into a political showdown aided and abetted by some powerful countries," he added, without naming countries.

He also urged the international community to refrain from taking measures that will worsen the situation in the impoverished southeast Asian country, also known as Myanmar.

Public anger, which ignited Aug. 19 after the government hiked fuel prices, turned into mass protests against 45 years of military dictatorship when Buddhist monks joined in.

Soldiers responded last week by opening fire on unarmed demonstrators, killing at least 10 people by the government's account.

Nyan Win said he was "greatly disturbed" by media campaigns accusing his government of human rights violations and countries imposing sanctions on Burma, calling the actions "counterproductive" and bound to worsen poverty.

Burmese general to meet UN envoy

Also Monday, Burma said its top general has finally agreed to meet with the United Nations special envoy, who hopes to deliver a stern message from the international community over the junta's crackdown on recent protests.

Ibrahim Gambari has travelled to northern Burma twice since arriving in the country only to be rebuffed at the isolated jungle headquarters of the military regime.

But on Monday, the government issued a statement saying Senior Gen. Than Shwe will meet Tuesday with Gambari.

On Sunday, Gambari met Burmese opposition leader Aung San Suu Kyi, a key symbol in the country's pro-democracy movement, which has been quelled by a huge deployment of soldiers in at least two major cities.

The meeting took place at a state guest house in Rangoon, the country's commercial centre and former capital. Suu Kyi was taken there from the residence where she has been held under house arrest.

Diplomats said the meeting lasted about 90 minutes and can be viewed as something of a concession by Burma's military rulers.

However, the military's occupation of Rangoon has successfully stifled any demonstrations for the past two days, and observers say the regime may already feel it has won.

"Unfortunately, the military have regained the momentum now and it's going to be difficult. There'd have to be a major new dimension emerge for the situation to alter again," Sajjan M. Gohel, director of international security at the London-based Asia Pacific Foundation, told CBC News.

On the streets Monday, troops removed road blocks and appeared to ease their stranglehold on Rangoon following the largest protests in two decades.

After days of intimidation that snuffed out the public demonstrations, soldiers and riot police redeployed from the city centre to the outskirts, but were still checking cars and buses and monitoring the city by helicopter.

Traffic was still light and most shops remained closed. Some monks were allowed to leave monasteries to collect food donations, watched by soldiers lounging under trees.

"It's outwardly quite normal at the moment. The traffic seems to be flowing, there's a lot of military tucked away in less visible locations," British Ambassador Mark Canning told the Associated Press. "They've obviously for the moment squeezed things off the streets."

– From CBC News, 1 October 2007

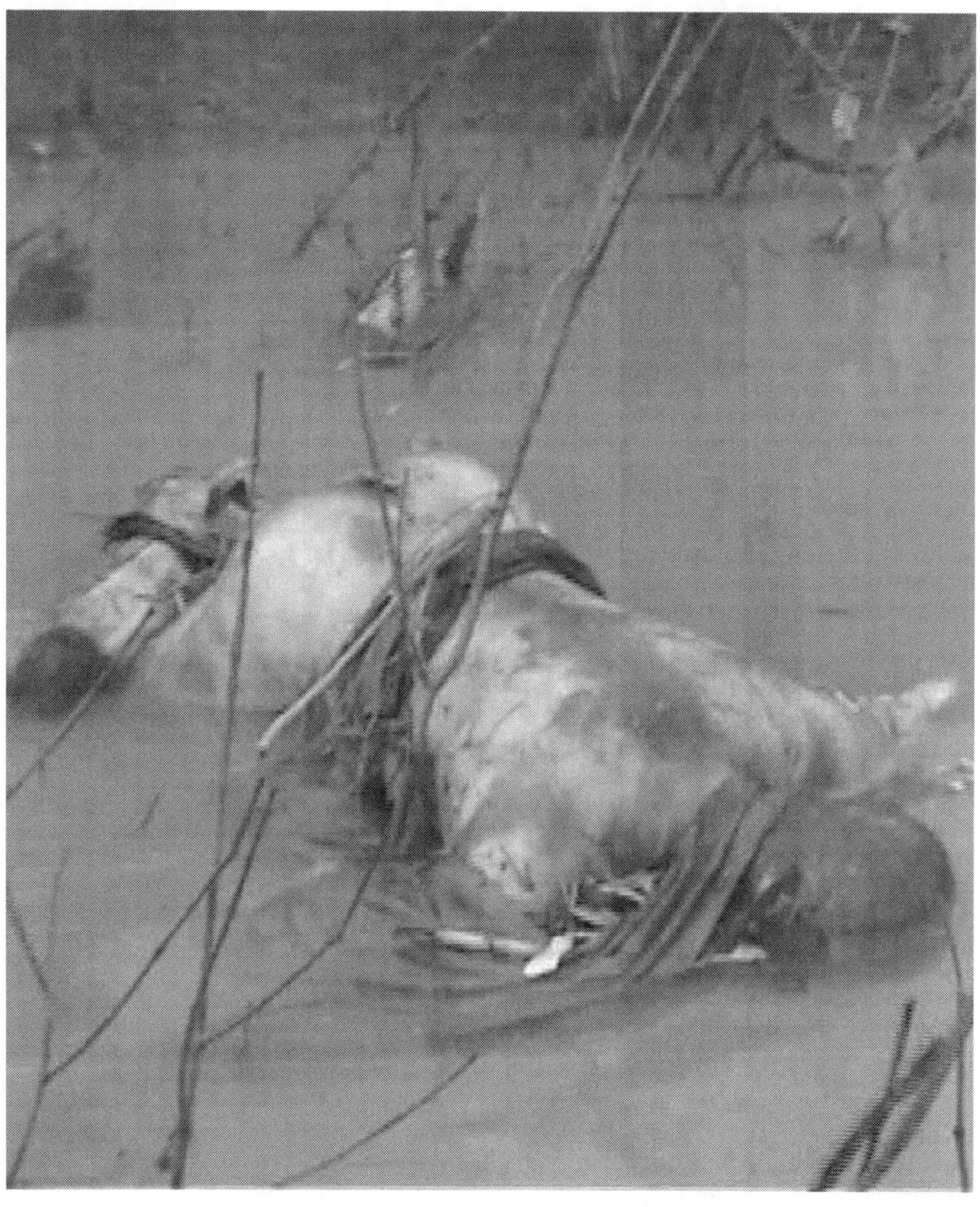

Item 41: Photograph of Buddhist monk murdered by the Burmese military junta on 30 September 2007

As news of the murderous military massacre of Buddhist monks in Burma gradually became known through the Burmese internet blogger Ko Htike in the face of massive media censorship, thereby revealing Burma's military junta to be a criminal government while exposing the United Nations as a feeble fraud, the entire world was shaken awake by the seismic shock of this outrageous atrocity.

At seven o'clock on the morning of 2 October 2007, I woke up with the following dream: I inform the manager of a restaurant that the cashew nuts which I have been served are infested with bugs that should be gotten rid of.

After breakfast, I turned on my computer and saw a revealing photograph of a haggard Aung San Suu Kyi with a distressed UN special envoy Ibrahim Gambari, followed by an equally revealing picture of the brutal General Than Shwe.

When I then checked my incoming email, what immediately attracted my attention was a CBC news report which had been sent to me by my friend Zepp Jamieson at 6:17 that morning and which bore the shocking headline: "THOUSANDS OF PROTESTERS EXECUTED IN BURMA" (See Item 40).

I immediately transmitted that CBC news report to my list of friends around the world (including my new friend Ko Htike), prefaced with the following message.
Dear Friends:
    Here is one of several reports on the murderous response by the criminal military regime of General Than Shwe to the peaceful protest marches of 100,000 Burmese citizens led by 10,000 Buddhist monks in Rangoon and Mandalay during the past week.
    In Love's pure Light,
    All-is-one Heartsong
    www.planetaryascension.net

I next read a carefully spun BBC news report that misled the world with the following sanitized words.
"UN special envoy Ibrahim Gambari has met detained Burmese opposition leader Aung San Suu Kyi for a second time, hours after talks with military rulers.
"The meeting took place on Mr. Gambari's return from the new capital, Naypyidaw, where he conveyed to General Than Shwe concerns over a violent crackdown.
"At least ten people were killed, possibly many more, when troops ended days of pro-democracy demonstrations...
"Mr. Gambari's meetings suggest he is trying to establish some kind of dialogue between the government and the opposition...
"The envoy is now on his way to Singapore. He had waited four days to see General Than Shwe before the chairman of Burma's State Peace and Development Council made himself available.
"No details have emerged, but Mr. Gambari was intending to urge the general 'to cease the repression of peaceful protest', release detainees, and embrace democracy and human rights, a UN

spokesman said before the talks...

"The general's reactions to Mr. Gambari's comments is likely to have been the same as that of Foreign Minister Nyan Win to the UN, says the BBC's Chris Hogg in Bangkok...

"Security forces, he said, had exercised 'utmost restraint' against an 'unruly and provocative' mob and 'normalcy' had been restored...

"The 47-nation council lacks enforcement powers, and is limited to focusing global attention on human rights offenders."

Instead of going for my usual morning walk, I spent the next hour recording my current experiences, after which I worked with Zepp from ten until noon organizing my manuscript from the portrait of Queen Nefertiti to the picture of Admiral Fallon.

Zepp then shared with me a current video clip of Keith Olbermann making fun of Bill O'Reilly's threat to 'hunt him down', which typifies the unfathomable depths to which Fox News has currently descended.

Feeling an urgent need to provide my body with the most nourishing lunch available, I next drove to Lily's Restaurant and ordered a bowl of vegetable soup followed by chicken pesto linguini, which lifted me up into a state of bliss. (Please note that, in 1991, Saint Germain specifically advised me to include chicken once a week in my otherwise vegetarian diet.)

While I was enjoying the soup, my friend Ron shared with me the story of his beloved dog. And while I was getting high on pesto, my friend Kim informed me that she was an experienced sky diver who had already done it three times.

After returning to my apartment and taking a short nap, I then turned on my computer and went directly to the website of Ko Htike, which now provided the following additional information (taken from an article in *The Australia* by Dennis Shanahan dated 2 October 2007)

"The savagery of an attack by the army and paid goons on Yuzana monastery in north Rangoon was so vicious that 3000 local residents living close by came out to protest the next day. Details are emerging of a sinister organization called Swann Arrshim, meaning strong force, whose purpose is to intimidate and beat anybody who steps out of line. Funded by a government body known as the Union of Solidarity Development Association, the gang is deployed across the country and comes under the control of Agricultural Minister Major General Htay-Oo . . .

"Bloggers, armed with digital cameras and software to dodge firewalls, have shown the uprising to the world, and the junta's bloodthirsty response. Now they have been silenced and forced underground.

"The junta has always kept a chokehold on internet users, licensing computers and issuing accounts through state-monitored internet service providers. Now, having failed to stop the cyber dissidents' broadcasting to the world, the authorities have switched off the internet.

"First they arrested individuals blogging about the protests and confiscated their computers. Then they blocked individual Burmese blogs and last Wednesday they blocked all of them. But the overseas sites were beyond their reach, and so on Friday they switched off the internet altogether."

The remainder of the day was devoted to proofreading the most recent additions to my manuscript and then catching up on my email correspondence.

At one o'clock on the morning of 3 October 2007, I woke up with the following dream: My friend Grace and I are the leaders of a small group of lightworkers within a larger community who are living very simply while quietly preparing for the awakening of humanity and the global transformation of Planet Earth that is about to occur.

During the next two hours, I then received detailed instructions from my higher self, telling my consecrated mind how to complete Volume One of *Channeling the Apocalypse*, requesting that I include the photograph of the murdered monk which I had seen on Ko Htike's website, and specifying that I should also include the CBC report dated 1 October 2007.

Last but not least, I was instructed to sell the gold medal of Andrei Sakharov (1921-1989), the Soviet nuclear physicist and human-rights advocate (a treasured memento which I had acquired at that moment in my life when I was a millionaire), so as to be able to pay Zepp and publish this book.

I woke up at six o'clock that morning feeling like an Olympic athlete on the verge of that major event for which I had been preparing.

After a quick breakfast, I decided to skip my morning walk in order to transmit the current message from Saint Germain, channeled by Mike Quinsey, which included the key words, "This is your last life in this dimension" and "Your sojourn is almost over."

By the time I arrived at Zepp's office, however, I realized that I was on the verge of exhaustion and was in no condition to make major decisions regarding the finalization of the last portion of my manuscript for Volume One. So I wisely decided to take the day off to rest and recuperate, my only work with Zepp that morning being to prepare the CBC report dated 1 October 2007.

After going to the bank to get some cash and walking to the market to buy some food, I fixed myself a tomato and cucumber salad and then took a nap to catch up on my sleep.

At 2:10 on the afternoon of 3 October 2007, I transmitted to my list of friends around the world a message channeled by Sheldan Nidle on 2 October 2007 (see Appendix J), prefaced by the following introduction.
Dear Friends:
    The Sirian Council of the Galactic Federation, channeled by Sheldan Nidle, has blessed us with a major message which describes the final stage of the end-game in the global contest between civilized lightworkers and uncivilized darkworkers that is now on the verge of CHECKMATE.
    The important thing to understand is that CHECKMATE will mean the permanent end of all criminal governments on Planet Earth.
    In Love's pure Light,
    All-is-one Heartsong
    www.planetaryascension.net

As a convenient means of recreation, I next made the decision to begin reading *Chronicle of a Pharaoh: The Intimate Life of Amenhotep III* (2000) by Dr. Joann Fletcher, which I had recently ordered through Amazon and which had just arrived in the mail.

My first impression was of a beautifully illustrated book that was expertly written. However, I soon began to encounter specific details where Dr. Fletcher's version of the Eighteenth Dynasty differs from mine, and, although such differences are not at all unusual in the field of Egyptology, they enabled me to understand why she had never even so much as acknowledged receiving the gift copy of my illustrated historical treatise which I sent to her on 24 May 2007.

The first major discrepancy to catch my attention consists in references to Tutankhamun as the grandson rather than the son of Amenhotep III on pages 25 and 27, the implication being that Tutankhamun's mother Kiya was mistakenly thought to be the secondary wife of Akhenaten, rather than the secondary wife of Amenhotep III.

The second major discrepancy, which occurs on page 35, consists in the nonrecognition of Joseph the Israelite and his Egyptian wife Asenath as Queen Tiye's parents, referred to in the Egyptian records as Yuya and Tuya or Thuya, the implication being that Dr. Fletcher did not want to risk being associated with the unorthodox Egyptian scholar Ahmed Osman, who deserves credit for publishing this brilliant insight in 1987.

Finally, the most important discrepancy of all, which occurs on pages 108 and 122, consists in the nonrecognition of Moses as Thutmose V, the elder son of Queen Tiye and Pharaoh Amenhotep III who subsequently became known as Thutmose the Sculptor, the implication being that Dr. Fletcher was unable to see through the cover story which Queen Tiye used to protect her elder son from being assassinated by the Amun priesthood, for whom a Hebrew-Egyptian pharaoh was anathema.

It only remains to add that, because I am acutely aware of the traumatic rejection which Dr. Fletcher suffered in 2003 at the hands of Dr. Zahi Hawass, the Secretary-General of Egypt's Supreme Council of Antiquities, I find it very easy to forgive her for not responding to what must have seemed to her like one more unwelcome set of problems. And I shall here record that these words are being written at ten o'clock on the evening of 3 October 2007.

At seven o'clock on the morning of 4 October 2007, I woke up, had a quick breakfast that included a toasted slice of Jewish rye for the sake of variety, and immediately turned on my computer to read a BBC news report that included the following passages.

"Scores of Burmese have been arrested overnight, as the country's military continues its crackdown following last week's protests, witnesses say.

"Security forces are said to be using recordings of the demonstrations to compile lists of activists for arrest.

"A source has told the BBC that as many as 10,000 people - many of them monks who led the demonstrations - have been rounded up for interrogation in recent days...."

"Residents of the main city, Rangoon, say the streets are quiet during daylight hours, with the police and army keeping a low profile.

"But during the overnight curfew, they say raids by the security forces continue.

"The BBC's Chris Hogg, in neighbouring Thailand, says if it is a tactic designed to scare people, it is working..."

"The Burmese regime - led by reclusive General Than Shwe - has been condemned for its actions across the world."

(Please note how the controlled media use the term "security forces" for what are in fact government criminals of a criminal government.)

That same day, the following article by Kenneth Denby was published by The Times UK:

"To the handful of monks still remaining at the Ngwe Kya Yan monastery – bruised, scared and in shock – it must have seemed that everything was over. The soldiers and police made their first swoop in the early hours, cracking skulls, firing rubber bullets, and dragging away more than 70 monks to secret detention centers.

"The ones who escaped returned at daybreak to their smashed and looted monastery, the blood of their brothers still glistening on the stone of the courtyard.

"By late afternoon, the soldiers and police returned to finish the job, but then something remarkable happened; thousands of men, women, and children emerged from the surrounding houses of South Okkalopa township, converged on the narrow streets leading up to the monastery and trapped the soldiers and police inside. For more than six hours, the unarmed crowd prevented security forces from taking the monks away – until they were dispersed in a onesided battle in which police reportedly shot dead at least two people.

"It was a scene repeated at monasteries and pagodas across Rangoon. At nearby Kyaik Ka San, Moe Kaung, and Mahar Bowdi, local people defended the monks with their lives . . ."

Shortly after nine o'clock, I sent the following email message to Lulu Distribution Services in another effort to resolve the problems that were delaying the distribution of my treatise which I had ordered and paid for on 21 August 2007.

"Reference number LTK91020846652X. In response to the message from Anne-Marie of Lulu Support received on 3 October 2007, we must deny on the grounds that we have not yet met the mandatory distribution requirements and must therefore request that our manuscript (ID 714890) be returned to edit mode on the revisions page so that the proper bar-code which we have created can now be placed on the one-piece cover before we approve for distribution.

"Our final question is: can we approve for distribution without having to order another proof copy or pay a revision fee?

"Many thanks for your help.

"Arthur Earl Jones, Ph.D."

At 10:30, I met with the local coin dealer, Paul Chabot, who paid me 705 US dollars (in the form of fraudulent Federal Reserve Notes) for the one ounce of gold contained in my Sakharov medal, which I immediately used to pay Zepp the $629 that I owed him.

Let history record that it was the unconstitutional creation of the Federal Reserve System in 1913, followed by the intentional induction of the Great Depression from 1929 to 1939, which enabled the Dark Illuminati to gain control of the Unites States federal government and then use it to wreak havoc throughout the world for the ultimate purpose of enslaving humanity.

Let history also record that the American people failed to heed this clear prophetic warning which was bequeathed to them by Thomas Jefferson: "I believe that banking institutions are more dangerous to our liberties than standing armies. If the American people ever allow private banks to control the issue of their currency, first by inflation, then by deflation, the banks and corporations that will grow up around (the banks) will deprive the people of all property, until their children wake up homeless on the continent their fathers conquered. The issuing power should be taken from the banks and restored to the people, to whom it properly belongs."

After lunch, I again turned on my computer and read the following news report.
"Burma's reclusive military ruler has agreed to meet the detained opposition leader Aung San Suu Kyi, it was reported today.
"The reports came as the Burmese regime admitted rounding up more than 2,000 monks and protesters during days of recent anti-government demonstrations.
"State media said General Than Shwe had told the UN envoy to Burma, Ibrahim Gambari, that he was prepared to hold historic talks with Ms Suu Kyi, with preconditions.
"It added that, during talks on Tuesday, he had insisted that the pro-democracy leader must publicly abandon her stance of confrontation with the regime.
"The Burmese military leader is thought to despise Ms Suu Kyi to the point where he will not even tolerate mention of her name in his presence. This is the first time he has said he is willing to meet her..."

(Please be advised that, at the request of my higher self, this enlightening insert has been added to Volume One of *Channeling the Apocalypse* on 16 October 2007. To arrive at an enlightened understanding of the Burmese tragedy, I recommend that you see the film *Beyond Rangoon*, which provides a vivid portrayal of the courageous leadership demonstrated by Aung San Suu Kyi during the earlier national uprising in 1988. What is more, this film reveals how the Burmese people unwittingly play the duality game by dividing up into two opposing factions that are completely polarized between military soldiers who are unenlightened darkworkers and Buddhist monks who are unenlightened lightworkers in that, rather than believing in a loving Creator of all humanity, they believe instead that, by its very nature, life is suffering.)

I then spent the remainder of the afternoon recording my current experiences and proofreading the most recent material for my manuscript.

That evening, after asking for guidance as to what film I should watch, I reviewed my video copy of *Network* yet again, which served as a useful means of keeping in touch with the collective consciousness of humanity.

At seven o'clock on the morning of 5 October 2007, I woke up with three dream fragments: 1) I am informed that there will be five more days before the change (which I interpret to mean the ending of Volume One and the beginning of Volume Two); 2) I levitate in the presence of a Japanese man that I am assisting (which might refer to the Japanese reporter Kenji Nagai who was shot dead at close range by a soldier of the criminal government at the height of the military crackdown on marching protesters in Rangoon approximately one week ago); 3) I am feeding bread crumbs to two hungry ducks (which may be an expression of my compassion for the millions of human beings who are currently starving to death all over the world.)

After doing my morning exercises, the first thing I did before getting dressed and having breakfast was to ask Saint Germain to overlight and orchestrate the imminent meeting of Aung San Suu Kyi with General Than Shwe (which never took place).

Next, as I was turning on my computer to check the news, I reaffirmed my choice to be a humble servant of spirit.

Then, between 10:30 and 11:30, guided by my higher self, I wrote the conclusion for this book with effortless ease.

From 11:30 to 1:30, I worked with Zepp through the lunch hour to get items 24, 25, and 26 in place, using illustrations from Dr. Fletcher's book, *The Search for Nefertiti*, which had finally arrived in the mail two full weeks after I had ordered it through Amazon.

It then became necessary to revise all of the subsequent item numbers in the text, which was a task that turned out to be far more time-consuming than we had anticipated, so that, by 1:30, both of us were starving.

However, after a late apple-banana-and-nut lunch followed by a brief nap, I had fully recovered by the middle of the afternoon and felt grateful for what we had accomplished.

Not until that point did I have an opportunity to contemplate this email message from my younger daughter:

Hi, Dad,

My latest batch of medical tests came back and indicate that I have two chronic and difficult-to-treat (because they can hide out inside cells) infections. ...Right now the plan is long-term antibiotics, but there is a possibility of using herbs and colloidal silver...Good luck with completing your book.

Love, Cinnamon.

Instead of responding immediately, I decided to wait until I had clear guidance from my higher self as to how best to continue the ongoing conversation with my beloved daughter.

By the time I had recorded my current experiences, it was after six o'clock and time to select a video that would help me relax my mind and facilitate a good night's sleep. *Groundhog Day* served as an easy choice for the umpteenth time.

On the morning of 6 October 2007, I woke up at 7:30, ate a quick breakfast which included a whole wheat English muffin for the sake of variety, and turned on my computer to read the following BBC news report, which began with the headline: GLOBAL RALLIES TO PRESSURE BURMA.

"Campaigners in 30 cities around the world have staged a series of rallies against the bloody crackdown on anti-government protests in Burma.

"The day of marches began in New Zealand, then moved to Asia and Europe and then North America.

"UK Prime Minister Gordon Brown met marchers in London and vowed to keep 'pressure for change' and push for more EU sanctions against the regime...

"'I want the EU to impose further sanctions on the regime to make it absolutely clear we will

Item 42: The ascended master Saint Germain

For a magnificent full-color reproduction of this current portrait of Saint Germain, see p. 196 of *The Seven Sacred Flames*, by Aurelia Louise Jones.

not tolerate the abuses that have taken place,' he told the delegation.

"The marches came as Western powers at the UN make moves to condemn the junta.

"Diplomats have circulated a draft statement at the UN denouncing the 'violent repression' of pro-democracy protests.

"The US, France, and the UK called for immediate dialogue with opposition leaders, while the US suggested it would push for sanctions on Burma.

"But China and Russia remain opposed to sanctions, saying the situation in Burma is an internal affair that does not threaten international peace and security...

"Demonstrations were scheduled to take place at noon local time in Austria, Australia, Belgium, Canada, France, India, Ireland, New Zealand, Norway, South Korea, Spain, Thailand, the UK, and the US."

In response to this news report, I devoted the next hour to the task of first recording it and then sending Love's pure Light to darkworkers as well as lightworkers around the world, knowing from my personal experiences as a deep-trance facilitator that darkworkers become totally confused, completely disoriented, and absolutely bewildered when confronted with the transformative power of Love's pure Light.

The remainder of that morning was spent enjoying a leisurely walk in the sunshine, followed by another delicious tomato and cucumber salad.

Having been informed by my friend Wayne Kingsbury that my friend Aurelia Louise Jones had just published a new book titled *The Seven Sacred Flames*, and having immediately acted on this information by purchasing a copy at the local book store owned by my friend Kathy Lancaster, I then proceeded to focus my full attention on the process of exploring Aurelia's masterpiece for the specific purpose of testing its accuracy.

Instead of beginning at the beginning, which would have been the conventional thing to do, I immediately turned to Chapter Seven at the back of the book and began reading about the ascended master Saint Germain, Chohan of the Seventh Ray, which is the Violet Flame of Transmutation.

There, to my delight, I found on pages 198 and 199 a comprehensive list of Germain's key incarnations prior to becoming an ascended master: 1) the Old Testament prophet Samuel (c. 1105-1015 B.C.), 2) Joseph, the husband of Mary and the father of Jesus (c. 35BC - 20 AD); 3) Saint Alban of Verulam (c. 300 AD); 4) Merlin Taliessin (c. 550 AD); 5) Roger Bacon (1220-1292 AD); 6) Christopher Columbus (1451-1506 AD); 7) Francis Bacon (1561-1626 AD); the only important omission being Germain's prehistoric incarnation as Noah, the High Priest of Atlantis (c. 10,500 BC), who salvaged the DNA codings and organized the surviving seed colonies in Egypt, Peru, and Tibet prior to the sinking of Atlantis.

I next turned to Chapter Six and found on page 165 the names of three Israelites thought by Aurelia to be Sananda's key incarnations prior to his final lifetime as Yeshua ben Joseph, who became known as Jesus the Christ: 1) Joseph the Israelite (c. 1443-1333 BC), who was chosen by Pharaoh Thutmose IV to be the governor of all Egypt; 2) Joshua (c. 1330-1220 BC), who was selected by Moses to lead the Israelites into the Promised Land; 3) King David (c. 1040-970 BC), who was selected by the prophet Samuel to be the king of Israel.

At this point, I wrote the following email message to my friend Aurelia, which was

Item 43: Aurelia Louise Jones

transmitted at 3:54 that afternoon.

Dear Aurelia Louise Jones:

I have just discovered your newly-published masterpiece *The Seven Sacred Flames*, have immediately begun the process of reading it, and wish to express my heartfelt gratitude and sincere congratulations on your magnificent accomplishment in the service of spirit for the benefit of humanity.

All-is-one Heartsong
also known as Arthur Earl Jones, Ph. D.

Here is the email message that I then sent to my list of over ninety friends around the world.

Beloved Friends:

Please be advised that my treasured friend Aurelia Louise Jones has just published a new book titled *The Seven Sacred Flames*, which contains priceless information about the spiritual hierarchy governing Planet Earth, and invaluable guidance for all those who wish to facilitate their participation in the planetary ascension process which is now taking place on Planet Earth.

In Love's pure Light,
All-is-one Heartsong
www.planetaryascension.net

Shortly thereafter, I transmitted the following message to my younger daughter at 4:23 that same afternoon.

Beloved Cinnamon:

If you wish to use spiritual methods to heal your body, I recommend that you immediately obtain a copy of the book *The Seven Sacred Flames* by Aurelia Louise Jones, which has just been published and which is capable of greatly facilitating your personal process of becoming an ascended master.

Your father who loves you.

After receiving guidance from my higher self to include all of these experiences in this book, I asked for guidance as to which video I should watch before going to bed and was immediately advised to review *Whale Rider* one more time before recommending it to my list of friends around the world.

At four o'clock on the morning of 7 October 2007, I was awakened by my higher self and directed to get out of bed for the specific purpose of recording in this book some of the key incarnations of the other five chohans of the seven rays.

Thus, in Chapter Five of *The Seven Sacred Rays*, it is recorded that the ascended master Hilarion, chohan of the fifth ray, had key incarnations as the Apostle Paul (c. 4-67 AD) and Saint Hilarion (290-371 AD).

In Chapter Four, we discover that the ascended master Serapis Bey, who is chohan of the fourth ray, had key incarnations as Pharaoh Amenhotep III (c. 1409-1358 BC), the father of Moses and Akhenaten, and as King Leonidas of Sparta (c. 515-480 BC).

In Chapter Three, we learn that the final lifetime of the ascended master Paul the Venetian, who serves as chohan of the third ray, was the Italian Renaissance painter Paolo Veronese (1528-1588 AD).

In Chapter Two, we are informed that the key incarnation of the ascended master Lanto, who has long served as chohan of the second ray, was the Duke of Chou (c. 1100 BC), better known as the Yellow Emperor of ancient China.

And, last but not least, it is revealed in Chapter One that the key incarnations of the ascended master El Morya, who serves as chohan of the first ray, include Abraham (circa 1500 BC, as one of a soul group composed of seventeen souls, according to Archangel Gabriel Benu), Melchior (one of the three wise men attending the birth of Jesus), King Arthur (c. 550 AD), Thomas Beckett (1118-1170 AD), and Sir Thomas More (c. 1478-1535 AD).

After devoting the entire morning to this task of recording and refining these key incarnations of the seven chohans, I celebrated with another three-cheese omelet for brunch at Lily's Restaurant, and then took a long walk in the sunshine on what had turned out to be one of the most beautiful days of this whole memorable year.

As I was walking down Russell Street on my way back to Orem Street, I was surprised to see a beautiful table lamp sitting on the sidewalk, together with several other items and a handwritten sign which proclaimed: "Free stuff. Please take."

Because I had been planning to buy a much-needed lamp for my living room, I immediately recognized that spirit was again demonstrating its capacity to provide for my needs and quickly decided to accept this beautiful lamp as a gift from the universe.

After carrying it home, I plugged it in and discovered that it worked perfectly.

In accordance with the guidance that I had received from my higher self on the previous evening, I next transmitted the following email message to my list of treasured friends around the world.

Beloved Friends:

Even if you have seen it before, I heartily recommend that you celebrate this pivotal point in the history of humanity on Planet Earth by reviewing the cinematic masterpiece WHALE RIDER (2003), starring Keisha Castle-Hughes and Rawiri Paratene; written and directed by Niki Caro; based on the book by Witi Ihimaera; music by Lisa Gerrard.

When the heir to the leadership of a Maori tribe dies at birth, his twin sister is misperceived by her grandfather as being incapable of taking his place, until her natural ability to communicate with the higher consciousness of whales when she is only twelve years old proves otherwise.

What makes this film so incredibly powerful is the fact that the natural ability of this young girl to communicate with the higher consciousness of whales exemplifies our natural ability as human beings to communicate with our own higher selves.

It is a sign of the times when this cinematic masterpiece ends with the words: "I'm not a prophet, but I know that our people will go forward all together with all of our strength."

In Love's pure Light,
All-is-one Heartsong
www.planetaryascension.net

I spent the remainder of that afternoon proofreading the most recent material for my manuscript and coordinating the list of items with the text.

When I turned on my computer around three o'clock to check for email messages, I was amazed to find a magnificent poem titled *Truth*, which my brother had just posted on the open forum at The Rumor Mill News Reading Room. (See Item 44)

I immediately transmitted the following request to my brother in the Hawaiian Islands, who promptly responded with the two words: "Permission granted."

Dear Bob:
I just read your magnificent poem and would like to request your permission
to include it in my new book that will soon be published, the basic theme of which
is the love of truth.
Your brother who loves you

Around seven o'clock, I stopped working on my manuscript and spent about an hour in silent meditation before watching the concluding portion of *The Toast of New Orleans* for the umpteenth time.

At six o'clock on the morning of 8 October 2007, I woke up with the following dream: I am an experienced psychotherapist with a psychopathic patient who puts me to the ultimate test by systematically wreaking havoc with my office and soiling my coat. I quickly recognize that his destructive behavior is intentionally designed to provoke me, and I immediately make the empowering choice to respond with unconditional forgiving love rather than fearful anger. I then say to him: "I am you, and you are me, and we are one." As I wake up from this extraordinary dream, I realize that the psychopathic patient represents the lower self, that the psychotherapist represents the higher self, and that in reality they are simply two different aspects of one being.

When I got up and went into the bathroom to wash my face, I discovered that I was having a nose bleed, to which I responded without fear by simply elevating my head until the nose bleed subsided and stopped.

After doing my morning exercises, I began preparing breakfast and, when I realized that there were no more oranges in my refrigerator, I quickly decided to instead make a smoothie with frozen strawberries, frozen blueberries, some pineapple-coconut juice and a small helping of whey protein powder.

I next turned on my computer and, after quickly checking the world news, I proceeded to transmit the current update by Germain, prefaced by the following introduction:

Dear Friends:
Channeled by Mike Quinsey in England, the ascended master Saint Germain,
who is overseeing our planetary ascension process, has today blessed us with an

Item 44

TRUTH

by
Robert Howard Jones

Truth is what we search for
        In this journey through our life,
But for many of life's travelers,
        It's a road of grief and strife.

Without truth we lose direction,
        And the seas of life get rough;
We create our pains and problems
        By not seeking truth enough.

Truth will light your way in darkness
        When all else may seem to fail;
Truth will lead you out of bondage
        And in time will lift the veil.

For within each person's true self
        There is wisdom so profound,
That the mysteries of the ages
        Are revealed when truth is found.

Truth empowers us and frees us,
        Just like love, it brings the light;
Keep your focus on these virtues;
        They will guide you with their might.

Turn within for God to guide you,
        For within the answers lie,
And this truth is universal:
        God, when asked, will not deny.

Truth and love will give you freedom,
        As the masters all agree;
It's been said down through the ages,
        That the truth will set you free.

update that includes the following passages:
"Never lose sight of the fact that absolutely nothing can prevent the coming of the end times."
"It is an event that has been decreed by the Creator."
"The process of change is speeding up and is bringing in a series of events that are taking you to completion."
"The coming of the Christ is a collective energy that will carry you into the higher energies through Ascension."
"Have we not told you that you are gods in the making, and that that is your true destiny?"
"Stay calm regardless of what is going on about you."
"It will serve you well in the coming period, when the dark have their last fling to avoid their inevitable defeat."
"I am Saint Germain...and I shall lead you into the New Age."
"The way has opened up, and Ascension is your ladder to success."
In Love's pure Light,
All-is-one Heartsong
www.planetaryascension.net

I then took a leisurely walk in the sunshine, during the course of which I celebrated Columbus Day by expressing to Germain my heartfelt gratitude for his presence in my life.

After enjoying an avocado and salsa lunch, I finally got around to preparing the captions for items 25 and 26.

The rest of the day was spent organizing the material between item 24 and item 34.

I woke up at six o'clock on the morning of 9 October 2007 with the clear realization that this would be the last recorded day of Volume One.

After a quick breakfast, a short walk, and a careful survey of world news on the Internet, I worked with Zepp from ten to twelve on the task of finalizing my manuscript all the way from page 46 to page 160.

By the time we broke for lunch, I felt completely exhausted; but I quickly revived after an apple, banana, and cashew nut lunch, followed by a short nap.

However, when I observed that my sinuses were signaling the potential beginning of a cleansing cycle, I realized immediately that it was time to break out of my focused work routine by introducing some refreshing recreation.

What immediately came to mind was the recently released metaphysical film *Next*, which had just been brought to my attention by Sangeeta Handa, one of my email correspondents who lives in Bombay, India. So I walked over to Village Video, where my beautiful friend Tracy Zylstra informed me that I was due to receive *Next* as a free gift.

Refreshed and invigorated by this welcome synchronicity, which was further enhanced by Tracy's lovely smile, I next decided to stop in at Berryvale for the purpose of purchasing some organic rolled oats and currants with which to enliven my breakfasts as the weather turned cold.

Then, when I got back to my tiny apartment, I made the radical decision to complete this revolutionary departure from standard procedure by watching *Next* next instead of waiting until that evening.

What I quickly discovered is that *Next* is a film about a man who was born with the psychic gift of precognition which enabled him to foresee the immediate future two minutes in advance and to explore the various options and their potential outcomes within that framework.

Although I was acutely aware of the contrast between his supernormal ability to foresee the immediate future and my supernormal experience of absolute knowing about the ancient past, it was unmistakably clear to me that my higher self had intentionally orchestrated for me to see this particular film at this particular time.

So it was that, after viewing this film once, I decided at seven o'clock that evening to watch it again for the specific purpose of asking my higher self to show me exactly why it wanted me to have this particular experience at this particular time.

As I began viewing it for the second time, the realization suddenly dawned on me that my higher self was using this film as a convenient way of reminding my consecrated mind that government intelligence agencies have a history of trying to recruit people with supernormal psychic abilities for their own nefarious purposes.

Knowing that life is always a choice between fear and love, I quickly recognized that this reminder was actually a test, to which I responded by making a very conscious choice to love rather than to fear.

And since it is highly probably that these words of mine will come to the attention of some government intelligence agency sooner or later, let me take this opportunity to state very clearly that, when Archangel Gabriel and the ascended masters Saint Germain and Yeshua Esu Sananda are one's closest friends, one knows that there is absolutely nothing to fear.

It only remains to add that, for the most part, *Next* is a typical product of psychopathic third-dimensional consciousness engaged in immature adolescent fantasy that revolves around unenlightened human beings endlessly killing one another.

For this reason, I definitely do not recommend that you see this film.

Instead, before we conclude Volume One of *Channeling the Apocalypse*, I wish to cordially invite you to read and contemplate two very simple poems, one of which is dedicated to all darkworkers who fear the truth (Item 45) and the other of which is dedicated to all lightworkers who love the truth (Item 46).

CONCLUSION

As I prepare to conclude Volume One of *Channeling the Apocalypse*, with the understanding that I will then begin Volume Two for the purpose of continuing to record my personal experiences at this pivotal point in human history, let me briefly summarize my orientation, which also constitutes the source of my motivation for devoting my time and energy so wholeheartedly to this project.

I am, quite simply, a lover of truth who has chosen to pursue the path of revealing the truth, the whole truth, and nothing but the truth, so help me God.

To be more specific, I have made the empowering choice to place my consecrated mind in the service of my higher self so as to allow the enlightened sixth-dimensional aspect of my multidimensional self to guide my limited third-dimensional mind, which functions as its humble servant.

The resulting format of this book, as a truthful record of my personal experiences from 10 October 2006 to 9 October 2007, is intentionally designed to effectively rule out any possibility of a lack of integrity on the part of its author.

Thus, the only question that remains to be answered is that of the author's sanity.

Because the contents of this book happen to revolve around the channeled testimony of Archangel Gabriel, this particular question will inevitably be a source of considerable controversy, and I therefore choose to leave the answer for each of my readers to decide for themselves.

For those agnostic readers who prefer to doubt that Archangel Gabriel could possibly be the source of the revelations and confirmations contained in this book, I propose that we simply regard them as working hypotheses.

In short, it is for you, the reader, to decide for yourself what it all means.

EPILOGUE

I would now like to conclude this record of my personal experiences, during one unforgettable year at this pivotal point in human history, by sharing with you my own perspective regarding the ultimate significance of this grand drama in which we have chosen to participate, not only as actors, but as playwrights.

What I envision for our future is that all of us will eventually come together for a heavenly cast party where we will all have a good laugh together regarding the various roles that we played in this grand human drama, including heroes and villains alike.

For, the reality is that, like sunbeams radiating outward into the darkness from one central sun, we are all equal when viewed from the perspective of our Creator-Source, regardless of whether, at any given moment in the divine process, we happen to be darkworkers who are looking outward into the darkness of separation consciousness or lightworkers who are looking inward into the light of unity consciousness.

Thus, the key thing to understand is that, when we are in judgment of one another or of ourselves, we are in an unenlightened state of being, whereas practicing unconditional forgiving love toward one another and toward ourselves means that we are in an enlightened state of being.

Consequently, while I honor the right of each one of us to make a free-will choice as to which orientation we are going to base our lives on, I myself have chosen to fly into the sun so as to become one with the sun through the simple act of choosing to practice unconditional forgiving love toward others as well as toward myself, knowing that, in reality, all is one.

I would therefore like to emphasize the fact that, although this book has been written for all of us, it has been written most especially for those of us who have lost their way in the darkness and are still in a state of confusion regarding the question of who they really are and what this divine

Item 45

POEM FOR DARKWORKERS

Most people believe
only light can reveal,

And it follows from this
that the dark must conceal;

Yet the stars are concealed
by the light of the sun,

While the darkness of night
doth reveal every one.

Item 46

POEM FOR LIGHTWORKERS

When darkness claims
  a victory in its fight

To conquer all
  that's free and true and right,

Then be the sun,
  whose love transmutes the night,

For we are in
  this world to give it light.

drama called life is really all about.

Without exception, I recognize all of you as my brothers and sisters; and I invite each and every one of you to join with me in blessing ourselves by celebrating our true identities as spiritual co-creators with our beloved Father-Mother Creator-Source.

In the limitless love of the God I AM that we are,

Namaste.

Appendix A

Operation Apocalypse: End Timers & End-Game Strategy
By Captain Eric H. May

31 July 2006

Wolves in Sheep's Clothing

In the last week of July, just when the Israeli offensive was stalling against a tough Hezbollah resistance in Lebanon, Operation Apocalypse went into high gear in the United States. All at once the corporate media mouthpieces began to urge the American People to jump right into the quicksand war of Lebanon - and Syria and Iran, of course.

Monday, July 24, CNN began to run a story from Paula Zahn about End Times Christians who were predicting billions of dead in a war that had begun with Israel's offensive in the Holy Land -- and how this was what they were praying for. Within a day the same CNN crew crowed that the End Times "Rapture meter" was at its highest level since 9/11 -- and pretended to have nothing to do with it.

Tuesday morning the Houston Chronicle carried an essay by Zev Chafets, All quiet at Armageddon, but will it stay that way?, that praised the willingness of End Times Christians to see things in a one-sided, pro-Israel way, no questions asked -- to Kingdom Come, if need be. A bit later at breakfast, my dad handed me a brochure -- professional PR stuff -- passed out by thousands, paid for by pro-war money -- promising nuclear war before fall. The author, Yisrayl (Israel) Hawkins promised four billion dead and a sorting out of the elect from the remaining two billion.

The idea of Armageddon is gaining traction in every part of our global war media, which now treats World War Three as a foregone conclusion. Hannity and Colmes had a guest, Cham Dallas, who prophesied (five times in five minutes) that Al Qaeda and Hezbollah were going to nuke America to bring on the great, final contest of civilizations.

The nation prepares for the genocide and suicide of world war, and the media cheer-leads to doom like a Jonestown Cult. Operation Apocalypse has begun all right -- and there's no doubt in my military mind about it.

False Miracles

Last week's Lone Star Iconoclast presented an editorial showing that in the last decade -- particularly since 9/11 -- there has been a multifold increase in world seismic activity. It suggested that, as one possibility, the government's ultra-secret HAARP program, based in Alaska, may have been disturbing the earth's crust and climate.

My own induction into this irregular research of HAARP came last summer. One of the thousands who put in with Camp Casey in August, I was returning to my hometown of Houston from Crawford the Sunday night after Katrina plowed into New Orleans -- and the locals swore that there had been operatives dynamiting the levees to drown the poor folks. Watching the huge black clouds still menacing in the east as we drove home, I told my wife that Katrina had removed Cindy Sheehan from the news for Bush. For the first time a suspicion formed and I added, "Was it meant to?"

Back home, I began to examine the most irregular meteorological data behind Katrina, and in a few days had seen enough research to conclude that it was a HAARP-induced event. Rita came next, and like Katrina followed a very distinct hot water trail across the Gulf of Mexico, as if someone had been pouring the energy it fed on into the Gulf waters ahead of it to lure it onward. It, too, served the political convenience of the Bush administration, since Cindy Sheehan was then blasting away against the war in a Washington, D.C. rally -- on the very Saturday when Rita slammed into the Texas/Louisiana coast.

Like Katrina before her and Wilma after her, Rita was a category 5, and those three of them, in one season, meant that there were more super-hurricanes in 2005 than in all the previous 100 seasons combined. The three weird sister storms struck the Gulf Coast hard, resulting in record profits for the oil allies of the Bush administration. Catastrophes of convenience.

Four Terror Scenarios

Operation Apocalypse looks to this officer like an End Times extravaganza to launch us into the truly "global" part of our global war, rigged to explode now that Israel, our "special friend," has gone into action to clear out their ungodly Arab enemies.

In order to keep the spirit of war booming along, there must be more national terrors in the near future, more proofs of End Time Armageddon for the faithful followers. My cyber-associates and I have analyzed four types of created terror. Each has its direction, and its element:

Western Earth: Many believe that the Jakarta tsunami of Christmas 2004 was induced by HAARP tectonic warfare. I didn't believe it when it occurred, but do now. Further, the Pakistan quake of 2005 occurred in the middle of the three weird sister hurricanes. What are the odds?

For the last half year we've been following FEMA and Homeland Security exercises along the West Coast, all of them simulating once-a-century earthquakes and tsunamis. One media outlet after another has been selling us on catastrophe programming. Disaster-industry companies are increasing their personnel in anticipation of a mega-quake that someone in the government is telling them will come soon. Does it seem like they know something we don't?

Northern Wind: The Windy City of Chicago has long been in the cross hairs for a "terror" attack, as was supposedly planned as part of 9/11. When King George and Mayor Daley met in late June it made many of us think that the set-up is still on.

It is interesting that two days after the Bush/Daley party, Central Illinois media and officials issued a bird flu alert, urging the public to prepare for an outbreak in September or October. State officials I contacted couldn't explain why there was this sudden and sure warning of a pending bio-terror. They couldn't say why there would be an outbreak in Central Illinois, of all the areas in North America. They couldn't say who it was who sent out the alert -- though, alarmingly, they said that they'd been rehearsing the bio-terror scenario for over a year.

Eastern Water: The Internet research community chats about the man-made hurricanes as HAARPicanes. Before the three weird sisters of 2005, there was the "Florida Four" of 2004, all of which defied all odds to hit Brother Jeb's state -- including Ivan the Terrible, which hit the state, did a circle in the Atlantic, then hit it again. The weather warriors who run the HAARP program can put the HAARPicanes where they want them, and the Florida Four show that they tested them in 2004 before getting down to business with the three weird sisters in 2005.

This is bad news for New York City, where federal and local officials have been preparing for a once-a-century New York hurricane in 2006. Some officials are so sure of the pending event that we who follow weather war believe they know it's coming. If it happened, the storm surge could wash away as many impediments to urban development (i.e., poor people) as Katrina's did. People who knew it was coming would clean up on the redevelopment, of course.

Southern Fire: Worldwide petrochemical powers have profited from King George's reign, beyond all reckoning, and control the Houston area. With failed-war political pressures building toward a November election eruption against Republicans, the powers that be could turn things around immediately with a staged terror attack in a Texas petroleum town, afterwards paying off well the parties that sponsored the deed, while blaming it all on Al Qaeda or Hezbollah -- to lead the country to world war.

In recent weeks the Iconoclast has published my analysis of a two-year string of petrochemical explosions in Southeast Texas, from Beaumont through Texas City and into Houston. I urge it on anyone concerned that there may be more.

8/8 and 8/28

In previous columns, I have explained the code analysis of terror event dates, and how disasters seem to frequently occur on dates with embedded numeric codes. With that in mind, the next dates to be watched are 8/8 and 8/28, for all areas, all scenarios.

It's a tough road to salvation in these twilight zone days of the American Republic, in the face of Operation Apocalypse, the diabolical plot to pull together all the dark forces of our greed, fear and hatred to start a world war and call it God's Will.

Captain Eric H. May, MI/PAO, USA
CO, Ghost Troop, 3/7 Cybercav+
Mission of Conscience / Patriots in Action

Appendix B

A Message from God
Channeled by Suzanne Ward

1 August 2007

MATTHEW: Along with loving greetings comes my farewell for a while. My mother, Bob and their dog family are relocating, and traveling, moving preparations, resettling and collaborating on a book as part of an expanded mission will occupy all of my mother's time for an indefinite period. I ask that you please not write to her as her inbox is overflowing; during the past many months she has had little opportunity to answer emails, and those as far back as March will receive her attention first.

God and I discussed that this is a fine time for Him to speak to you via this means, and to give space for this as well as address the two subjects most prevalent in your emails, I shall comment only on those, and briefly. The first is the concerns about President Bush's executive order that permits the arrest of dissenters with his war policies and confiscation of their property. When you put that order into the context of what you know through our messages; the Internet's widening exposure of evidence of the administration's deception and wrongdoing; and the facts that major media are being forced to report because of growing public awareness and outcry, you can see that FEAR is the real intent of the desperate ones who conceived of the order. They know that there is no possibility whereby its wide-scale coverage can be achieved; however, they will try to entrap some individuals to "show-case" in an attempt to create fear throughout the populace. We urge you, DO NOT GO INTO FEAR! Remember what we have told you, that a lot of information, including on the Internet, is false and its intention is to create fear. Trust your intuition as to what is true and what is not, and do NOT fear ANY forthcoming grave-sounding projections or developments—we also have told you that you are innately well prepared to navigate bumps along the way. Everything in your world is moving in accordance with the energy invested in it, and whatever is based in darkness is facing a short and increasingly bleak existence.

Second, and related to my previous sentence, is that the events known as "Fire the Grid" and "7-7-7" so successfully accomplished their purpose that Earth is glowing brilliantly in the profusion of light that you generated jointly with our benevolent space family. The light streaming to Earth from myriad points in the universe and mingling with your own has reached unprecedented measure, and while it may not soften the most hardened hearts and minds, the intensity is transmuting the remaining wisps of darkness and transforming its former strongholds into a global fortress of light.

God needs no words of introduction from me, and so now I leave you with the assurance that I and countless other souls in spirit and in body are lovingly and joyfully accompanying you every step of the way into Earth's Golden Age.

GOD: My dear Matthew, I too would like to think that I'm known well enough without any introduction, but certainly my thanks is in order for graciously letting me preempt your space, and to you, dear little Suzy, for your time in these busy days.

So then, good morning, all my beloved children! Call me whatever name you wish—I answer to all. Many of you have been wondering where I am while so much furor and ferocity is going on in your world. I am here to tell you that I'm right where I've been since Day One of this universe—everywhere!—and I have quite a bit to say about this.

To start, however paradoxical it may seem, the only constant anywhere is change. Your world is teeming with greater changes than ever before, and I assure you, you wouldn't want it any other way! Many who sensed a need to make changes are doing so confidently, but for some of you, moving out of the familiar space seems scary. "Whatever will happen if I change my job or location or even my mate? Oh NO, not my beliefs too?!" You'll get on with what you chose to experience, that's what will happen. Is that so bad, that you'll get yourself out of a rut and get on with Life's Adventure that you signed up for?

Of course not everyone needs to change jobs or mates or relocate, but many DO need to change beliefs, and here are the first two if you believe that (1) Your individuality means you're separated from everyone else, and (2) I am the cosmic superpower that makes everything happen. You're definitely a unique individual, but also you're an inseparable part of me and all others everywhere, and it's ALL of us in this universe who make things happen.

Hmmmmm. So you're a bigger deal than you thought and maybe I'm not such a big deal after all. Not exactly, my dear ones. WE ARE, together, ONE amazing powerhouse with infinite and eternal potential—so yes, you better believe I AM powerful! And it's not because I control you—I don't. It's because you and all other life in this universe are my BEing in all your experiencing forms—collectively WE ARE this universe!

I have more to say about beliefs, but let's talk about why I don't control you, which is much like your idea that I let bad things happen to good people. This is how it goes: Creator, ruler of the cosmos—that's all the universes—gave you free will to express whatever you want to and gave us universe rulers a law we have to obey: Stay out of your soul parts' choices! Eons later Creator made the one exception to that law: "No nuclear wars anywhere," so now we rulers have the authority to stop all efforts to do that.

Otherwise, it's your choices all the way, and actually, that's an excellent basis for your multiple lifetimes around our universe. If you stray from the path you chose in your soul contracts—those pacts you make before you are born so you can grow beyond that stage of evolution—I can't mess with that, and you wouldn't want me to. If your birthright to make your own decisions suddenly went pooooof and I started mapping out every one of your lives, I believe I would hear howls of protest.

I do have a hand in this, though. Creator thoughtfully put a loophole in that free will law that lets me put conscience as an ingredient of your souls, and that's what can keep you on your straightaway path if you want it to. Like everything else, it's your choice to pay attention to it or ignore it. Conscience should come with a warning: Ignore me and I'll become extinct. Well, just as you don't come with copies of your soul contracts, you don't come with a warrantee on your conscience either. You have instinct, intuition, inspiration and a sense of honor, too—those are other ingredients I put in souls that also help you know what's right and what's wrong for you.

But—sometimes "but" is necessary, and this is a big one—what you may think is right may be wrong and vice versa. You don't consciously know what's in your contract, and you sure don't know what's in anyone else's. Your contract is your part of the pre-birth agreement made by the souls who want to be in on the "give-and-take" lifetime of shared experiences. The agreements provide growth opportunities for every soul, so you can see that they're all-around win-win situations.

So think about this: You (or they) chose to be on one end or the other of "bad" things and you (or they) did it for one of two reasons, both of which provide experiencing that balances other lifetimes, and balance is essential for soul growth. One, you (or they) needed to feel what it's like to endure hardships and others volunteered to provide the circumstances that let you (or them) do that. Or: "Been there, done that" and this time around you (or they) are the volunteer(s). You can call this karma if you like—just don't interpret this opportunity to achieve balance as a reward or a punishment for yourself or anyone else.

Something else you need to know about those agreements is that unconditional love is the basis on which ALL the souls fill their various roles. Out of love, some agree to be the "heavies" for those who choose the "rough way to go"—I explained the reason for this see-saw experiencing. The thing is, you've been stuck for only I know how long on this bumpy see-saw of third density, where deceit, tyranny, violence and corruption are part and parcel of everyday life. You're sick and tired of it, so this time around you chose—again!—to get out of it, and believe me, you wouldn't want me sticking my finger in and doing anything that might keep you in it! You have no idea of the domino effect if I meddled in just a few lives, no matter how good my intention! I'm not allowed to do that anyway.

Now, some of my children aren't on Earth to wind up their karma—or if you prefer, call this universal law Divine Grace—they're there to HELP all the rest of you do it. And you'd better be grateful that they are willing to temporarily leave their families and homelands in higher planes to help you fulfill your pre-birth choice to deal with third density and be done with it.

Since doing that may require you to make some changes, maybe you'll welcome more suggestions for going about that. Pay attention to what Matthew said about DON'T GO INTO FEAR! I'll add this: If you think you have any enemies, you'd better know that fear's by far the worst. From my point of view, it's your ONLY one, and I strongly suggest you give my opinion of this careful thought.

Then there's what you could consider the other end of the spectrum from fear: pettiness, that clutter-clatter of attitudes, interests and activity that keep you preoccupied with trivialities that aren't worth even one bean in the hill, yet have the power to prevent knowledgeable, sensible evaluations and decisions. Of course I know what your petty stuff is—we are ONE, remember?—and I'm suggesting that you sort through that vast heap of mindless TV programs and gossip sessions; pointless tiffs and jealousies; nit-picking, nagging and griping; letting mere curiosity rather than core interests occupy your thoughts; and worries about "what if" and rumors of dire possibilities.

Now if those include your enjoyments, I'm not criticizing you—I'm simply giving you motherly-fatherly advice: Compare how much time and energy you spend in those pursuits with how much you devote to LIGHTening your mind, body and spirit. Say, to conversations or correspondence with like-minded folks, or to the silence and solitude that ease the pressure of daily responsibilities. Playing with your families and animals, smiling and laughing, listening to melodious music or reading something that expands your mind, or connecting with the beauty of Nature. Seeing and feeling thankful for the blessings in your life and going within your deepest self and listening to the song of your soul.

"But I'm already too busy!" won't cut it, my dear children. What I've just mentioned is restorative, rejuvenating, energizing and essential for balance in your days and within you. When you oust pettiness in its many forms, and I may have forgotten some, there IS time for uplifting experiences.

Another thing is, "Judge not…"—some things in the Bible are right. You do know that I don't ever judge you, don't you? "Judgment day"—I don't care much for that term—is when you review your past lifetime in the context of ALL your lifetimes, see where you need to improve things, and based on that you choose what to put in your soul contract for the next time around. Anyway, not judging is a key to helping self and each other evolve and so is gratitude. Feeling thankful for the help is as important as not judging the helpers. That doesn't ever mean approving of greed or viciousness or violence—you certainly don't have to do that! Gratitude is acknowledging and appreciating that some of you agreed to play the "heavies" because others need that to wrap up their last remnants of third density. It would be good, too, if you also feel thankful that you wanted and were selected to participate in this magnificent time of Earth's entry into the Golden Age.

"Golden" because only light will prevail on Earth, and how she will rejoice! She is a beloved part of me just as you are yourself, and what a price she paid to give her humankind many, many, MANY chances to get it right and "see the light"—it nearly cost her planetary life. I'll tell you more about that, but the point here is, she's giving all of you this one last chance to wake up and wise up. Part of that is, you have to stop confusing religion with spirituality, and that brings us back to beliefs.

I'm not saying that all of you are clinging to beliefs that are based on false teachings, but if you believe that your religion is better than all the others, listen up. My messengers whom you attach to the various religions didn't set those up. In a nutshell, the very concept of religion came from the thoughts of dark ones off-planet, and today's religious teachings are based on what a few of my self-serving parts on the planet said a long time ago: If you don't obey God—or some other name they gave me—you're doomed, and they said that was "My Word." Those few folks wanted to control everyone else, so they wrote the rules of "obedience" that spell "doom" to falterers. And I have to tell you, Christianity is THE major digresser from the truth that my messenger came to give.

Yes, the one you call Jesus, and oh my! how they changed his life from the actual to the fictional—it's hard to know where to begin to set the story straight.

The FACT is that Jesus was never put on a cross, so there was no crucifixion or resurrection. That rather blows the whole foundation of Christian dogma, doesn't it? For how, then, could it be that "he gave his life to save sinners"? Sinners means the whole lot of you, according to those who came up with the idea that everyone is "born into sin." Oh dear me! The only "sin," if you will, is interfering with the growth of a soul, your own or anyone else's, and the result is DEvolution with as many more chances as needed NOT to do that.

Then there's Mary Magdalene— how wretchedly the Bible portrays her! She was Jesus' wife and ultimate soulmate, and after the Sanhedrin flogged her husband and warned him to get out of their territory—they didn't want to make him a martyr as that would give impetus to his teachings—they went to the East where Jesus had spent the "lost" years learning from the masters how to perform "miracles" and where he knew his family was safe. He and Mary had a happy family there, and years later they all traveled to the West and settled in what now is France. Eventually Jesus returned to the East and along the way continued teaching My REAL Word—the Bible includes some of that, but everything in the early records didn't support the self-serving ones' cause got left out—and he lived to a ripe old age. Although in their later years he and his adored Mary were apart in body, they were so highly attuned spiritually that they were together then, as now and evermore, in spirit and celestial visitations.

Later leaders of the Roman Catholic faith made up absurdities like "the only son of God," "virgin birth" and "immaculate conception" and made layers of saints. They did that to put still more distance between "my ONLY son" and all my other children—and ME, who is ALL of you!—as well as making themselves the gate-keepers to heaven. Or hell. Actually, neither exists as portrayed, but that's another story.

Those leaders were greedy, too. In the centuries during and after Jesus' life, the same few people ran church and state, and along with unfair taxation of their poor countrymen, the church of Rome came up with a two-edged sword to cement their control: You can atone for your sins—they made those up too—if you confess and pay money, and a portion of everything you have must be given as well. That spread to other churches and you know it as tithing. Something else that church did now and again was demand of their priests sexual abstinence, as if denying that strong nature in humankind made them more "saintly," and you know what that led to. Then there were all those wars and inquisitions and brutal killings in my name!

Later movers and shakers of the Roman Catholic religion decreed that birth control is a sin and more recently, so is abortion. With the wanton killings they've caused or sanctioned throughout the ages, it's hardly sanctity of life that interests them. No, it's to keep the population growing that financially supports them and bows to their authority. From Day One of the papacy, the appointed one and his close circle have lived in opulence that has been paid for by the masses they brainwashed into believing that the church's rules came from ME.

If it sounds like I'm picking on that religion, it's because its headquarters, the Vatican, has been the biggest hotbed of darkness from its beginning. No other religion has it all right or all wrong either—strands of truth are in the "holy books," but the Bible is by far the most seriously distorted to keep unquestioning followers mesmerized. And while the original basis of individuals' faith may have been pure long ago, fanatical elements have defiled that purity to the extent that some of you think they represent the religion itself.

Realizing that EVERY soul is a precious and EQUAL part of me and I love each and every one unconditionally, let's look at the collective soul-selves "religiously." Fundamentalist Protestants say that unless you accept Jesus as your "lord and savior," you'll burn in hell for eternity—I notice that they tend to leave me out of it. Some congregations have split over accepting or scorning my beloved children who are homosexual by birth choice, and they choose it for good reason: It's an advanced stage of balanced masculine and feminine energies, and all my children experience those lifetimes as they progress toward androgyny. Islam is seen as rewarding its followers for "killing the infidels," and my women children are deemed inferior to my men children. Zionism, a political militant movement, hides behind the skirts of Judaism and cries "anti-Semitism"; and the pacifist Far Eastern religions, which have adhered most closely to my messengers' teachings, are deemed by the others as out of touch with reality. As if those painful departures from SPIRITUALITY aren't enough, this whole situation has become so befouled that even Satanism with its diabolical tortures and human sacrifice is an established religion.

It's been like the plaintiff wail of a broken record but with far harsher, far sadder effects as generation after generation, my Earth soul-selves have been mind-controlled by religious "authorities." Once the people were stuck in those clutches, governments and all other institutions that impact life on Earth easily became authority figures too. Souls come in with amazing intuition and the capacity to use common sense and reason wisely, but the collective influence of "authorities" dulled those abilities. My children bought into the rhetoric and obeyed the instructions, even when it meant being sent off to war after war, where billions have killed and been killed.

How did that whole sad state of affairs come about? It was the work of the off-planet dark force that is without conscience, without light except the spark of viability. That force "captured" my weak-willed children of Earth who got caught up in the lure of power and money and, performing as the force's puppets, they kept all the rest of my children in the bondage of fear, poverty and ignorance. The souls' need for balanced experiencing kept it going until now—that ages-old merry-go-round is stopping. There's more to say about that, but I want to give you a good example of ignorance.

"All life began in the sea and apes are humans' ancestors." OH?! I'm not saying that primitive sea life and apes and their relatives aren't parts of me, but can't you see how DEMEANING the very idea is that that is how I started you, my HUMAN souls?! You credit me—well, some of you do—with making you "in my own image," and I assure you, my drawing board didn't start with you as amoebas, some of which I "inspired" to move to dry land and grow into apes, and then I picked which ones of those I wanted to become humans. Your ancestors are such highly spiritual and intelligent beings that you can't even imagine it! Yes, your "theory of evolution" was in there somewhere, but not as you understand it. Nothing's "black or white" the way you think.

Now about the price Earth paid for enduring the darkness throughout the millennia of the insidious workings of religions and other sources of near equal dark persuasion. She kept giving her own light to sustain the lives of her humankind as they slaughtered each other and destroyed and polluted her Nature until all the bloodshed and devastation nearly claimed her own body, your planet home. Her soul, which stayed in its high plane of origin as her body spiraled downward into low third density, was in deep sorrow and despair. Her planetary self survived because she cried out for help and my children in civilizations far advanced from you spiritually, intellectually and technologically—yes, some are your ancestors!—rushed to infuse Earth's body with their light so it could survive. She wanted to give you this one last chance to open your minds, "light up" your consciousness and shake free from the shackles of that dark force.

And this brings us to why that LONG merry-go-round ride that you're sick and tired of is stopping. So is my beloved Earth fed up with it! She's on the fast track out of third density where, until recently, the darkness has been quite successful, but its time is up—the dark force "has left the building," so to say. Only the lingering effects of its influence on its Earth puppets remain and those are fading fast. The truths "coming to light" are exposing once-hidden agenda, and by the impartial law of physics regarding form and frequencies, the puppet's refusal to accept the light will cause their demise along Earth's ascension path. Your dear planet is homeward bound to her soul's blissful plane, and all who go with her will live in harmonious cooperation with your benevolent "space" family. The trip ticket is free, but with strings: You need to know and live the TRUTH of who WE ARE. This isn't complex—it's as simple as paying attention to what your soul is telling you! "Going within" automatically connects you consciously with soul-self—that's you and me—and all the rest follows naturally.

I never take sides—how could I when I'm ALL of you!—but I do have my druthers, and I'd love to have all my children choose to live together peacefully. So I hope you will believe what I've said and act on it, but I can't make you—it's always been your choice to believe what you want, do what you want. All I can do is add my voice to the messengers who have told you the very same things through their Earth receivers. What will happen if you don't believe us? What will happen to the souls who will never know about our messages? They will go to a placement attuned to the energy they put forth in deeds and motives throughout the lifetime.

Some will journey with Earth because they are living in "godly" ways simply by heeding their souls' messages. They live from their hearts, where unconditional love, kindness, honor, truth, compassion and desire to help others lie.

Some will go through it again—the tyranny, violence, corruption, lies, the hold of religions—and they'll come in with the brain power to question and reason, yet another chance to break free of dark control. But not on Earth. There are other third density places in our universe where rampant disrespect for life will go on until all my soul parts know the truth of their god- and goddess-selves.

And some will DEvolve and start over from scratch. They're the ones who persist in choosing darkness over LOVE, the same Creator Source energy as light. Constantly light will be beamed to those souls, who will start with only basic instinct, and when they accept the light, they'll recall a smidgeon of intelligence. As they accept more light, they will remember a modicum of reasoning ability, and so on and so on. This isn't punishment, it's a chance for those parts of me to start over without even a hint of darkness.

It's quite a lot to think about, isn't it? There is time, my beloveds, but frankly, not much, to decide what you want. Whatever that is, I will honor it, and if it's help, ask and it shall be given!

Appendix C

PROPHETIC MESSAGE #1 FROM KRYON
Channeled by Nancy Tate
27 August 2007

Dear Friends:

I invite you to read and reread and contemplate this mysterious message from Kryon, channeled by Nancy Tate on 27 August 2007.

It appears to be predicting the occurrence this autumn of a non-catastrophic catastrophe which will have the effect of momentarily traumatizing and then awakening humanity.

Let us therefore prepare ourselves for an apocalyptic revelation in the immediate future and know that all is well regardless of appearances to the contrary.

In Love's pure Light,

All-is-one Heartsong
www.planetaryascension.net

Kryon

My dear ones of the golden light, I am here this morning to take you on a journey, one that will captivate you and hold you in its charm for hours to come. In this journey, there may be some surprises and a few known parts of the story. Shall we begin? I am Kryon, and I have come back to this one's field today to give you this gift.

Long ago in the days of the Nibiruan's descent to earth there was a lone being on the planet who knew of their coming. He knew for in his state of remembrance he was here in the capacity to welcome them to a time when they would have great influence not only on their lives, but on the planet as well. This person was a lightbeing of the highest magnitude. and with this greeting he prepared for the visitors from the cosmos, there was an advent of a new way of life on earth that would begin with one of the most remarkable of events that had ever taken place on this new planet.

As the ship descended to the surface, this being, whom I will identify now as Lucifer, for this being was a furtherance of the soul who was to enter the embodiment of Lucifer, stood among the reeds, and watched as the ship bearing those who would deliver unto earth the pioneers of the next segment of life forms unto the earth, approached the landing area and set down.

As the occupants of the ship emerged from the vessel, they looked around and hesitated only moments before stepping onto the hard ground. This was not the first time that people from Nibiru had descended to this planet. There had come before a lone man who had set the stage for the onset of the new age of creation. These ones who came now came with a direct reason that connected their home planet with this one. They came for the gold, and for the ability to repair the atmosphere on Nibiru.

What they did not know at that time was that their destiny on earth was multi-faceted. They wereto follow urgings and inspirations that came from their inner knowing of what was to take place on the earth and within it. They, surely as there is now a re-emergence of their heritage, came to set forth on a journey that would bring them to this present day, and beyond. The beyond part of this journey is the one that I take you on from this point in this message.

You all know the story of Adam and Eve, the Biblical history of what took place and the progression unto this day. I will not review this for you, for there have been many interpretations of that history. Each of you carries within your field the actual accounting of how those times transpired. That is a story for another time, when you are able to access it for yourselves and to share your own individual parts of the story with each other. A day of days that will be!

Now, I am here to take you beyond this day and into the New Golden Era of peace and love. I take you now into the immediate future, for in these coming days there will be a great revival of the idea of truth in the eyes of the world. There is coming a demand worldwide for the truth of your history to come forth and be revealed. This will come with the onset of the fall on earth, and I speak of the autumn months when I say fall.

In these coming months, there will be an event that will so traumatize the people of earth as to render them speechless and unable to bring to their awareness the brevity of what they have witnessed. This will last for only hours and then the actual truth of what they have witnessed will call out to them to demand an answer that speaks of the times past and the times that lay in the shadows. The people will rise out of their stupor and will take to the streets and the capital places of the world to demand an answer to not only what has taken place, but what has come about in the years and other catastrophic events that led to this final one that took humanity over the edge.

My dear ones of earth, you are about to embark on a journey so profound as to reckon the premises of truth to the door of every person on this earth. The reverberations will be felt worldwide and will bring many to their knees and then to their feet to rise in truth of what they have remembered from the cavities of their long forgotten memories of their lives on earth. They will 'know' on a depth of knowing that what they are witnessing and living now rings as a memory of times long ago.

This time, though, it will be an event that carries with it an empty danger, for in the energy of the event will be revealed that intervention has been bestowed upon the life of earth, and the catastrophe does not carry with it the consequences that it did those years ago. The result of this event will carry only the trigger to the remembrance of the energy of betrayal and the ability to walk out from the cloud of deceit and into the freedom of choice according to the intent of The Creator.

As this wave of truth sweeps across the surface of the planet, there will come an emerging from the center of the earth. That emergence will take on the form of the communication of the truth throughout the world, and the action needed to deliver the truth in manifestation to all parts of the globe. Those responsible for this mighty event will be delivered to their final place of destiny. They will be given the opportunity to divest their destiny in a way that represents the truth of the Source in a way that bespeaks the Grace that is the final outcome of all life.

More importantly, the people of earth will then begin their journey into the new age of life in the light of truth. There will be a time when there is a great upheaval on earth. It will come in the form of single events that will serve to uphold the ideals and intentions of building a new life on earth that will serve all who came to earth on that ship eons ago and held in their minds and hearts the secret longings for a new life on earth.

These ones who pioneered this human life on earth came with a secret desire, instilled in them by the Source, to come and divest their energies in the investment of bringing paradise to earth forevermore. They knew not the path it would take and the living of the destiny that was ordained by The Source, Creator of all.

As life is begun anew in the energy of rebuilding the promise of life on earth, it will be the enactment of life on earth as was seen in the souls of those early pioneers. You see, they were enacting what they knew to be their roles on earth in the physical. They too lived their consciousness and through the energies of earth, which represented only a fraction of the awareness of The Creator, they laid the foundation and erected the buildings of the duality experience on earth.

Those early pioneers are here on earth once again. They are here embodied, accompanied by their evolved souls in order to play out the last and final vestiges of the old ways of being and doing. The final playout of the beginnings are underway, and as they emerge and take shape on earth, the ones who lived it before will live it once again, with a difference. They will take what was and change it. They will live the different result of that which was, and they will change the course and story of the history of man in the ending that represented the downfall of humanity after that first catastrophic ending those thousands of years ago.

This is a soul dance that will take place all over the globe. Even the place of origin can be seen by all to be in its final stages of the playout that will bring it all full circle. This time there will be a different outcome and as the smoke clears there will be a wellspring of love and compassion so great that it will sweep across the globe and enter into every heart on the planet. As the clouds are lifted from the hearts of man, there will be a unification of input for the rebuilding of the earth in the destiny that was envisioned so often in those early days.

I tell you all this now my dear brave ones, for you are the early pioneers. You all were here when the clouds and waters spilled across the lands and desecrated your lives. You have all aspected your souls and divided the experiences of those times so completely so as to reach every part of the globe with your intention for a life as was first envisioned. Your numbers are multiplied and your intentions are heightened and represented in every race, every culture, and every way of being on planet earth. What was once expressed and experienced within on that one part of the globe is now widespread and living in the hearts and souls of all life on earth.

This will manifest in the times to come. Hold on to that promise you have made to yourselves and know that as you do, you are assuring the destiny that frees you, once and for all, to reach the Promised Land that opens the door to Foreverland, and into eternity. Keep the knowledge strong and sure in the times to come, for in these times, you will be asked to hold on to that truth. You will ride the waves of change and challenge for a very short time, and then it will be freedom and joy for the rest of your days.

The best way to be in that strength is to live your life, right now and for the times to come, in the joy that is around you. See those with whom you share these times as the family and friends who chose to be with you, and you them, at this time, and realize the strength of unity that you share. There is no better place for you to be right now than where you are, and as the next days, weeks and months come and slide by, you will know deep within that this is so.

I take leave now and leave you to your journey. I thank Hatonn for inviting me to this journey and to this messenger, with whom I have alliance. We have traveled far and wide, all of us, and I never am away from any of you, for you are my family, as I am yours. Trust in yourselves and know that as you rise to what is coming, you allow the God within to step forth and be heard and lived. For within is the abiding place of all freedom and love, joy and peace. Know it as you are, live it as you do.

And so it is.

Thank you dear Kryon,

Love, Nancy Tate

Appendix D

PROPHETIC MESSAGE #2 FROM KRYON & HATONN
Channeled by Nancy Tate
29 AUGUST 2007

Kryon or Hatonn, please would you elaborate on what you told us in the message of August 27?

My dear ones, there is nothing to fear. There is coming an event, a spectacle of immense proportion. This will come according to the star nations results of bringing a part of the plan into readiness. As the star nations have been in alliance with the Galactic Federation, there is a determination that is being made as we speak to bring about an event that will rock the rafters of heaven, so to speak and allow the things that have been hidden to be revealed in the droppings that will come from this rocking.

We are here to advise against any fear that will surface from these reports. As the pieces fall into place there will be sentries along every corridor who will be there for those who find themselves in fear. These sentries are people of earth with whom we have been working to stand by and assure the people that there is more to what is being displayed than meets the eye. The people will be told the truth about what is taking place, and as they realize the depth to which the present regime will go to place before them a fearful display, they cannot overcome the trail of truth that is waving across the globe.

Truth will out, and the tables will turn on the efforts of the cabal to present an atmosphere in which they can gain more power. This ploy of theirs will not work, and as we employ all of our emissaries around the world to inform the people with incontrovertible truth, they will see that there is nothing to fear in the skies above and certainly nothing to fear on the ground.

There will be a time when those who have not been approached will find the fear jump into their field. This is when they will be approached, for it is within the scope of that fear that the emissaries will tune in and realize their place for the easing of that person's fear. It will be an immediate presence, and one that the person will trust, that will come to the side of that person, and advise them of the truth.

Understand that this is all part of the destiny of these people who will be helped. It is part of the opening that will take place; they will have called it in on a soul level. This is their time for the remembrance of who they are and what they are here for. It is the time for them to step out of the suit of forgetfulness and into the raiment of full recall.

This can happen most times in families; there can be one person in a family who will come to the others and tell them of the awakening that has taken place. It can also be in communities where the combination of societal events and called for meetings will reveal the truth. This will all come from trusted members of the families and the communities.

These emissaries have been working in their sleep time, and some of them in their waking hours to be ready when the time comes. There is no reason for anyone to fear earth calamities or catastrophic political upheavals, for what is to take place will be of epic proportions and will be well monitored by the star nations and the Galactic Federation.

Some of you have questioned what are the star nations and how are they in co-operation with the Galactic Federation. Realize that there are a number of sects that comprise the cosmic family, just as there are earth sects in the governance, and military as well as other parts of the society of earth. In these sects there is an entwining of communication and co-operation and each one is in constant contact with the other. As these operations on earth wind down to the eleventh hour, and the operations here in the cosmos interact with each other, we are in constant contact with all that is taking place on earth.

We are aware of the energies that are building with every aspect of earth life. We are in total and complete compliance with the Creator, and with all levels of this communication and undertaking. The cabal is under the impression that they are immune to all of our ministrations; that is the extent of their arrogance and the realm of denial of what their position is in this whole scenario. Despite numerous and myriad talks we have had with them, they still are dealing in their own ideas of what they can do, for they have so immersed themselves in their own deceit that they cannot see the source of it, or the ending of it. It has indeed become who they are, and they do not deny themselves.

As we enter into these times that are upon us, we do so with full authority from humankind. We also do so with the full authority from The Source of all. Coming into this time is like opening up a box that has had stored within it for generations, the treasures and trinkets of past experiences. As each one is brought forward there is a remembrance that takes precedence in ones' mind for the moment of discovery. As the items are brought forth and laid upon the table, they impart a certain energy.

This is what has been taking place with all of the clearing that is going on around the planet. As all of you clear out past emotions and energies of the experiences you have accumulated over the lifetimes, those energies of memory are touching in with those of the present. This brings on a series of repercussions that, given enough focus, serve to manifest once more and give those involved the opportunity to say yes, this is now, or no this is old energy and has nothing to do with today.

That is what you all are being given right now. You are being given the opportunity to see the relevance to your present life of what is coming forth emotionally and physically at this time. This is taking shape in all kinds of ways, and as they come forth to be examined, they are assessed and allowed to flow forth into transmutation, or they are held onto and made to manifest once more into the reality that is present.

This is what is happening with the cabal. They too are re-experiencing all of the old energy of war, and conflict, and the need to attain and retain power over the rest of humanity. As they do this, there are the ones who are experiencing this emergence of old energy and saying no, this is not today and I allow it to flow on by into the light of clearing. This is stepping up, as the energy of truth is strengthened more and more, it is overcoming the darkness that has pervaded so much of humanity.

This is why, with the event that the cabal tries to bring about, there will be an overriding of what is presented and this will allow the way for our contact with all of you. First, you will be presented with a preview, by the cabal. You will know in your hearts and souls that this is not representative of your origins. You will know, for you will not hear our language of love in your soul, and you will know that what is being presented to you is based on illusion, not on truth. You will then know that there is a truth that will come and present itself, and it will come when you are ready for it.

There is no stepping back now and allowing your inner knowledge to fight with the presentation that is staged for you. You will watch their performance, and you will know that it is not what you recognize as truth. There will be some on earth who will cower and who will believe what they are being told by the cabal. Those people will come to no harm, and they will be told the truth by our emissaries. As they are brought to their own truth, through their free will, they will follow their inner guidance, or they will experience that soul decision that they have made for this time.

Dear ones, this is a pivotal time in the life of humanity and earth. This is the time when all of the cards that the cabal have created are out on the table. There can be no more deceit and coverup, for it will not stand your scrutiny. There are more and more of you who are standing up for what you know and feel to be your rights as citizens of this planet earth. Those who still have their blinders on will find their new place to be in the time to come. Know that they operate on soul contract and that they are fully exercising their free will and the inherent right to make their choices.

Those who choose to experience something other than what others on earth will experience will find their way made clear for living out their contact in a place that suits their intent. There is no one who will be left behind anywhere. Everyone on this planet will be residing in the exact place where he/she chooses. This is the truth of the universe and is ordained and decreed by The Source, Creator of all.

There is only one way to be, and that is the truth of choice. There is no other way to express except for that of individual choice. As we wind down to the final bell in this game of choice, we are finding more and more have crossed the line and are standing in glory in their Light of truth. They are giving their all to support that which they know to be the way of love, and as they join in harmonic toning, they ring out to the rest of existence that all is one. That reverberates throughout all of life, giving every particle of life, every atom, the opportunity for total and complete oneness in the intent of that particle of life, that spark of The Creator.

As you go into these next days, weeks and months, know that your every wish is what you will receive, in the time you call for on a soul level. Know that your life and that of those around you is precious and fine to all of us. We are pledged to do what it takes to make sure that this is all carried out as is ordained by The Source. Your wish is in command. Humanity has spoken, and as the bell tolls on into the hearts ands souls of all of you, know that the song that is sung throughout heaven is your song of the rebuilding of heaven on earth, and that it is being prepared as we speak in the realms to which you are ascending.

Hold on to your hats for just a little while and watch, as would an interested bystander, as the cabal brings forth its final play to an audience that has left the theater. Have compassion for them, for this is their last farewell, and the theater will ring no more with the sounds of their toning. It will ring with the tones of love and joy forevermore.

Thank you dear Kryon and Hatonn,

Love, Nancy Tate

Appendix E: Business Proposal
by Arthur Earl Jones, Ph.D.

My higher self has asked me to organize a creative team of business associates for the specific purpose of facilitating the awakening and enlightenment of humanity by means of the distribution of seven different works of mine.

The seven works will consist of five books, one CD, and one DVD.

The five books will be: 1) *The Bible's Cover-Stories Revealed: The Golden Keys That Unlock History*, which is an illustrated historical treatise that was self-published in April of 2007; 2) *Channeling the Apocalypse: From the Eighteenth Dynasty to the Current Incarnations (Volume One)*, which is almost completed and scheduled to be self-published in October of 2007; 3) *Channeling the Apocalypse (Volume 2)*, which will be written and self published during 2008; 4) *Illustration of Spiritual Awakening: A Brief Autobiographical Account of My Spiritual Journey During This Lifetime*, which was written in 1998 and can be prepared for self-publication at any time, and 5) *The Book of Choices: Keys to Enlightenment*, which was written in 2000 and can be self published at any time.

The CD will be titled *The Wake-Up Song* by Allisone Heartsong and will consist of the title song, which was composed in the spring of 2003 (consisting of twenty-four stanzas, and scheduled to be performed and recorded by Rebekah in the very near future), together with a hallelujah chorus titled *The Epiphany*.

The DVD will be titled *Birthing the Era of God; A Message to Humanity From the Divine Mother* and will consist of a channeling by Claire Heartsong, together with an introduction by Allisone Heartsong, an inspired musical accompaniment by the world-famous New Age musician Michael Hammer, and a spectacular visual accompaniment consisting of abstract kaleidoscopic color imagery by the masterful Ken Jenkins, all of which was manifested in 1993 and can now be prepared for publication whenever the time is right.

The creative team of business associates will consist of 1) the author (Arthur Earl Jones), who will be responsible for paying 2) the word processor (Zepp Jamieson), 3) a manager with legal expertise who will be responsible for paying 4) an accountant to handle the bookkeeping, and 5) a promoter (Bernie Nelson?), who will be responsible for promoting the distribution of the seven works.

This creative team of business associates will operate on a contingency percentage basis, which will be different for each of the three categories as follows.

For the books, the author will receive half, the manager will receive one quarter, and the promoter will receive one quarter.

For the CD, the author will receive one quarter, the performer will receive one quarter, the manager will receive one quarter, and the promoter will receive one quarter.

For the DVD, Allisone Heartsong will receive one quarter, Claire Heartsong will receive one quarter, Michael Hammer will receive one eighth, Ken Jenkins will receive one eighth, the manager will receive one eighth, and the promoter will receive one eighth.

The key steps in the formation of this creative team of business associates will be 1) the selection of a manager by the author, 2) the selection of a promoter by the author, and 3) the negotiations by way of correspondence between the manager and the promoter for the purpose of facilitating this project.

Appendix F: Admiral Fallon versus General Petraeus
by Gareth Porter*

WASHINGTON, 12 September 2007 (IPS) - In sharp contrast to the lionisation of Gen. David Petraeus by members of the U.S. Congress during his testimony this week, Petraeus's superior, Admiral William Fallon, chief of the Central Command (CENTCOM), derided Petraeus as a sycophant during their first meeting in Baghdad last March, according to Pentagon sources familiar with reports of the meeting.

Fallon told Petraeus that he considered him to be "an ass-kissing little chickenshit" and added, "I hate people like that", the sources say. That remark reportedly came after Petraeus began the meeting by making remarks that Fallon interpreted as trying to ingratiate himself with a superior.

That extraordinarily contentious start of Fallon's mission to Baghdad led to more meetings marked by acute tension between the two commanders. Fallon went on to develop his own alternative to Petraeus's recommendation for continued high levels of U.S. troops in Iraq during the summer.

The enmity between the two commanders became public knowledge when the Washington Post reported Sep. 9 on intense conflict within the administration over Iraq. The story quoted a senior official as saying that referring to "bad relations" between them is "the understatement of the century".

Fallon's derision toward Petraeus reflected both the CENTCOM commander's personal distaste for Petraeus's style of operating and their fundamental policy differences over Iraq, according to the sources.

The policy context of Fallon's extraordinarily abrasive treatment of his subordinate was Petraeus's agreement in February to serve as front man for the George W. Bush administration's effort to sell its policy of increasing U.S. troop strength in Iraq to Congress.

In a highly unusual political role for an officer who had not yet taken command of a war, Petraeus was installed in the office of Minority Leader Mitch McConnell, a Republican from Kentucky, in early February just before the Senate debated Bush's troop increase. According to a report in The Washington Post Feb. 7, senators were then approached on the floor and invited to go McConnell's office to hear Petraeus make the case for the surge policy.

Fallon was strongly opposed to Petraeus's role as pitch man for the surge policy in Iraq adopted by Bush in December as putting his own interests ahead of a sound military posture in the Middle East and Southwest Asia -- the area for which Fallon's CENTCOM is responsible.

The CENTCOM commander believed the United States should be withdrawing troops from Iraq urgently, largely because he saw greater dangers elsewhere in the region. "He is very focused on Pakistan," said a source familiar with Fallon's thinking, "and trying to maintain a difficult status quo with Iran."

By the time Fallon took command of CENTCOM in March, Pakistan had become the main safe haven for Osama bin Laden's al Qaeda to plan and carry out its worldwide operations, as well as being an extremely unstable state with both nuclear weapons and the world's largest population of Islamic extremists.

Plans for continued high troop levels in Iraq would leave no troops available for other contingencies in the region.

Fallon was reported by the New York Times to have been determined to achieve results "as soon as possible". The notion of a long war, in contrast, seemed to connote an extended conflict in which Iraq was but a chapter.

Fallon also expressed great scepticism about the basic assumption underlying the surge strategy, which was that it could pave the way for political reconciliation in Iraq. In the lead story Sep. 9, The Washington Post quoted a "senior administration official" as saying that Fallon had been "saying from Day One, 'This isn't working.' "

One of Fallon's first moves upon taking command of CENTCOM was to order his subordinates to avoid the term "long war" -- a phrase Bush and Secretary of Defence Robert M. Gates had used to describe the fight against terrorism.

Fallon was signaling his unhappiness with the policy of U.S. occupation of Iraq for an indeterminate period. Military sources explained that Fallon was concerned that the concept of a long war would alienate Middle East publics by suggesting that U.S. troops would remain in the region indefinitely.

During the summer, according to the Post Sep. 9 report, Fallon began to develop his own plans to redefine the U.S. mission in Iraq, including a plan for withdrawal of three-quarters of the U.S. troop strength by the end of 2009.

The conflict between Fallon and Petraeus over Iraq came to a head in early September. According to the Post story, Fallon expressed views on Iraq that were sharply at odds with those of Petraeus in a three-way conversation with Bush on Iraq the previous weekend. Petraeus argued for keeping as many troops in Iraq for as long as possible to cement any security progress, but Fallon argued that a strategic withdrawal from Iraq was necessary to have sufficient forces to deal with other potential threats in the region.

Fallon's presentation to Bush of the case against Petraeus's recommendation for keeping troop levels in Iraq at the highest possible level just before Petraeus was to go public with his recommendations was another sign that Petraeus's role as chief spokesperson for the surge policy has created a deep rift between him and the nation's highest military leaders. Bush presumably would not have chosen to invite an opponent of the surge policy to make such a presentation without lobbying by the top brass.

Fallon had a "visceral distaste" for what he regarded as Petraeus' sycophantic behaviour in general, which had deeper institutional roots, according to a military source familiar with his thinking.

Fallon is a veteran of 35 years in the Navy, operating in an institutional culture in which an officer is expected to make enemies in the process of advancement. "If you are Navy captain and don't have two or three enemies, you're not doing your job," says the source.

Fallon acquired a reputation for a willingness to stand up to powerful figures during his tenure as commander in chief of the Pacific Command from February 2005 to March 2007. He pushed hard for a conciliatory line toward Iran and China, which put him in conflict with senior military and civilian officials with a vested interest in pointing to China as a future rival and threat.

He demonstrated his independence from the White House when he refused in February to go along with a proposal to send a third naval carrier task force to the Persian Gulf, as reported by IPS in May. Fallon questioned the military necessity for the move, which would have signaled to Iran a readiness to go to war. Fallon also privately vowed that there would be no war against Iran on his watch, implying that he would quit rather than accept such a policy.

A crucial element of Petraeus's path of advancement in the Army, on the other hand, was through serving as an aide to senior generals. He was assistant executive officer to the Army Chief of Staff, Gen. Carl Vuono, and later executive assistant to the chairman of the Joint Chiefs, Gen. Henry Shelton. His experience taught him that cultivating senior officers is the key to success.

The contrasting styles of the two men converged with their conflict over Iraq to produce one of the most intense clashes between U.S. military leaders in recent history.

*Gareth Porter is an historian and national security policy analyst. His latest book, "Perils of Dominance: Imbalance of Power and the Road to War in Vietnam", was published in June 2005.

Appendix G: Message from Adama
Channeled by Nancy Tate
13 September 2007

Beloved Friends:

Channeled by Nancy Tate, the ascended master Adama of Inner Earth, has today blessed us with a momentous message that deserves our top-priority attention.

I regard this message as a sure sign that the divine plan for the radical transformation of our beloved Mother Earth has been activated and is now underway.

This divine plan will culminate in our planetary ascension during the next five years.

In Love's pure Light,

All-is-one Heartsong

Adama Channeled by Nancy Tate

My dear ones, this is Adama of the Galactic Federation. I am on special mission at this time from Inner Earth to bring to you a resumé of kindness for the upcoming times. With this resumé there is contained a nucleus of a ready-made agenda to continue with the present mode of travel in the cosmos.

I address this particular agenda because there has been an abundance of late of interference from the Earth minions, and their attempts to subvert our activity of assistance has failed completely. In fact, it has caused a meltdown in their communication between themselves, and in so doing has caused them to avert many of their plans and dislocate the parts of their plans and the areas that they have set up to work from. They have seen that there is no longer a feasible place from which to operate in these various places around the globe; therefore they have not only shut them down, they have cleared away any evidence that they were there.

This has caused us to reveal to you the operations that they were engaged in, and that are no longer a threat. We have seen to this and are operating in your best interest and the best interests of the rest of your solar system. At this time, there are twelve of these former stations that are dismantled and cleared of all trace of the overt operations. We have seen that they have followed our instructions to the letter. Their nuclear capability has been obliterated in those areas, and they are presently working on dismantling the rest of the stations that are in their network of nuclear capability on planet as well as off. We are seeing to the dismantling, and are overseeing the procedure by which it is taking place.

I am able to bring this news to you through the complete communication and acceptance of the Earth allies. We have come together in this venture for the express purpose of rendering the ministrations of the plans for nuclear destruction that have been long in place to be no longer possible. We have found all of the stations that they have created and in addition are in the process of searching the caverns and underground bunkers to assure that there is no trace left of the ancient places where the explosive devices have been kept since time immemorial.

During my tenure in Telos, I have been overseeing the protection of and the present dismantling and removal of these warheads. My associates and I have seen to their neutralization and their return to the ships for disintegration. First, we are removing any programming from them that was instilled at the beginning. These warheads were actually brought to this planet thousands of years ago by off-world beings who felt the need for the protection that the presence of those warheads on Earth afforded them. We were not authorized to remove them before this time, for the free will that has been in place has not allowed for their removal, since those beings who brought them were the Annunaki, who began the present human race on Earth. At this time, we have obtained permission from The Creator and are following the process outlined by the overlords of the Angelic realms.

As for the events of the day and how they relate to this, we are telling you that the attempts to instill fear in the hearts and minds of the people is being stepped up, for as we dismantle and remove any capability of nuclear calamity on Earth, they are trying to bring about a third world war that would serve to present another means by which they can reduce the world population. They produce feared scenarios that have no basis in fact. They create stories that are filled with supposed veracity, and are empty when researched by those who do not buy into the content.

We advise you all to look upon what you are hearing and reading and allow yourself to go to your center and realize what is contained there that will reveal the truth to you. Your inner guidance has a clear stream to the truth of what is taking place at every moment. There is no way that you can receive misguidance as long as you call in the Light of your oversoul and the subsequent information that is contained there.

We are with you every moment. At this critical time in the evolvement of Earth, Gaia, and humanity, we are steering the momentum toward full and complete ascension in the various stages that are set in place. You are receiving complete communication at all times, and when you, in your purity of intent, go within and listen to the reassuring voice of your inner knowing, you will be able to hold your peace and your equilibrium of thought and being. Fear cannot survive within the consciousness of knowing who you are and being in that knowing every time you begin to go to fear. Instantly replace that fearful question with a gentle request to receive the truth, and you will have it.

We of the Galactic Federation are with you through every step in this process and stage of your ascension. We are replacing the timeworn energies of hands off with the timely allowance of intervention when it is clear and called into acceptance by humanity that the decrees that are set down by The Creator are followed to the last word. One of those decrees is as is stated here; "There shall be no life lost on Planet Earth in the energy of nuclear war, or in the premise of retaliation according to the old decrees of allowance unto the days of Armageddon, and complete destruction of the planet. Those energies are no longer valid and have been completely removed and obliterated from the celestial record."

I, Adama, of Telos and the Galactic Federation, envoy to the people of inner and surface Earth do stand by and remain in service to the total and complete removal and obliteration of the nuclear energy on Earth for now and in the future. As Earth is restored to her perfection any and all of the presence of nuclear energy at this time and at any other time on the history of this planet will be obliterated and cleared from the energy of Gaia, Earth Mother of All. We stand in readiness to celebrate with you when the Earth is ready for the restoration and jubilation of the New Golden Age.

Hold your light and love, with peace in your heart and joy in your step as these last days, weeks, and months bring to a close this chapter of the book of dreams for the ascension of Earth and all life within and on her surface. In the name of the Christed Energy, we leave this transmission and honor your coming to this time and stage of your new way of being.

Thank you dear Adama, of Telos and the Galactic Federation,
Love, Nancy Tate

Appendix H: Letter to Lulu.com
13 September 2007

Dear Bob Young, CEO:

    Let me say at once that I have been very happy with my choice to use the services provided by Lulu up to this point, but that I am not happy with the current hassle that has arisen during the past few days, which is, I am confident, a solvable problem.

    In May of 2007, I gave my approval to the seventh version of my illustrated historical treatise, The Bible's Cover-Stories Revealed (ID #714890), and placed orders for over one hundred copies to be distributed by me, using my own ISBN 978-0-9794139-1-9.

    On 21 August 2007, I then decided to try out Lulu's "Published by You" distribution service, for which I placed Order #1507710 and paid $50.

    On 29 August 2007, we received a notification from Lulu (Reference #LTK91020846652X) informing us that Lulu required a different ISBN 978-0-6151-6074-0, and requesting that we revise our document and then approve a proof copy of the revision.

    After revising our document by replacing my ISBN with Lulu's ISBN on page 2 and on page 36, we then ordered a proof copy for our approval (Order #1572208, for which we paid $12.49 on 31 August 2007), assuming that Lulu would take the responsibility for replacing my bar code with Lulu's bar code on the back cover, for the simple reason that Lulu's bar code was not in our possession.

    On 10 September 2007, we received the proof copy that we had ordered and paid for, but when we discovered on 11 September 2007 that Lulu had not replaced my bar code with Lulu's bar code on the back cover, we immediately notified Don C. at Lulu Support on the evening of 11 September 2007 that our proof copy of this twelfth version was defective and unacceptable because Lulu had not replaced the bar code on the back cover.

    We were then told by Don C. that Lulu would replace my bar code with Lulu's bar code if we would revise our document again by sending two separate images for the front cover and the back cover.

    On 12 September 2007, when we discovered that the condition of our document was such that we could not revise it as requested, we contacted Josh at Lulu Support, who first suggested that we pay a revision penalty fee but then advised us to send an email to distro@lulu.com requesting help for the purpose of resolving this problem.

    Sincerely,
    Arthur Earl Jones, Ph.D.

Appendix I: How to Destroy a Nation

By Judith Moriarty

The Eve Of Destruction
19 September 2007

If I were given unlimited power, money, and the unknowing assistance of multitudes of pawns, players, shills, toadies, lap dogs, etc; to take down a nation, how would I do it?

Common sense says, first I would want to control that nation's monetary system with the unlimited ability to tax the population (incurring massive debt) into servitude. I might name my monetary system with an official-sounding title that would fool the multitudes into thinking I was an official governmental agency - and not a private banking cartel.

I would institute various programs of entitlement to entrap and make the citizenry dependent on various handouts - thus killing their incentive to work, but most of all to control dissent. One doesn't bite the hand that feeds them.

I would give robber barons and various corporate entities, through lobbyists and campaign contributions to key legislators, the power to write their own meal tickets, excusing them from various taxes, regulation, liabilities and accountability. I would set up off-shore accounts and various trusts to protect the wealth of the favored elite. Only the working cogs will pay strangulating taxes.

I would kill unions. Unions are not cost-effective for companies whose sole purpose for existence is 'profits'. Unions are a hindrance with their silliness of demanding livable wages, safe working conditions, medical benefits, pensions, vacations, etc. I would initiate a PR campaign to discredit and label those who had any thoughts of organizing. I would threaten to close down local industries and ship them overseas if workers balked at lower wages, or resented being mere cogs in the machine. In the event of a strike, I would call in scab workers and security guards to handle unruly vocal workers. Maybe I'd kill the leaders - just as a lesson.

Next, for quicker servitude, I would shut down the mills, the various plants, machine shops, manufacturing, auto companies (livable wage jobs), and send them to foreign lands, where labor costs (no benefits - no safety standards) are mere pennies. I would grant tax incentives, subsidies and create consulting firms to assist companies in making a smooth transition to less restrictive lands.

I would direct Congress to vote legislation (various visas) to import tens and more tens of thousands of foreign workers who would be paid one-half to one third of American wages (no benefits, no job security) to work at resorts, hotels, restaurants, in the medical field, engineering, teaching, and in Information Technology. I would propagandize the gullible public, telling them that Americans 'won't do' those jobs - or that there are not enough trained Americans to fill the positions. Congress will be instructed to reinforce this lie in various scripted messages (media - campaign trail - speeches in Congress).

Slowly and insidiously, I would remove most of the major decision-making to the Executive Branch under the guise of national security. Presidential Directives, and Executive Orders will replace the messiness of having decisions held-up, or argued in Congress. Most importantly, the public will remain mostly oblivious.

I would open the borders to allow millions of the dispossessed (due to trade agreements) south of the border/others, to work on corporate farms, as maids, laborers, construction workers, roofers, etc. I would encourage illegal immigration, so as to keep these unsuspecting people in a constant state of apprehension - should they insist on a livable wage, or complain, when unscrupulous contractors leave them unpaid, or injured without compensation. I would organize massive marches (making them appear as grassroots uprisings) pitting victims (American workers) against victims (immigrants) - so as to keep the focus off of the various trade agreements (constructing a global plantation). The more venom, rancor, hatred and chaos, the better. The workers of the world must never see these issues as pertaining to class......but rather intolerance, racism, and bigotry. Victims blaming victims, never the elite behind the curtain.

I would limit any real choices in voting, keeping the field limited to a two-party (monied) system - where only the wealthy (poor candidates ignored) and chosen need apply. Again, I would encourage animosity between the reds and the blues, never revealing that they are playing (these political parties) good cop - bad cop (depending on who is in power). Both parties will be given their scripted talking points, which per usual, will promise the world...and deliver nothing. They must not address the real issues facing Americans and instead distract by sniping and snipping amongst themselves. I would turn over the responsibility (to assure the outcome) of voting to corporate entities with their easily-compromised voting machines with no paper trails (such as even local ATM machines provide).

I would keep up the pretense of a 'representative democracy' in Foggy Bottom with a lot of bickering, the blame game, and senseless tedious hearings (always after the fact) of scandals, the lack of response to disasters, sex, etc. This gives the 'appearance' of being busy and on top of things.

I would set up a dysfunctional Department of Education, that would dictate to the states (thus parents) various insane mandates, regulations, and policies, for the sole purpose of dumbing down (through tests, not teaching - whole language etc) the future generation. A dumb population is an easily-controlled population. These various edicts, will have the dual purpose of putting more and more costs on work-a-day property owners who are unable to absorb the demands for higher and higher taxes (to meet these demands). Thus, everyone will be made to work two or three jobs to keep up with the newest tax bills, and so on. All of this will result (as planned) in turning out functionally illiterate students, fit for the local widget factory, Wal-Mart, Home Depot, garbage man, prison guard, or cannon fodder for war. None of these vocations demand calculus, or being educated in literature, or world affairs.

The teachers of old will be replaced with 'change agents' who will focus on group think, hive mentality behavior modification, and social engineering - not teaching. Pre-school will become mandatory. The younger the child, the easier it is to mold them into non-thinking dolts conforming to authority. Parents (unread - easily intimidated) will be convinced that little Johnnie or Jane is 'learning disabled, or hyper active', and thus needs to be drugged into compliance. Mental illness centers will become a major part of education - with soon nearly everyone being found at risk.

"There's no earthly way of knowing
Which direction they are going!
There's no knowing where they're rowing,
Or which way the river's flowing!
Not a speck of light is showing,
So the danger must be growing,
For the rowers keep on rowing,

And they're certainly not showing
any signs that they are slowing........."

--Robert Dahl - Charlie and the Chocolate Factory

DRUGS - I would saturate the land with drugs, pills, LSD, marijuana, prescriptions, designer drugs etc; till the land was awash with mind-numbing, brain-damaging chemicals making crime rampant, destroying families/communities, and creating a private prison industry (the largest in the world). The costs, to states and various communities will bankrupt many - with peace officers, renamed law enforcers and gradually becoming militarized. People will be conditioned to FEAR the police, not welcome their presence.

I would allow the HMOs, Pharmaceuticals, and Insurance companies to ravage and destroy what was once an affordable medical system. They will write the legislation relieving them of any liabilities, and making doctors mere technocrats in the 'machine', dictated to by some HMO/Insurance drone in a far away cubicle as to what treatments their patients are ineligible to receive. The focus will be on 'profits' with ever more exotic drugs being offered in lieu of preventive medicine. Pollution, food additives, chemicals, and Frankenstein crops will be added to create even more ill health. The Hippocratic Oath will become as antiquated as the Geneva Convention. Being on constant vacation and with their own (taxpayer subsidized) health insurance, granting them the best in prompt treatment (prescriptions), the people's representatives will, as usual, protest feebly and do nothing. Pharmaceutical companies will be granted legislative authority to charge top dollar for needed medicines, with Congress voting to prevent more affordable medicines (made by the same companies) from being imported to the U.S. from Canada and Japan. Profits over people is the corporate mantra of the land.

I would make (except for legislators and the judicial and executive branches with their obscene pensions) retirement an impossibility for seniors. On fixed incomes, or minuscule pensions (if not already looted), they will be unable to afford rising taxes, the cost of medicine, rent, food, home heating, or medical treatment. Many will die in the land of plenty of hypothermia, cancers, malnutrition, and once treatable medical conditions that they can no longer afford to deal with (while their well-to-do neighbors sing Amazing Grace at the village church). If they don't die fast enough, they will be encouraged to embrace 'death with dignity' - an Orwellian term for execution.

WAR - I would institute perpetual war, thus killing off the best and brightest, bankrupting the country (borrowing billions for destruction) while filling the coffers of corporate gangsters, the favored, and the military industrial complex. I would privatize most of the military, hiring mercenary troops at lucrative salaries for international and domestic crises. Soldiers, when returning home (due to privatized bureaucracy), will be made to jump through hoops (for benefits) and forced to prove that missing limbs, depleted uranium poisoning, and brain damage will hinder them from living happily ever after.

"Don't you understand what I'm trying to say?
Can't you see the fear I'm feeling today?
If the button is pushed, there's no running away,
They'll be none to save with the world in a grave"

I would see gentrification by disaster and eminent domain, tearing apart communities and making the dispossessed all wanderers in the land of their birth. With shuttered downtowns, concrete box stores, sprawl malls, fast food, plastic booth slop joints, consultants, and appointed committees replacing local government, etc, I would destroy the known and the familiar. Thus scattered, unity and the security of small town America (ethnic neigborhoods) makes strangers struggling to exist...not to live.

"I can't twist the truth, it knows no regulation,
handful of Senators don't pass legislation"

TRAVEL - The wealthy and chosen need have no fear. With private jets - they will not be subjected to the humiliation put upon the masses. Citizens held captive in rushing to business, a vacation, a funeral, or medical emergency, etc will be scanned, groped (by rent-a-cops) made to empty innocuous liquids, questioned, etc - not for security purposes but for behavior modification...conditioning them to obedience and compliance. No one will mention the incoming cargo containers not searched - millions of containers from foreign lands sitting on docks and then embarking on trucks to every corner of the unsuspecting nation. In a world of announced terrorists, all become suspect (minus the favored few)...even the babe and senior in his wheelchair. Examples will be made of those daring to question or object. Travel will thus be discouraged.

"Hate your neighbor next door, but don't forget to say grace".

FEAR - Waco, Ruby Ridge, school shootings, hijackings, serial killers, child rapists, imploding towers, danger stranger, assassinations, road blocks, taser attacks (by police), roaming gangs, identity theft, SWAT teams (getting the wrong address), invading Arabs (threat), color-coded fear days, video cameras, security alarms, schools invaded with police, and drug-sniffing dogs, beating/arresting dissenters, etc. All these and more will be used to cause confusion, anxiety, suspicion, and paralyzing fear resulting in evermore draconian controls, laws, and violating the rights of a once carefree population. Who's watching the watchers...is nobody's business.

MEDIA - Information, education, rational discourse, and debate on all sides of an issue will be limited or prevented. Citizens will be encouraged to take sides - i.e., abortion, gun rights, immigration, gay marriage, funding religion with taxpayer dollars, graphic sex education for young elementary children, etc. Issues will be kept to the superficial and emotional. Corporate control of the media (all media) is mandatory (thus Clinton's Telecommunications Act - giving away the airwaves) with entertainers, not newscasters, giving their fluff and nutter reports of the day: OJ, Paris Hilton, pit bulls, Rosie O'Donnel, the runaway bride, the diapered astronaut, etc. PR hirelings will be presented as 'experts' be they mothballed generals or think tank suits. Citizens will be instructed what to think - not how to think. Limits will be put on speech, in public hearings, local council meetings/gatherings, letters to the editor, etc. Facilitators, stakeholders, and consensus will take the place of the democratic process (the outcome pre-determined).

ECONOMY - Trade agreements, unread (some are hundreds of pages) and not debated, will be voted on with the results being massive unemployment, bankrupt farms, imported suspect food stuffs/products, echoing steel mills, foreclosures, homelessness, etc. Language in these various 'agreements' will take precedence over all local zoning laws and environmental protections. Elected representatives, (federal/state) will find these agreements almost impossible to understand with their legalese and loophole language.

PRIVATIZATION - I would give away the Commons to private industry and foreign investors, including water, medical care, the infrastructure, roads, schools, utilities, bridges, rivers, waste disposal, and lands (under the guise of nature preserves, parks, heritage sites, biospheres and buffer zones, etc). As collateral for the trillions in debt, I would post the people's land with countless signs reading "Keep Out" and "No Trespassing" and "Private" etc.

I would keep the multitudes entertained (distracted) throughout the years with ball games, gladiator (well-paid) sports, concerts, theme parks, shopping malls, expensive automobiles, theater, the arts, movies, various awards ceremonies, electioneering debates (senseless), arguments on war (to surge or not to surge, to invade or not to invade), liposuction, breast implants, Viagra readiness, exotic vacations, designer clothes, the newest must-have electronic gadgetry, air-headed starlets doping and drinking it up, NASCAR, horse racing, soccer, golf, environmental activism (safe not threatening industry), etc.

Meantime, I would see to it that government agencies were slowly and inclemently dismantled, with the work farmed out to private contractors. Positions of authority and decision-making will have corporate interests appointed to them. Food protections, health, and safety, and environmental regulations, will be under-funded or disregarded - favoring corporate interest (profits) instead. Federal and state environmental agencies will be mere rubber stamp mouth pieces for industry, paying no heed to polluters or to the protection of various community health issues (SuperFund sites).

All of this and more, I would do, if I were given permission (generously-compensated, of course) to destroy a nation. I would make sure that all of these various entities, and non-governmental agencies, were compartmentalized (thinking they were about the people's business) with no one (even within these agencies) having a clue as to the final objective. It is comparable to the worker in the eastern European factory thinking he is building baby carriages. Stealing a piece a week (he couldn't afford to buy one) for his expected child. He finally has them all, and assembles it on the living room floor. To his surprise, he sees an M-16 in his hands.

The greatest conspiracies aren't hidden - just fragmented into different pieces - like a puzzle. Right before people's eyes.

Whistle blowers, of course, will be dutifully dealt with, making an example for others. Most of the masses - worried about their jobs, promotions, benefits and pensions - will 'follow orders.' The few who object and fail to conform to the dictated, carefully constructed 'norm' will be labeled 'conspirators, crazies, fringe extremists, communists, queers, un-American, and traitors', etc. This has always worked down through the centuries - it's the old herd instinct. Identified as 'other' has those protesting or objecting marked as 'other' and therefore blackballed, to be avoided and shunned. Nobody wants to be labeled 'other' - not in group-think. That would make him or her much like the mad cow discovered in a dairy herd - a turd in the punchbowl of society.

"Ah you don't believe we're on the Eve of Destruction?"

[For further insight, see *Protocols of the Learned Elders of Zion*.]

Appendix J: Update from the Galactic Federation
Channeled by Sheldan Nidle
2 October 2007

6 Men, 8 Tzotz, 3 Manik

Selamat Jarin! We come before you once again to inform you about your world. The final battle between the dark's last minions and our Earth allies rages on. The open deceit, avarice, and arrogance of these shadowy ones are now very plain to see. Their strategy for victory still contains within it the seed of their inevitable defeat. Those fleet personnel assigned to monitor them have noticed increased caution and suspicion among them in the past few days, but their actions continue to confirm that they intend, by any means possible, to take the bait and its, as yet, undetected death trap. However, their natural leeriness has kept them from lunging outright for their intended "prey." So, the game is still afoot, and we believe the moment we are waiting for is drawing near. During this time, our Earth allies are in the midst of subtle negotiations with this dark cabal to iron out any remaining difficulties. On another front, another set of talks is focusing on a more forceful implementation of the Agreement of 1998.

The untold wealth of the dark ones is their most powerful weapon; another advantage is the iron-fisted stranglehold on all major financial transactions that the present US regime gives them. Their bankers and financial allies are making it difficult to move large monetary resources around unless one belongs to their privileged circle. These conditions have both positive and negative aspects to them. It is essential to understand this point and to use one's acquired influence to ensure that needed funds are dispatched in approximately the same timeframes as planned. Our Earth allies are pulling out all the stops to put our joint end game into a position to succeed. The dark's wariness only slows down the timetable and does not put the operation on hold, and intelligence gathered by our fleet during this same time span confirms this. Therefore, the many arms of this operation are closing in for the coup de grace. The trap is ready to be sprung, and those intended for its jaws are getting closer every day.

This game of cat and mouse is truly amazing: We have not seen this amount of deceit and caution since the days of the now-defunct galactic wars. Even our former adversaries are most intrigued by what is going on. According to them, the behavior of these dark ones is typical of the modus operandi of the draconian empire, a former primary constituent of the ex-Ancharan Alliance. And it is this obvious affinity that makes them certain that the unbounded greed of the cabalists will trump their present circumspection. The amount of gold, natural resources, and territory involved are too tempting for them to pass up. The prospect of increasing their power and wealth to such a degree constitutes the perfect bait, which their arrogance will induce them to take. Once the trap is sprung, the many new enterprises, created to replace the dark's institutionalized control framework of the last five centuries, can come on line. Then the rapid redistribution of wealth and power among the peoples of Earth can build a firm foundation for your global democracies.

This future coalition of global democracies is a bedrock necessity for the many activities required of you by the Divine. Global cooperation and combined political will can permit you to solve your crises of pollution and shortages of water and energy. The release of technologies currently suppressed or hidden from you can make a difference, but their deployment relies on an unprecedented degree of international collaboration. Technology transfers, financial transactions, and governmental pacts must happen swiftly, without hindrance. Of equal import is the subject of preparing your world for first contact: a series of formal announcements, which ends the UFO cover-up and reveals our benevolent presence, is required on the part of the mass media and those government agencies that presently use fiction and innuendo to instill in the collective consciousness an effective jumble of denial and images of "monsters from outer space"! Wiping the slate clean on this subject prepares the ground for our own first contact announcements and allows us to overcome the current mass prejudice about who we are.

While all this is going on, we can move the initial phase of the off-world technology transfers through the major governments of your planet. In this way we can remain anonymous and use our special position to assure the Divine that the intent of Heaven is being carried out on your world. Heaven desires only your success. They have done much over the past 13 millennia to get you to where you are now, and our role has been to put into play certain consciousness patterns that, in the last decade, have eased your move toward your future goal. We are wrapping up this procedure now and preparing you for the actual first contact events. This move toward first contact is as much a consciousness operation as it is a physical one. We are making it possible for you as a people to make a collective leap toward full consciousness. As we mentioned before, this involves a leap of several centuries of evolution and is mandated by the Divine.

What this amounts to is your reunion with your full spiritual Self. You are to become a fully conscious Being destined to perform many sacred acts. These acts can permit the divine plan to unveil the next parts of this Creation. Hence, your move forward in consciousness is inherently necessary. This divine momentum sent us here well over a decade ago. We answered this clarion call and assembled the first contact fleet that is now parked throughout your solar system. While keeping most of our ships cloaked, we revealed enough of our fleet to your dark cabal so that they can see that we do not intend to leave until first contact and its attendant goals are fully effected. And so to the present, and the issues we discuss with you. It is time, dear Ones, for many miraculous things to happen!

You are not here to continue on down this grim and forbidding path; you are here to create a new world redolent of the Light, which fulfills the divine plan. This takes for granted a number of basic conditions, starting with the cornerstone of immense physical, mental, and spiritual abundance for all. In such a context, the insidious manipulations of the dark simply evaporate, along with greed, judgment, ignorance, and strife. In their place will come universal prosperity, a sense of connectedness, wisdom, and above all, an overt reverence for all Creation and, especially, the Creator! In a magnificent transformation, you are to become privy to the divine Truths of Heaven and Creation. You will become physical Angels, created to unfold the many wonders that constitute the divine plan.

This realm that we describe to you is getting close. Multitudes of likeminded beings join us in watching the progress of events on your world. We all see the shift in your reality that is quickly taking you toward your divine destiny. The break-up of your present global order is the usual way for a reality to transform itself into a new one. While this happens, its inhabitants can experience anything from mere frustration to great distress. Although we stand outside the often-overwhelming conditions of your world, we truly understand what you are going through. We deeply wish to assure you that this seemingly endless operation is coming to an end and that marvelous things are about to manifest! Together, We are indeed Victorious!

Today, we continued our discussion about what is happening around you. As usual, we ask you to remember that much is happening behind the scenes and preparing to appear before you. Be patient, centered, and joyously focused on your most deeply desired goals. The greatest of wonders are almost upon you! We now retire. Know in your Heart of Hearts that the perpetual Supply and infinite Abundance of Heaven are indeed Yours! Selamat Majon! Selamat Kasitaram! (Sirian for Rejoice! and Be Blessed in Heavenly Love and Joy!)

TO ORDER BY EMAIL: fearorloveorders@austin.rr.com

Retail price: US$29.95 plus shipping

ISBN 978-0-6151-6204-1

First Printing: 31 October 2007
Third Version: November 2007
Printed in the United States of America

www.ingramcontent.com/pod-product-compliance
Lightning Source LLC
Chambersburg PA
CBHW081214230426
43666CB00015B/2722